THE **boat**
REPAIR BIBLE

A COMPREHENSIVE
REPAIR GUIDE FOR
POWER AND SAIL

THE **boat**
REPAIR BIBLE

A COMPREHENSIVE REPAIR GUIDE FOR POWER AND SAIL

Adlard Coles Nautical
London

Published by Adlard Coles Nautical
an imprint of Bloomsbury Publishing Plc
49–51 Bedford Square, London WC1B 3DP
www.adlardcoles.com

Copyright © Adlard Coles Nautical 2012
First edition 2012

ISBN 978-1-4081-3321-7

The right of the authors to be identified as the authors
of this work has been asserted by them in accordance
with the Copyright, Designs and Patents Act, 1988.
A CIP catalogue record for this book is available from
the British Library.

This book is produced using paper that is made from
wood grown in managed, sustainable forests. It is
natural, renewable and recyclable. The logging and
manufacturing processes conform to the
environmental regulations of the country of origin.

Produced for Adlard Coles Nautical by Ivy Contract.

Project editor: Nic Compton
Project designer: Lisa McCormick
Designers: Alistair Plumb and Luke Herriot

Typeset in Veljovic Book and Bliss
Printed in China by RR Donnelley South China Printing Co.

Note: while all reasonable care has been taken in the
publication of this book, the publisher takes no
responsibility for the use of the methods or products
described in the book.

Contents

Welcome to Boat Repair

Essential repair skills
Safety   12
Surveying your boat   14
Essential tools   18
Essential spares & materials   20
Setting up a portable workshop   22

Hull & deck repairs
Fibreglass skills   26
Impact & surface damage   28
Cracks, voids & crazing   30
Treating osmosis & delamination   32
Core damage   34
Resealing the hull to deck joint   36
Moulding from a sister ship   38
Cutting & polishing after repairs   40
Rudder damage   42
Replacing rudder bearings   44
Weeping keel   46
Lifting keel problems   48
Damaged bulkhead   50
Re-bedding loose fittings   52

Repairing teak-finished decks 54
Leaking windows or hatches 56
Replacing a hatch 58
Sheered or bent guardrails 60
Upgrading aluminium fittings 62
Refurbishing old fittings 64
Replacing anodes 66

Wooden boat repairs

Woodworking skills 70
Dealing with minor hull leaks 72
Repairing a damaged deck 74
Doubling up fastenings 76
Replacing damaged or rotten planks 78
Replacing a sawn frame 80
Making a laminated deck beam 82
Making & fitting a graving piece 84
Caulking & paying methods 86
Refurbishing solid teak decks 88
Resurfacing a leaking coachroof 90
Dropping keel bolts 92
Repainting after a repair 94

Steel & ferro-cement repairs

Metalworking skills 98
Welding new panels 100
Shot blasting & painting 102
Replacing deck fittings 104
Repairing ferro-cement hulls 106
Working with ferro-cement 108

Domestic repairs

Repairing upholstery 112
Relaminating interior surfaces 114
Repairing interior linings 116
Fixing domestic water pumps 118
Tracing & fixing water leaks 120
Tracing & fixing gas leaks 122
Replacing gas piping & fittings 124
Troubleshooting diesel heaters 126
Troubleshooting for manual heads 128
Troubleshooting for electric heads 130

General mechanics

Mechanical skills	134
Freeing seized fittings	136
Freeing seized seacocks	138
Replacing through-hull fittings	140
Split fuel & water tanks	142
Stripping a seized manual windlass	144
Leaking hydraulics	146
Repairing wind vane self-steering	148

Electrical repairs

Electrical skills	152
Replacing damaged wiring	154
Soldering & replacing connectors	156
Tracing connection problems	158
Earth leaks	160
Navigation instruments	162
Autopilot repairs	164
Windscreen wiper repair	166

Engine repairs

Engineering skills	170
Starter problems	172
Blocked fuel pipe & water in fuel	174
Bleeding an engine	176
Adjusting the belt drive	178
Water pump repair	180
Heat exchanger problems	182
Beating the diesel bug	184
Water & oil contamination	186
Broken or loose engine mounts	188
Damaged engine controls	190
Replacing cutlass bearings	192
Dripless shaft seals	194
Propeller evaluation	196
Prop & bracket damage	198
Replacing the prop & shaft	200
Clearing a fouled propeller	202
Fitting a new engine	204
Troubleshooting engines	208
Troubleshooting diesel engines	210
Troubleshooting petrol engines	212

Motorboat repairs

Fitting trim tabs   218
RIB & centre-console boats   220
Repairing an outdrive   222
Repairing duo props   224

Sailboat repairs

Rigging & sailmaking skills   228
Aluminium mast repairs   230
Glue failure in a wooden mast   232
Repairing rot in a wooden mast   234
Repairing seized blocks   236
Repairing seized winches   238
Repairing seized roller furling   240
Installing or relocating winches   242
Sail repairs   244
Halyard repairs   248
Rigging terminal repairs   250
Damaged hardware   252
Pop riveting   254
Replacing standing rigging   256
Making a new mast boot   258
Making a solid wooden spar   260
Making a hollow wooden spar   262

Dinghy repairs

GRP dinghy repairs   266
GRP hull repairs   268
Buoyancy tank leaks   270
Refastening loose fittings   272
Wooden dinghy repairs   274
Inflatable dinghy repairs   276
Trailer mechanical repairs   278
Trailer body & other fittings   280

Outboard repairs

Diagnosing starting problems   284
Replacing gearbox oil seals   286
Faulty outboard controls   288
Fuel blockage & contamination   290
Descaling waterways   292

Glossary   294
Index   300
Acknowledgements   304

Welcome to boat repair

The ideal boatowner would be a boatbuilder/sailmaker/mechanic/electrician/plumber/welder who also happened to know how to navigate a boat! Of course, none of us have all those skills, so when things go wrong with our beloved boat we invariably have to call in an expert to help with some aspect of the work. And that can use up precious cruising funds. This book aims to empower boatowners with the knowledge to fix the damage themselves and to reduce the need for outside help. That way, there will be more in the kitty to go cruising – which is where the fun really starts!

Above **Learning to fix your engine can make the difference between a day out and waiting in the marina for the mechanic to arrive.**

Left **Don't be put off wood because you don't have all the skills. It's a forgiving material which most boatowners can learn to master.**

Essential repair skills

Start here for basic tool skills, advice on essential spare parts, setting up a portable workshop, and surveying your own boat. Why spend money on a surveyor when you can do it yourself?

Hull and deck repairs

Crunch! This is the bit where those big hull repairs are carried out, covering everything from filling scratches in the gel coat to treating osmosis, and even replacing a section of hull. There's also important information on repairing damaged rudders, checking keel bolts, and replacing deck fittings.

Wooden boat repairs

Wooden boats are like a good wine: they get better as they get older – but they can also become 'corked'! Specialist knowledge includes how to use woodworking tools, replacing rotten planks, doubling up fastenings, and resealing a coachroof.

Steel and ferro-cement repairs

Key skills are welding and plastering, but there's a whole host of other factors to consider if you own a steel or ferro-cement boat, such as getting paint to stick to the hull, and how to replace deck fittings.

Domestic repairs

Damage that happens below decks can crucially affect your sailing comfort. Learn some essential plumbing and upholstery skills, and how to keep the cabin warm.

General mechanics

Seized-up seacocks can be inconvenient as well as dangerous – but different brands have different solutions. And there are some vital tips on keeping the oil flowing through your hydraulics, too.

Electrical repairs

Tracing an electrical fault can test the patience of a sea saint. Find out how the electricians do it and how to deal with specific problems, such as autopilot and windscreen wiper failure.

Engine repairs

There are whole books written about engine repairs – but have you got time to read them? This chapter covers all the essentials, from dealing with air locks to fitting the right propeller, plus comprehensive troubleshooting.

Motorboat repairs

Vital information for petrolheads, including fitting new trim tabs, refastening a RIB console, and stripping down a sterndrive.

Sailboat repairs

Ripped sails, seized winches, corroded masts – this is the price we pay for the pleasure of voyaging under sail. This chapter suggests ways of dealing with spar, sail and rigging damage.

Above **You know it's serious when you have to drop your boat's keel. This yacht was reassembled and is now sailing the Med.**

Dinghy repairs

The smaller the boat, the bigger the pleasure, they say. But you still need to know how to patch up the hull, refit loose fittings and keep the trailer wheels turning.

Outboard repairs

This chapter shows how to get a stubborn outboard started (clue: it might be your posture), plus advice on repairing faulty engine controls, getting water out of the system, and descaling your waterways.

A job done well should enhance your boating experience.

Left **Learning to use polyester resin and fibreglass cloth is essential for tackling hull repairs on most modern yachts.**

Essential repair skills

Safety

When undertaking any boat repair project it's vitally important to create a safe and efficient working environment. If it is done properly it will not only minimise the risk of injury, but will speed up the workflow and help to produce a neat and professional job.

A hazard assessment is key to creating a safe working environment. At sea all skippers are accustomed to being constantly on the lookout for hazards, and this is a skill that can be easily transferred to the boatyard. Before starting each project identify all the potential risks, and ensure you're prepared to handle each one.

Ladders and staging

Many boatyard accidents occur when unsafe ladders or temporary staging are erected to allow you to work on your boat's topsides. Ladders should be placed on level ground, at an angle of 15 degrees to the vertical, and should be tied to a strong deck fitting to prevent them capsizing or slipping away from the boat.

At the very least, when working your boat's topsides, staging should be laid on substantial trestles, again on level ground. The minimum recommended safe width for such staging is 2ft (60cm) and a toe board on the outer edge should be included.

Don't be tempted to carry items weighing more than 22lb (10kg) on a ladder. Instead, use a rope to lower items to the ground or heave them on board. Extra-heavy items can be lifted on board yachts using the boom and mainsheet or, on a powerboat, the davits.

Above **Disposable gloves are essential when dealing with paints, solvent or resins – but make sure they are suited to the job. Check the specifications on the packaging.**

Below **When working aloft ensure a quality bosun's chair is used, that the halyards used are in good condition, and make sure no tools can be dropped onto the deck.**

Electrical dangers

It is important to be aware of the inherent dangers of using mains power tools outdoors. The risk of electric shock is raised if the tools get wet, and so extension leads should have all-weather connections to keep them dry. It's also worth considering using cordless power tools instead – most are now available for a modest price from DIY stores.

Safe handling of tools should quickly become second nature, yet many people working outside the discipline of large organisations take potentially dangerous shortcuts. In particular it's vitally important to keep hands behind and clear of any cutting blade, whether it's a chisel or an electric saw. Make sure that any item you are working on is held securely before you start drilling, cutting or planing. A portable workbench incorporating a vice, and three or four clamps, should be sufficient for this.

Paints, solvents and resins

Many boat interiors are small spaces that are poorly ventilated, so a build-up of noxious fumes from these products is a very real possibility. In addition to the health hazards, some solvents pose a risk of fire or explosion. This should be considered when storing these products, so make sure they are kept well clear of heat sources.

Above **Metal work is hazardous to eyes and ears. Even if working outside, the best protection you can get is vital.**

Apart from falling off ladders and the incorrect use of tools, dust is the largest health hazard arising from boat repairs. Whatever the construction of your boat, it's inevitable that you will be exposed to harmful particles at some stage, so buy the best dust mask you can find – and make sure it's the right mask for the job. A dust mask offers no protection against fumes, for example. Check the specifications on the packaging.

You should also use a sander with an effective vacuum extraction system. Even then, antifouling coatings must never be dry sanded.

Above **Don't cut corners if you need to work above ground level when the boat is ashore. There's no substitute for proper staging.**

Above **Never underestimate the dangers of sanding dust. An effective face mask and dust extractor are essential.**

Surveying your boat 1: The hull

Most people have their boat surveyed once, when they buy it (if it's secondhand), and never again. But if you want to avoid nasty surprises, it's a good idea to conduct your own survey at least once a year. Here are some things to look out for.

To get a reliable appraisal of the condition of your boat, you need two surveys: one in the water and one out. The in-water survey will allow you to run the engine and check for obvious leaks. The out-of-the-water survey will allow you to check the structural integrity of the hull and underwater fittings such as rudder, propeller(s) and seacocks.

Starting with the out-of-the-water survey, make sure the hull is thoroughly cleaned off and you have good all-round access. Before getting stuck into the nitty-gritty of surface testing, stand back and make a

general appraisal. Are there any obvious signs of damage? Any cracks in the gel coat? Any hard spots on the hull which might indicate that it is being stressed against an internal bulkhead (see page 50)? Any rust lines coming from the keel/hull join, which might suggest the keelbolts need to be dropped (see page 46)? If you spot any bubbling on the surface, use a scraper to remove the paint. If the bubbles are under the gel coat, the boat probably has osmosis, which may require considerable work to rectify (see page 32).

(see page 50)

(see page 46)

(see page 32)

TOOLS OF THE TRADE

Plastic hammer
Bradawl
Scraper
Torch
Moisture meter

Testing methods

There are two main methods for testing the soundness of a GRP hull: a hammer (percussion) or a moisture meter. A hammer is used to tap the hull at intervals of about

Right **Bubbles on the surface of the hull are a sign of osmosis. But you need to strip the antifoul paint off to confirm the diagnosis.**

Below **Crazing in the gel coat is common on older boats and relatively easy to treat. No need to panic!**

6in (15cm) to 'sound out' any damage. A sharp sound indicates the laminate is good; a hollow sound indicates a void; a soft, muffled sound suggests the GRP may be saturated with water. But don't jump to any conclusions. Bulkheads and fittings on the inside of the hull may also create different sounds. Make a note of your findings and check the corresponding position inside for any offending items.

A more reliable way to test for moisture (and therefore possible osmosis) is to use a meter. This instrument indicates the moisture content of the GRP without removing any paint or gel coat. Readings of up to 10 per cent are usually acceptable, but bear in mind the bigger picture. An older boat will usually have a higher reading, as will a boat that's moored afloat all year round. The best method is to take a reading from an area known to be sound, and use that as a basis for comparison.

While you are under the boat, check the seacocks for signs of corrosion and the hull around the fittings for saturation (see page 136). Check the rudder fittings for corrosion and excessive play. Hold the rudder firmly with both hands and move it fore and aft and sideways. If there's too much play, you may need to replace the rudder bearings (see page 44). Also, check the propeller(s) for corrosion and the propeller shaft for alignment.

TALK TO THE EXPERTS

If in doubt, get the advice of a qualified surveyor. Their national body in the UK is the Yacht Brokers, Designers & Surveyors Association (YBDSA). In the US, contact the National Association of Marine Surveyors (NAMS) or the Society of Accredited Marine Surveyors (SAMS).

Left **Using a moisture meter to check for osmosis. Treat the readings with caution as there may be other factors at play.**

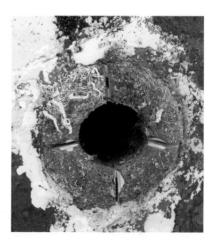

Above **A corroded seacock could shear off and sink your boat. This one has been cut and is ready to be knocked out.**

Surveying your boat 2: On board

On deck

You can learn a lot about a boat just by walking around her while she's afloat. For a start, how does the deck feel underfoot? If it feels springy it may not be adequately supported, or water may have got under the fibreglass and damaged the core (see page 34). Use a light hammer or screwdriver handle to do a 'percussion' test, as described on page 14. It should produce a sharp sound; if not you'll need to investigate further. The deck around the chainplates is particularly vulnerable as the stress exerted by the rigging may cause movement that could turn into a leak.

Check the deck fittings. Are they rusty or, in the case of aluminium, pitted? Both are sure signs of neglect. Less obvious is whether they were

adequately supported in the first place. All deck fittings should have some reinforcement (eg wooden pads) inside the boat. If not they are liable to pull through at a crucial moment. While you're checking that, check for leaks too. Re-bedding loose deck fittings is possible but can be tricky if repairs to the deck's core material need to be made first (see page 52).

Above **The smell of a boat's interior can give clues about its structural condition.**

Look closely at the standing rigging. If it's rusty or kinked it will probably need replacing (see page 256). The swage terminals can be a source of problems, as water trickling down the rigging creeps in and degrades them (see page 250). Use a magnifying glass to spot any hairline cracks.

Below **Water ingress around coachroof and deck fittings can affect the core structure. Check the fastenings are properly supported inside by washers and/or pads.**

Below decks

The first thing to notice when you go below decks is the smell. Does it smell musty? That may indicate poor ventilation. Does it smell of diesel? That may mean there is a leak in the engine fuel pipes or even a split tank (see page 142). Try to work out the source of any smell and decide whether it's significant or not.

Check the bulkheads are secure. Ideally, they should be attached to the hull and deck on all four edges with fibreglass tape – although some boatbuilders don't bother attaching the top edge. It's good practice to place a 'cushion' of foam or similar between the bulkhead and the hull to prevent hard spots developing. If water is allowed to accumulate in the bilge it's likely to seep into the bottom of the bulkheads and cause delamination, in which case they may have to be cut out and rebuilt (see page 50).

Lift the floorboards and examine the bilges with a torch. Make sure all the seacocks are operational and not corroded. If you can, locate the keelbolts and check the condition of the nuts. If washers are rusted or missing the keel may have dropped down slightly, creating a leak and applying wracking strains on the hull when heeled over. Dropping keelbolts is not for the faint-hearted, though (see page 92).

The engine

Surveying an engine is a skill in itself, but at the very least make sure it's running smoothly, that cooling water is coming out of the exhaust, that the battery is charging, and that there is no excessive rust on the engine and associated parts.

Above **The end grain of this wooden samson post is vulnerable to rot. Fitting an extra cleat is simpler than trying to replace it.**

Above **Check all the equipment is in working order. Fitting replacements can be surprisingly expensive.**

Above **Don't be put off by a bit of verdigris. Old bronze fittings such as these have plenty of life left in them.**

Above **Most rust on stainless steel is harmless enough, but check for cracks in the metal which might indicate a weak spot.**

Essential tools

Over the past couple of decades tools have become significantly cheaper. Many can now be found secondhand, too, so there's no longer any excuse for not having the best tools for each job.

Hand tools

The starting point is a decent set of hand tools – it's possible to do any job with these, they will never break down and they won't run out of power. With hand tools a 'one size fits all' philosophy never works – a wide range of sizes and types of screwdriver and spanner, for example, are typically needed so that you have one to fit every fastening on the boat, engine and electronics.

Proper maintenance of your tools is vital, especially for those kept on board. Make sure you keep your boat's interior as dry as possible, either through good ventilation or by using a dehumidifier if mains power is available. And don't keep them in a damp locker.

In addition, all moving parts should be lubricated with a light oil to prevent them seizing up; this will also help to keep rust at bay. Tools

HAND TOOLS

Essential hand tools
Screwdrivers
Allen keys
Spanners and sockets
Pliers and mole (vise) grips
Wire cutters
Bolt cutters
Wire stripper/crimper
Hacksaws
Files
Wood saws
Chisels
Oil stone
Hammer and mallet
Sharp knife
Paint scrapers
Sanding block
Mastic gun
Tape measure

Desirable hand tools
Torque wrench (for major mechanical repairs)
Plane
Consolidating roller (for fibreglass repairs)
Impact driver (for removing stubborn screws)
Vernier gauge and micrometer
Try square
Pop-rivet gun (long arm or a concertina-type for rigging repairs)

Left **The right tools make each job quicker to complete and result in a better finish, even when working in less than ideal conditions.**

should be kept sharp too – chisels and planes benefit from being kept super sharp, although in today's throwaway society we tend not to sharpen drill bits or handsaws.

Power tools

These help speed up progress enormously, as well as removing much of the physical effort required when using hand tools. The tools needed will vary according to the type of work being undertaken, but by far the most useful on-board electric tool is the cordless drill/screwdriver. Indeed for many projects it's worth having two – one for drilling holes, the other

as a screwdriver – as this eliminates the time needed to repeatedly swap between drill and screwdriver bits. For a big project consider getting a model that's sold with two batteries so that you never need to wait for one to recharge.

Next on the list for most boatowners are electric sanders. A good starting point is a standard random orbital sander; although many boatowners eventually collect a range of models, including a triangular detail sander for work in intricate corners. Beyond this, serious fibreglass repairs often require an angle grinder, while jigsaws and circular saws are useful for projects involving woodwork.

Above left **A comprehensive mechanical repair kit is vital to fix engine problems. This is in effect part of the safety kit of any sea-going vessel.**

Above **Many boats develop electrical faults. A basic tool kit will facilitate diagnosing and rectifying problems.**

POWER TOOLS

Essential power tools

Cordless drill and drill bits/cordless screwdriver

Sanders

Electrical multimeter

Desirable power tools

Jigsaw

Portable circular saw

Hot air paint stripper gun

Pressure washer

Inspection lamp or other high-power lighting

Angle grinder (used extensively in fibreglass repair)

Polisher

RCD safety device (for using power tools outside in damp conditions)

Left **Fibreglass repairs demand specialist tools. However, these are readily available and not expensive.**

Essential spares & materials

Ensuring you have the correct spares and materials to hand is just as important as having a comprehensive toolkit. While some items are needed for specific tasks only, many spares are used frequently and so are worth keeping in store.

Engine and electrical spares

The spares kept on board a boat will vary according to its use, especially how far it ventures from its home port and the availability of spares in the places visited. However, some items are essential for all boats – a complete set of fuses and spare bulbs for navigation lights being an obvious example. Less obvious perhaps, but equally important, are service kits for all the pumps on board. The failure of a fresh-water pump, heads pump or bilge pump can result in anything from embarrassment to loss of the vessel, no matter how close to home you are.

Similarly, carrying a small number of basic engine spares will mean you're immediately equipped to deal with most causes of engine failure, including fuel contamination, a failed water pump impeller or a broken alternator and/or water pump drive belt. Boats venturing further afield should also take additional spares such as a head gasket set, engine oil and filters, spare cooling hoses, a water pump and alternator diodes.

ESSENTIAL SPARES

Fuses
Stainless steel hose clips
Cable ties
Electrical connectors
Pump repair kits (bilge and water pumps)
Heads service kit
Monel seizing wire
Shackles
Split pins
Engine spares (fuel filters, water pump impeller, and drive belts for alternator and water pumps)
Variety of electrical and waterproof tapes
Inflatable dinghy repair kit

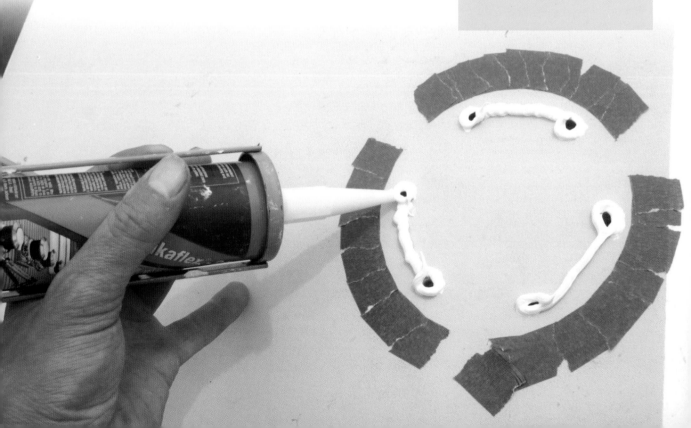

Fibreglass repair materials

Polyester or epoxy resins, woven rovings and chop strand mat, fillers such as colloidal silica, microfibres and microballoons, and gel coat are needed for repairs to fibreglass boats. These are readily available from many chandlers, although products sold as gel coat filler should not be confused with proper flowing gel coat. If these products aren't readily

Above **Electrical spares should include all bulbs – there may be several different types on board – plus connectors and tape.**

available to buy, it's worth keeping a supply in store to deal with any damage incurred.

Keep track of the shelf-life of these materials too. Although some will last almost indefinitely others may degrade after a couple of years, especially in a hot climate. This is particularly true of adhesives, resins and sealants. If storing paints, it's important to keep them somewhere without extremes of temperature – solvent-based paints can be a fire risk if exposed to excess heat, while water-based types should not be exposed to frost as this can cause the paints to solidify or separate.

Above **The spares kit must include an ample stock of fuses of all sizes used on board.**

Right **Basic materials for fibreglass repairs will enable boats that cruise in remote areas to undertake temporary repairs without disrupting the planned schedule.**

Left **The consequences of deck leaks are such that fittings should be bedded onto a quality marine adhesive sealant. Any compromise is likely to be a false economy.**

Setting up a portable workshop

A well-ordered workspace is essential to be able to work quickly and safely, so the time spent organising your tools and materials for each project is often repaid many times over.

Few boatowners have the luxury of being able to work on their vessels at home, with full workshop facilities on site. For most, creating an efficient work area is therefore a major challenge. Don't be tempted to skimp on this stage, though. A decent workshop makes a huge difference to the time it takes to complete a job and to the quality of the finish that can be achieved.

A proper on-site workshop
Most well-funded racing yachts have shipping containers fitted out as fully equipped workshops and stores, enabling their crews to fix almost any type of damage overnight. Not many boatowners have the resources for this kind of facility, but for a big project it's worth looking at ways to create a proper workshop. With a bit of planning, it's possible to create

Above **A portable workstation on deck speeds up repair work and reduces the dangers associated with repeatedly ascending and descending a ladder.**

Below **A large wheeled tool chest facilitates the organisation and transportation of tools.**

Right **Erecting shelter over the boat is worth the time involved, but never tie tarpaulins to the shores supporting the vessel.**

space for labour-saving items such as table saws, bench drill presses and even lathes.

The easiest option for this is a 'Tow-a-Van'-type trailer, which can be fitted out with workbenches, power tools and storage. Much of the capital cost of buying a trailer can be recovered by selling it at the end of the project, although fitting out an inexpensive old caravan in a similar manner might reduce the upfront costs. Similarly, the cost of parking the trailer in a boatyard is often recouped through finishing the project more quickly.

Creating a shelter

Unless the boat is in a shed it is also worth spending time building a decent shelter around it. In hot climates this will give protection from the sun, allowing you to work

more energetically, and in the case of wooden boats help to prevent them drying out too much. In cooler regions a shelter will keep the rain off and the wind out, and allow the work area to be heated in cold weather. Another alternative, if using staging,

is to build a shed on a scaffolding platform – this has the advantage of the workshop being on the same level as your work, which can save an enormous amount of time.

For a smaller project, it's possible to create a portable yet practical workstation based around a folding workbench, which can even be set up on deck if necessary. Transporting tools to and from your boat can, however, be a headache – it's all too easy to find you've left a crucial item at home – so it pays to keep them well organised. Fortunately, large toolboxes on wheels are now readily available, and this makes it much easier to travel with a complete set of tools, and even by public transport if necessary.

Above **Many raceboats use containers or trailers as a workshop and a store – ideal when close to hand and properly organised.**

Above **For a big project it's worth building a freestanding and all-encompassing shelter that can double as a workshop.**

Hull and deck repairs

Fibreglass skills

Most modern boats are built of fibreglass – Glass Reinforced Plastic (GRP) – a polyester resin strengthened with closely packed strands of glass. This type of construction makes a damaged hull very simple to repair because the materials bond easily, are fairly cheap and are very forgiving.

The ability to work effectively with resin is very important, but the skills are easy to acquire. With a little experience, a DIY enthusiast can make an invisible repair and make the structure stronger in the process. The materials are widely available from a number of trade and retail outlets, and practical courses, books and how-to DVDs are available from colleges and resin suppliers.

Resin
Polyester resins are 'pre-accelerated' so they slowly cure after manufacture, and have a finite shelf-life of around six months to a year. When you want to use the resin, a catalyst is added to increase the curing time to around half an hour.

Gel coat
Gel coat is a clear resin that can be infused with a pigment to form a coloured outer layer to a hull or moulding. Flow-coat, or topcoat, is another polyester resin that can be used to line the insides of lockers with a smooth, wipe-down coating. A little styrene wax is added to help the curing process.

Below **The outer skin of a GRP boat is made of a layer of coloured gel coat that can fade with age. Here, it is being restored with the application of a mild abrasive treatment.**

Above **Catalyst is added to resin to produce the basic ingredient. Make sure you only mix as much as you need.**

SAFETY

Splashes of polyester resin will sting exposed skin and could damage unprotected eyes. When handling resins, especially neat catalyst, always cover up with old clothes or overalls, and wear eye protection and gloves.

Reinforcement

The most common reinforcement material used is chopped strand mat (CSM), which is available in various thicknesses and quantified by weight (grams per square metre). It cuts easily with a sharp knife or scissors, but being only loosely bound can fall apart easily. Tape and cloth reinforcements are stronger and hold their shape better, so are more effective for some applications such as seams. All reinforcement material is designed to soak up the activated resin and provide structure when it sets.

Gel coat and flow-coat

Two layers of gel coat are usually painted onto the inside of a pre-waxed mould and the reinforcement material is then laid up behind it. Flow-coat is simply painted on as a thick layer of resin. Both are activated in the same way as ordinary resin except a higher percentage (usually 2 per cent) of catalyst is used, and it is applied at about the thickness of a business card. The second layer of gel coat should be applied when the first is tack dry.

Activating the resin

✪ Decant as much resin as you can safely use in half an hour.

Above **The cloth is 'wetted out' with activated resin, and a consolidation roller is used to force out any air bubbles.**

✪ Carefully measure out the recommended percentage of catalyst (usually 1 per cent) by volume, and pour it into the resin.

✪ Mix thoroughly, and use immediately – especially in warm weather when the curing time will probably be faster than usual.

Wetting out

This involves saturating the cloth with activated resin and using a disposable brush or roller to work it in. Sometimes the cloth is wetted out on a plastic sheet and then carried to the hull, but usually the dry material is placed where it is needed before the resin is applied.

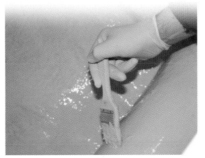

Above **Flow coat is resin mixed with pigment, styrene and wax. It behaves like thick paint, and sets into a hard, wipe-down finish.**

Above **By adding a bulking agent such as silica and microballoons, resin can be made into a thick paste, which can be sculpted.**

Filleting

Resin can be used as a glue to join two surfaces together and also, with a bulking agent, can be used to form a cove-shaped fillet along seams or corner joints. Epoxy resin is far more adhesive than polyester resin, but both can be used for filleting. To do this:

✪ Activate a small batch of resin and then add the bulking agent – colloidal silica, microfibres or microballoons – until the mix is the consistency of peanut butter.

✪ Run the mix along the two surfaces that need to be joined together or bulked out, preferably after they have been pre-wetted with activated resin. Allow to cure.

Impact & surface damage

Repairs to gouges and blisters can normally wait until a convenient time. However, impact damage, unless it is very minor, will need to be repaired quickly to prevent further damage or even loss of the boat.

Gouges

Gouges that don't penetrate beyond the gel coat are purely cosmetic, and their repair may be delayed to any convenient time. Repair is carried out using gel coat filler as described in the panel opposite.

To prevent water penetrating the lay-up, gouges that penetrate into the reinforced layers should be treated as soon as possible by applying an polyester filler to the gouge. When convenient, remove enough of the surface layer of the polyester repair so that gel coat filler can be applied, then finish and polish as outlined on pages 30 and 31.

Blisters

Blisters normally occur because of some form of hydraulic pressure under the gel coat. They can be an early indication of osmosis – particularly if located near or below the waterline – but may just be caused by an accumulation of solvent in the lay-up. If the blister is small and isolated, grind it out and treat it as a void, as explained on pages 30 and 31.

Below **Sometimes shallow scratches can be polished out using a polishing mop and cutting paste.**

Impact damage

The impact damage will need to be ground away, and it is likely that the inside surface will require reinforcement, so gain access to the inside of the structure to assess the damage. This may require some internal structure or fittings to be removed. The more that's removed, the easier it will be to carry out the repair and to finish it off so that it's invisible from the inside. Then proceed as follows:

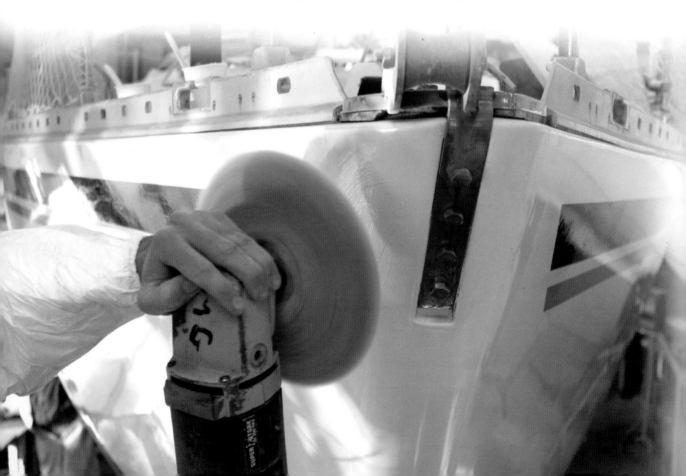

✪ Grind away any damaged lay-up, ensuring that no distressed structure remains.

✪ Chamfer the lay-up so that the layers can be built up gradually. If you chamfer on the inside, there will be a smaller area to fair in.

✪ Clean inside and out with acetone.

✪ Lay up some glass mat on the inside to make a reinforcing layer.

✪ When this layer is stiff, lay up extra layers, each over an area about 2in (50mm) wider than the previous layer. Leave overnight.

✪ On the outside, use a straight edge to ensure that none of the reinforcement is within about 0.25in (6mm) of the finished surface; grind a little away if it is.

✪ Fill the surface until it's just proud of the finished surface, and allow to cure.

✪ Grind the surface back and fill with gel coat, mixing some wax into it, or it won't dry in contact with the air.

✪ Rub down with wet and dry sandpaper used wet to fair the surface, compound it, then polish with wax polish.

✪ Finish the inside with gel coat to complete the repair.

Filling scratches and gouges

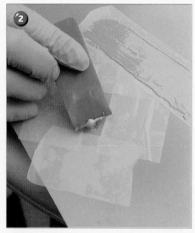

These gouges need to be filled, so first remove any loose or flaking material with a gouge or small grinder.

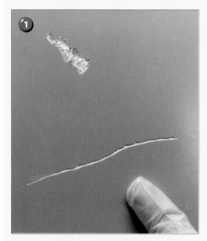

Mask up the area, mix the gel coat filler, and apply with a spatula, ensuring that the filler stands proud of the surface.

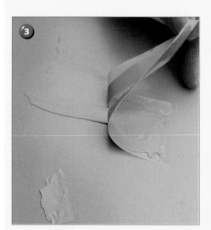

Peel off the masking tape before the gel coat has cured. The raised patches are clearly visible in the picture.

Grind the area flat, refilling if necessary. Then cut and polish the area as described on pages 30 and 31.

Cracks, voids & crazing

Small cracks in fibreglass may be no more than cosmetic blemishes, but it is also possible that they may indicate a part of the structure that is under too much stress. If the latter is the case, then the cause of the overstressing needs to be removed.

Stress cracks and crazing

Cracks may be caused by an overloaded structure, as well as flexing due to normal use. Once the cause of the cracking has been determined and (if necessary) removed, the cracking itself can be tackled in this manner:

- Use a small, high-speed rotary drill with a small engraving cutter to open up the cracks. Ensure that you get to the bottom of the cracking – usually this will mean drilling all the way to the bottom of the gel coat.
- Drill a small diameter hole 0.04in (1mm) at the extremity of each crack. This acts as a stress relief to stop the crack spreading.
- Clean the area with acetone.
- Mask around the area with masking tape.
- Fill the opened-up cracks with gel coat filler.
- Once cured, rub down with 'wet and dry' abrasive paper used wet, starting with 240 grade and finishing with 600 grade on a sanding block. (The masking tape is there to limit the abrasion to the area being repaired.)
- Refill and rub down again if necessary, until the area is completely smooth.
- Remove the masking tape.
- Cut the surface with a finishing compound to make it smooth.
- Polish with a good wax polish.

Above & left **These stress cracks indicate that some below-deck strengthening is required before making the repair.**

Filling voids

Voids are sometimes found at angles in a moulding, usually because an air bubble has been trapped during lay-up. To fix the problem:

- ✪ Use a small, high-speed rotary drill with a small engraving cutter to open up the void, ensuring that all loose material is removed and the whole void is exposed.
- ✪ If the void is large, fill it with polyester resin.
- ✪ Remove excess resin with the rotary tool and cutter.
- ✪ Fill with gel coat filler.
- ✪ Rub down the filler to make a smooth, faired surface. If the void is in a corner with a tight radius, you may need to wrap the wet and dry sandpaper round a suitably sized dowel in order to be able to rub down.
- ✪ Polish the area with compounding paste, and then wax polish.

Colour matching the gel coat

Matching the colour of the gel coat can be difficult, even if it's white, because there are many different tints and shades. Some boatbuilders have their standard colours and they may supply matching gel coat. Some resin suppliers have gel coat colour-matching kits available (for various hues), but it's a trial and error exercise to get a good match. Thin crack repairs don't need as good a match as a larger area.

Treating gel coat cracks

The gel coat needs to be ground out all the way down to the laminate and small holes drilled at the end of each crack before you start filling.

Fill the cracks with gel coat filler of the appropriate colour. Use masking tape to protect any adjacent woodwork or metal fittings.

When cured, rub down the filler with a fine grade abrasive paper used with water. Check the gel coat filler is flush, and refill if necessary.

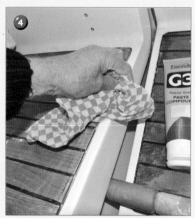

When the gel coat is completely flush, cut back with cutting paste to bring back the gloss. Finish off with polish, unless it's a surface which is going to be stood on.

Treating osmosis & delamination

Early onset of osmosis indicates either poor build quality or shoddy materials and, unsurprisingly, it is generally considered a catastrophic event. Nor is the treatment cheap – but if it is done properly, the boat will probably end up better than it was to begin with.

Above **Until you explore further, it's impossible to tell if this is paint blistering or osmotic blistering.**

Below **Osmosis isn't the death sentence it once seemed. This yacht has been treated and repainted and looks as good as new.**

What is osmosis?

Gel coat is not completely waterproof, so water molecules can diffuse through it to the GRP lay-up. If voids are present in the lay-up, the moisture dissolves any compounds in the building resin that have not cured properly, expanding the cavities. These show up as blisters on the surface. In extreme cases, with many voids, large areas of the hull can be severely weakened and can lead to structural failure.

Diagnosis of osmosis

High readings from a moisture meter alone are not a clear indication of osmosis. Fibreglass hulls will always absorb moisture, but osmotic blisters will only occur if the resin hasn't cured properly. If a blister is pierced and the emerging liquid smells vinegary, osmosis is strongly indicated. Ideally, an experienced boat surveyor should be engaged to diagnose the complaint and prescribe suitable treatment.

Localised blisters

Small blisters can be ground out and washed with clean fresh water to remove any contaminants. Ensure that all areas of any delamination are removed back to sound lay-up. Once fully dry, the void can be filled with epoxy filler and the area finished off as detailed on pages 28 and 29.

Treating large areas of the hull

The gel coat will first need to be removed, and this is most easily achieved using an electric gel-plane. Practice is required to ensure that only the gel coat is removed and no deep gouges occur. This will expose the blisters and areas of delamination, which must then be ground back to sound lay-up. If too much material has to be removed, a new lay-up will be required and professional advice should be sought.

Having removed all suspect areas of lay-up:

○ Thoroughly wash all the ground-back areas with fresh water. Steam cleaning is even better, as it will dissolve and remove any

remaining residues and their by-products. This needs to be done as soon as possible after grinding back.
○ Allow the old lay-up to dry. This process can be accelerated by using infra-red heating. The aim is to get a moisture content as similar as possible to the unaffected parts of the hull, so you'll need to regularly monitor

Above **A moisture meter is used to measure the moisture content of the laminate. This can be compared with a dry part of the hull.**

the hull's moisture readings using a moisture meter.
○ Prime with two coats of epoxy primer.
○ Fill and fair with an epoxy filler, sand, and refill any low spots. Continue until the surface is completely fair, checking with a long straight edge (fairing board).
○ Prime all the refinished area with an antifouling primer, and then antifoul.

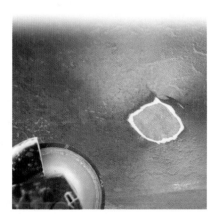

Above **This blister was confirmed to be osmotic, so has been ground out to remove all the damaged lay-up.**

Above **Once the lay-up is dry and free of any remaining traces of solvent, it can be filled and sanded smooth.**

Core damage

Many modern production boats are built using a sandwich construction, which usually consists of a layer of foam, plywood, honeycomb or balsa wood between two skins of fibreglass. This makes a yacht very light and strong, but also more difficult to repair. However, it's not beyond the ability of a competent DIY enthusiast.

Lightweight sandwich construction tends to be favoured for fast cruisers and racing yachts, as well as some powerboats. The most common sandwich material used is 'end grain' balsa core, so named because it is made up of hundreds of finely cut balsa squares. These squares are orientated in a sheet so that the end grain of the wood is exposed to readily soak up resin.

If the outer skin of the boat is fractured, or a deck fitting works loose and leaks, then the balsa core can soak up water, which may lead to a spongy feel to the hull and possible delamination.

When faced with major hull damage, it is very important to first determine the full extent of the core's saturation. If the crack has gone untreated for a while, the amount of saturation could extend well beyond the immediate impact site, and the balsa core may be rotten over a wide area. Some older trailable motorboats have a foam core to the cockpit sole that, over time, can soak up water, adding weight and leading to structural

Below **Once the core has been replaced (see panel opposite), the outer skin can be re-bedded and any unnecessary holes filled.**

TIP

If the inner hole is inaccessible a flexible backing plate can be made out of three layers of glass cloth wetted out in epoxy. To do this:

- ✪ Make a pattern for the backing plate that is slightly larger than the inner hole.
- ✪ Cut the biaxial cloth to shape and then add a self-tapping screw in the centre. Attach a wire to this screw.
- ✪ Clean the inside of the hole as far as you can. Wet it out with activated epoxy. Add thickened epoxy to the backing plate, and slip it inside the hull.
- ✪ Position it over the hole and then pull it up tight with the wire. The screw can be removed once the epoxy has cured.

Repairing core damage

Cut out the affected area using a jigsaw or router and lift off the GRP skin.

Scrape or chisel out all the damaged core back to firm dry material.

Repair any damaged areas of the inner skin using mat and resin.

If plywood is used instead of foam, shallow cuts on one side will make it easier to bend.

Spread thickened resin on the inner skin and the bottom face of the core sections.

Bed each section level with its neighbour, using weights to keep it all in place.

failure. To fully investigate, open up the outermost skin around the damaged area and see how far the saturation extends. You may find yourself replacing a much larger area than the damage suggests. The good news is that core material is relatively inexpensive and repairs are fairly simple to do.

Repairing damage to the core

✿ Use a router to open up the hole on the outside of the hull as far as the outer limit of the damage. Make sure the router doesn't penetrate the hull's inner skin.

✿ Dig out the damaged core and clean the area with a solvent wipe. Then, using a grinder, open out a bevel to a ratio of 12:1.

✿ Cut out a new piece of balsa core that will fit tightly in the hole and soak with wetted epoxy resin. Add thickened resin to the underside and push into position.

✿ Clean up the bevel, wet out, and then build up the laminate with about six layers of resin and biaxial cloth. The widest layer should go onto the balsa first.

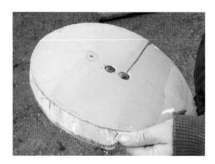

Above **A section of a balsa sandwich hull, cut out for a bow thruster tunnel. Note the two GRP skins, the end grain balsa, and how the thickness can be tapered.**

Resealing the hull to deck joint

On most fibreglass production boats the hull and deck are moulded separately and then sealed together. Occasionally, this important joint can fail, allowing water ingress and causing the deck to actually lift away from the hull. Repairs involve remaking the seal and mechanically strengthening the joint.

There are several ways that a production boat's hull and deck mouldings can be joined together, and some are more effective than others. The strongest joints involve using two flanges – one on the deck moulding and another on the hull. These are usually at right angles to the hull, either inwards or outwards, and are liberally covered with an adhesive sealant before being clamped together. The flange is then through-bolted to ensure that there is no movement and, as a final seal, a layer of fibreglass is sometimes laid up inside the boat between the two joints. On the outside, the joint is usually hidden behind a rubber or wooden fender strip. Another method is for the joints to overlap like the lid on a coffee jar, with the joint through-bolted from the side.

These joints tend to fail where fittings have been installed, in areas where not enough sealant has been applied, or if the bolts (or sometimes self-tapping screws) lose their grip due to the constant flexing of the hull. Occasionally, the deck can literally be pulled up off the hull by the running rigging, allowing water to run into the hull when the joint is immersed.

Below **Attaching a rubber fender belt to a hull to deck joint. The rubber fender has been immersed in hot water to make it more pliable.**

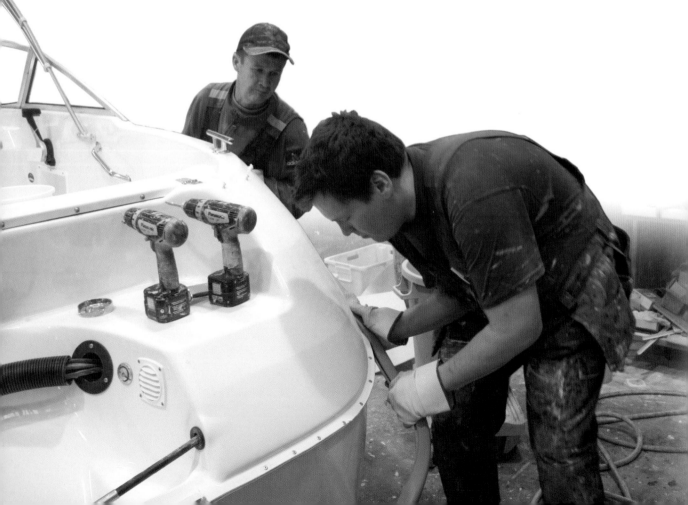

Repairing joint failures

❂ First identify where the water is actually coming in. This can be done by heeling the boat over to immerse the gunwale, or by blasting the area with a hose or pressure washer. Check that the leak isn't due to another fault, such as a leaking stanchion post, window or deck fitting.

❂ Remove the fender strip to expose the joint. You may see an obvious gap or, if the joint is accessible from inside the boat, you may see daylight through the gap.

❂ Prise open the joint as far as possible by removing screws or bolts. Clean any grime or loose sealant from the surfaces. Using a fine nozzle on a sealant gun inject adhesive sealant liberally, push it in with a spatula and then clamp down with mole grips or G-cramps. Wipe off any excess sealant before it dries.

❂ Drill new holes and either pop rivet, screw or bolt new corrosion-resistant fastenings (stainless steel or monel) through the flange. Bear in mind how the fender strip will be reattached as fixings that stand too proud may interfere with it.

Repairing a damaged bulkhead

Once the fendering has been removed, drill out any surviving rivets.

Thoroughly clean out the join, and ensure it is dry so the sealant adheres properly.

Using a chisel or wooden wedge, prise the flange open and apply the sealant.

Clamp the join together, clean up excess sealant, and refasten with screws or bolts.

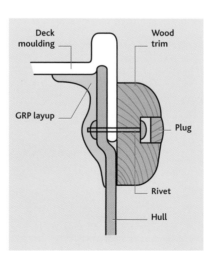

Above **The overlapping hull/deck joint.**

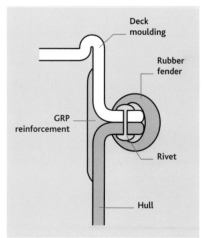

Above **The flange hull/deck joint.**

Moulding from a sister ship

Even a hole the size you can walk through in the side of a yacht can be repaired invisibly – which is just as well seeing as racing yachts regularly T-bone each other in the heat of competition! The trick here is to use a sister ship as a mould for the replacement section of hull.

Most modern production yachts of a class are built from the same set of moulds. It stands to reason, therefore, that they are all pretty much identical in terms of size and shape. If a large hole is punched in the side of a boat then it is usually possible to repair it by either laying up a new section using the production moulds, or by taking a mould from a sister ship.

First, the damaged boat is craned ashore and carefully supported so it won't distort, because a big hole can compromise structural integrity. The interior furniture in the vicinity of the damaged area is carefully stripped out, so that it can be reassembled after the repair is complete. The hole is then enlarged with a jigsaw and/or grinder until all of the stress cracks have been removed – this may result in it being considerably larger than the original area of impact damage. The area is then cleaned and the inside of the hull around the wound is ground back to a shallow bevel. The ratio should be around 12:1.

Find a donor

The hull is now ready for its donor mould and, once one has been located, the measurements of the damaged section are transferred to the corresponding area on the sister ship or production mould. This area is polished with release wax before gel coat is laid on top, followed by several layers of fibreglass and reinforcing batons. Once cured, the mould is removed and the donor yacht cleaned of wax.

TIP

Even quite obscure models of boat may have an owners' association, which may have members in your area who would be happy to lend their hulls as donors. Alternatively, the original moulds may still be in use. The section mould is best taken with the vessel out of the water, an obvious necessity if the damage goes below the waterline.

Above **This boat fell off a lorry on a motorway and sustained a great deal of impact damage and crazing. A write-off?**

Above **Not at all! The GRP repair specialist ordered a new section from the production mould, and grafted it in.**

The inside of the mould is then coated with release wax and carefully positioned over the damaged section. Gel coat is laid up against it from inside the boat, followed by several layers of a reinforcement material such as chopped strand mat or woven rovings that extends along the recessed area to give additional strength. The choice of resin depends on what finish is selected. Gel coat will adhere better to polyester resin; if the hull is to be painted, however, epoxy will create a stronger (if more expensive) repair.

Once the internal repair has cured the interior furniture can be refitted The mould is then removed, and the hull gently abraded before colour matching to the rest of the boat.

Left **If a boat is new, the production moulds may still be available from which a section can be cast. If not, the owner will need to find a sister ship to mould from – not a problem if the model was popular.**

The sister ship mould method

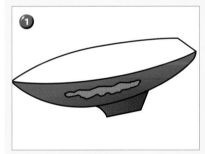

1 The first stage is to remove the internals from the hull in the vicinity of the hole, and check the extent of the damage.

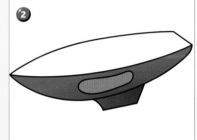

2 Using an angle grinder, the edges of the hole are cut back to sound substrate, and the inside skin is feathered back to a 12:1 bevel.

3 The measurements are transferred to the donor hull, which is taped, waxed, and laid up with gel coat followed by reinforcement.

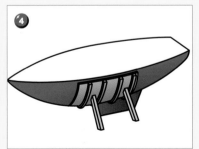

4 Once cured, the mould is placed over the same area of the damaged hull. The repair is then laid up from the inside.

Cutting & polishing after repairs

It is possible to make a fibreglass repair completely invisible, either by repainting the hull or by the more tricky method of gel matching and then cutting back. The latter method is more difficult, and therefore tends only to be undertaken by professionals, but the results can be staggering.

As we have seen, repairs to a fibreglass boat are relatively straightforward but hiding them afterwards is more complex. The main problem is that the materials used for making repairs don't always match the hull colour. 'White' gel coat, for example, isn't pure white. It can have all sorts of subtle shades in it, from yellow to blue grey or even red. Coloured or pigmented gel coats can also fade over the years and become chalky or blotched.

So, how do you make your repair invisible? The simplest way is to make sure the repair is completely flush, before lightly abrading the hull and then repainting it with

a tough two-pack paint system. Alternatively, you can have the hull professionally sprayed to get a superb, mirror-like finish. Repainting, of course, will give you the chance to completely change your boat's colour scheme.

Matching gel coat

If you want to preserve the original gel coat, you will have to 'gel match' its colour. First, polish the hull to reveal the true colour of the original gel coat around the repair. Use a variable-speed polisher and an increasingly fine series of cutting compounds to cut back the oxidised and contaminated outer layer of gel coat.

If you're filling a relatively small gash or scratch, the trick is to add pigment to the new gel coat so it will blend in to the surrounding hull. For

Above **White is never white, so for a correct colour match small amounts of one or more pigments have to be added.**

the more popular shades of blue, red or yellow, you can buy pigment kits, consisting of three pots of colour of different intensities. These are gradually added to clear gel coat (to a maximum ratio of 20 per cent) until you have the right shade. With white gel coat, the colour matching is more tricky, and most boatowners – especially those with newer yachts – tend to call in professionals.

Below **A professional gel coat specialist will carry a whole pallet of coloured pigments to effect a proper colour match.**

Right **The gel is applied in a stippling motion with a brush, and is left slightly proud of the hull so it can be abraded back.**

However, if you have an artist's eye for colour, you can still do the job yourself using a 'pallet' of several different pigments.

The repair procedure is the same for all colour matching:

✪ To find the correct match, start by experimenting with small samples of uncatalysed gel coat with minute amounts of pigment added. Smear these thumbnail-sized samples onto the gel coat near the repair and compare them for tint. You will need to keep a careful record of the pigment ratios so that you can replicate them when you make the final repair.

✪ Once you know the ratios (eg two dabs of red, one of blue), wipe off the samples with a clean cloth, and extrapolate the ratios to make two identical batches of coloured gel coat.

✪ Mask off the area outside the repair, and then apply the coloured gel coat with either a brush for small repairs, or with a spray gun to larger areas.

✪ When the gel coat has cured, remove the masking tape, sand back any protruding lips, and go over the whole area with a compounding system. This will flatten back the build-up of colour-matched gel coat, and give the hull a brilliant shine.

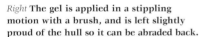

Above **Tiny amounts of pigment are mixed with uncatalysed samples of white gel coat on the hull to achieve the correct shade.**

Above **Once cured, the gel coat is abraded back before being polished for an invisible, colour-matched repair.**

Rudder damage

Although rudders are relatively vulnerable to impact damage, it's usually water ingress through poor seals or splits in the laminate that leads to corrosion of the metal tangs. This could potentially result in a loss of steering – usually, of course, when you need it most.

Most fibreglass rudders are made in the same way. A stainless steel stock has a series of three or four horizontal extensions called tangs welded to it. These form the skeleton of the rudder and exert internal force on the blade. Around this skeleton is the blade itself, which is usually made from two hollow sections of fibreglass and foil-shaped for efficiency. The tangs are bonded to the fibreglass skin, and then the voids are filled with expanded foam.

This arrangement usually works well, but over time water can find its way into the structure through the joint where the rudder shaft enters the blade. Impact damage on the leading edge of the rudder can also create leaks. This water will be soaked up by the foam and might cause corrosion of the stainless steel. Eventually one or more of the tangs will part from the stock and the rudder may begin to flop around on the shaft.

Temporary repairs are almost impossible, so the rudder assembly has to be removed from the boat. Ideally the fibreglass skins are preserved, but sometimes the damage is so bad that a new moulding is required.

Repairing a water-saturated rudder

⚙ Remove the rudder from the boat (see page 44) and drill a series of holes at the base to drain out the water. A clean cut should be made along the leading and trailing edges so the rudder can be split open with the two halves intact. Once open, the full extent of the damage can be assessed.

⚙ Check the tangs, especially where they enter the shaft, and renew if necessary. Reattach them to one of the fibreglass skins via a series of built-up layers of epoxy mixed with filler. These should then be glassed over for an even tighter seal.

(see page 44)

TIP

If you don't feel your boat is responding to the helm as well as it should, it may be worth checking whether your rudder could be modified to make it more efficient. Depending on its design, it could also be made self-balancing or deeper for more grip in a following sea. Blade area can also be increased. Manufacturers, owners' clubs or surveyors may be able to offer you some advice. Rudders are prone to osmosis, and this can be treated at the same time as any repair work or modifications are made.

Below left **This rudder has suffered from water ingress. An angle-grinder with a cutting disc was used to cut the rudder in half, revealing disintegrating foam and pools of water inside.**

Below right **The same rudder after a full repair.**

Above **Most modern rudders are made of a hollow fibreglass foil filled with foam. Metal vangs transfer the turning motion.**

✪ Fill the void with expanding foam and, when cured, grind back to create a level surface.

✪ Coat the fibreglass skin and the expanded foam with thickened epoxy. Join the two skins together using cramps and weights to ensure an even bond.

✪ Leave the epoxy to cure before fairing the blade back and coating it with epoxy. Finally, prime, antifoul and refit the rudder.

Above **With all the foam removed, this section of the foil has been placed back in a mould, which will make rebuilding easier.**

Above **The void is filled with thickened fibreglass instead of foam which will make the rudder less prone to water ingress.**

Replacing rudder bearings

Rudder bearings don't have an infinite life and should be checked for wear annually. They are generally easy and inexpensive to replace, providing the work is planned in advance.

Rudder bearings are usually made from a hard engineering plastic such as Delrin, although on older boats Tufnol may have been used originally. A degree of wear is inevitable over time, especially on well-used boats and ones where the steering isn't lashed or locked off when the boat is left on its mooring.

On tiller-steered boats, worn rudder bearings often become apparent at a relatively early stage – it will be possible for the helmsman to feel the play, and possibly even to see movement at the head of the rudder shaft. However, it's a different matter for wheel-steered vessels. On these, worn rudder bearings may not become apparent until wear is excessive.

The condition of the bearings can be checked with the boat chocked up in a boatyard by moving the bottom of the rudder blade from side to side. A small amount of play, up to $\frac{1}{16}$ in (1–2mm), is acceptable.

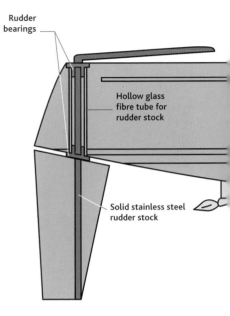

Rudder bearings

Hollow glass fibre tube for rudder stock

Solid stainless steel rudder stock

Dropping the rudder

Before starting work, discuss the best method of removing the rudder with the boatyard. In many cases, a yacht with a spade rudder will need to be lifted above a hard surface to gain the space needed to lower the blade and rudder shaft out of the boat. However, if the yard has an earth or gravelled surface it may be possible to dig a hole into which the rudder can be lowered.

Modern spade-type rudders are typically held in place with a two-part collet that prevents the rudder stock from sliding downwards. Before this is removed, the rudder blade must be supported so that it can be lowered gently to the ground.

Left **Using ropes to control a rudder being lowered from a boat. Most of the weight of this foil is in the solid stainless steel stock at the front.**

Above **Unscrewing the two-part collet that holds the rudder in a boat with tiller steering.**

Right **The rudder replaced, and ready for antifouling, with the black new lower bearing visible.**

Most spade rudders have a solid stainless steel rudder shaft – don't underestimate the weight of this, or the need to support the front of the rudder blade. Conversely, the relatively small rudders of most motorboats make this part of the operation much easier.

Long-keel boats

The process for removing the rudder is slightly different if it's mounted on a skeg or long keel – it may need to be lifted off the pintles, or have the bottom pintle unbolted from the skeg or keel.

Fitting the new bearings

Once the rudder has been removed, the rudder stock and its shaft can be measured with a Vernier gauge to determine the exact internal and external diameter of the bearings (see page 170), which can then be made up by an engineering workshop. New bearings should be coated lightly with a waterproof grease before fitting. The lower one is slid onto the rudder stock before replacing the rudder, while the upper one can normally be inserted once the foil has been lifted back into position.

Refitting the rudder is generally a reversal of removing it, although heavy spade rudders are inevitably more difficult to move upwards into the boat than to lower downwards. If this process is not done by the yard it's worth arranging for additional helpers to lend a hand if necessary at this stage.

Below **Looking downwards at the old top bearing as the rudder is dropped – the square head of the stock can be seen.**

Weeping keel

The ballast in a modern sailing yacht is usually made of cast iron, which is through-bolted to the hull. General wear and tear, as well as the occasional knock or grounding, can break the seal between the hull and the keel, and allow water in to start corroding the keelbolts. In worst case scenarios this may lead to the keel detaching.

Yachts and motorsailers usually have some kind of 'deep' ballast in the form of a metal keel. In performance yachts this will often be a metal fin with a bulb of lead on the bottom. Even traditional long-keel wooden yachts will have a large piece of iron or lead physically bolted to the bottom of the keel, which also gives protection when grounded.

The substantial bolts (or studs) that secure the keel on most modern boats are made of high quality steel and are well sealed, but over time the seal can be compromised. Once salt water has access to the bolts it will gradually corrode them and, if left too long without intervention, the bolts could fail completely. With fin-keeled yachts, a hard grounding or impact with a semi-submerged object can also break the seal, and even punch the trailing edge of the keel into the hull.

Bilge-keelers have the additional problem that a great deal of weight is exerted laterally on the keels when they sit ashore.

Spotting problems

Keel problems reveal themselves with tell-tale rust streaks from the keel to hull joint, which indicate the bolts are corroding. On traditional vessels it's common practice to occasionally 'draw' a keelbolt to check for 'waisting'.

Below **Attaching a fin keel. The suspended boat is lowered gently down onto the protruding bolts of its refurbished keel.**

TIP

Checking the keelbolts as soon as corrosion is detected could be a lifesaver. If you intend to check your bolts, ask the boatyard to prop your boat up well clear of the ground during your annual haul out. This is important for long-keel yachts, which have particularly long bolts that draw downwards. If your boat has hit a submerged object, it is well worth a lift out to check the area around the keel base for damage.

Left **Rust streaks around the keel-to-hull join are an indication that the keel bolts are waisting, and investigation is required.**

Right **A bilge keel can be partially detached, in this case to aid an impact damage repair to the hull at the keel's trailing edge.**

While both ends may appear intact, the corrosion is usually taking place in the middle (the waist), where the keel joins the hull.

Dropping the keel

When removing a keel, the usual procedure is to lift the boat away from it. The boat is supported by a crane or travel hoist, with the keel positioned over a special high-load hydraulic trolley. Locate the through-hull bolts in the bilge, and remove the nuts with a large spanner. The boat is then slowly raised to ease it clear of the keel, although some gentle persuasion using flat blades is often needed to break the keel-to-hull seal. For quick repairs, the keel can then be supported just clear of the hull, with the bolts only partly exposed to aid reattachment.

Checking the keelbolts

✪ With the keel removed it is possible to inspect the studs. If they are badly corroded or distorted in some way they can be removed from the keel (sometimes with difficulty), and new ones inserted.

✪ When the keel is reattached the keel stub should be liberally coated with sealant, and masking tape placed around the top of the keel to catch the excess when the nuts are tightened. It always pays to use far more sealant than is required to guarantee that the water stays out.

Above **Being in the bilge, keel fastenings are prone to rust. These are the nuts and bolts of a bilge keel, with hefty backing plates.**

✪ Once the yacht has been lowered back onto its keel, add the spacers and nuts and tweak down diametrically to avoid distortion. Following relaunch, you should check the bilge regularly to ensure there is no water coming in around the freshly tightened nuts. It is also important to monitor the bilge when the yacht is sailed for the first time.

Above **The studs are screwed deep into the metal of the keel, making them difficult to extract if replacement is needed.**

Right **Underwater sealant is applied liberally to the flat of the keel join, with masking tape placed to catch the excess.**

Lifting keel problems

Few lifting keels involve complex mechanisms; however, an annual inspection, and replacement of any defective parts, is vital to ensure there's no risk of losing the keel.

The lifting mechanisms of older boats with lifting keels are often poorly maintained. If buying one, therefore, it's sensible to factor in an overhaul of the system, unless it's clear the vendor has been meticulous with this aspect of the boat's upkeep.

A number of types of lifting keel are fitted to yachts and dayboats, although most divide into either a centreboard that pivots upwards into the boat or a daggerboard-type keel that slides near-vertically until it's above the water. In both cases, it may be necessary to inspect the components with the boat ashore and the keel in the lowered position – never assume all the underwater elements can be inspected with the boat on its trailer or in its cradle.

Centreboard pivots are prone to both wear and corrosion so they should be removed and inspected every year. If daggerboard-type keels have a mechanism for locking the keel in place while sailing, this should also be inspected annually.

Lifting mechanisms

At their simplest, these are a block and tackle, which has the potential to be long lasting and reliable. But don't be tempted to skimp on inspections – chafe of the rope and corrosion of the shackle or attachment point on the keel are common problems that can cause a complete failure of the system. In any case, the rope should ideally be replaced every five years.

Above **All aspects of a lifting mechanism must be maintained in good order. This removable crane is very easy to access.**

A wire taken to a captive winch was a device fitted to many boats in the 1970s and early 80s. As well as examining the attachment points at each end, the condition of the wire should be checked annually. It should be replaced if there is any evidence of stranding, and it's also worth renewing it as a cautionary measure every ten years.

Hydraulic and electric systems

Hydraulic systems add an extra level of sophistication but are much easier to use, especially on larger craft. The level of the fluid in the reservoir should be checked weekly (or every time the boat is used) with the keel raised, as this is when the level in the reservoir is at its maximum. Any leak in the system needs to be investigated

Left **Lifting keels are used on a wide variety of boats, from traditional classics to some of the latest racing machines.**

Above **The centreboard slot is prone to becoming clogged with mud or gravel, especially on boats that are kept on a drying mooring.**

Below top **A pivoting centre-board type of lifting keel – the pivot bolt must be inspected for wear periodically.**

Below middle **A dagger-board style arrangement.**

Below bottom **Boats fitted with ballasted dagger-boards may need bearings inside the case to allow the board to slide smoothly.**

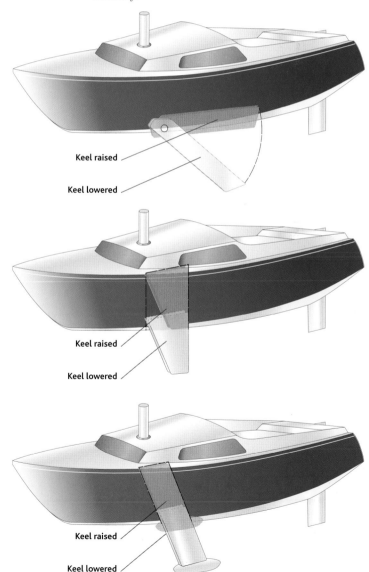

Keel raised

Keel lowered

Keel raised

Keel lowered

Keel raised

Keel lowered

and remedied. If the keel won't stay in its raised position but there are no external fluid leaks, this indicates a leaking seal around the hydraulic piston. The solution is to remove the piston, examine it for scoring, replace the seal and reassemble the unit, and then bleed any air out of the system. See page 146 for more on repairing hydraulic systems.

Some keels are also lifted via an electric motor, although this generally either drives a hydraulic ram or an electric winch. The motor will draw a large current, particularly when raising the keel, so ideally an extra battery should be placed near the unit. Electric cables should be oversized to minimise power loss through creating excess resistance, and the contacts kept clean.

Damaged bulkhead

Bulkheads are an integral part of the structure of most boats, whatever the construction of the vessel, but are prone to many different forms of damage.

Almost all bulkheads are made from marine plywood, so water saturation is the biggest source of problems. Deck leaks are by far the most common cause of water penetration – it's worth keeping a careful eye open for problems and dealing with them immediately by resealing fittings with a marine-grade adhesive sealant. In addition, the lower part of a bulkhead may start to rot if left exposed to bilge water for a long period.

Below **Bulkheads are prone to water damage from deck leaks, especially through chainplates.**

Water ingress

If a bulkhead has become wet, the first task is to allow it to dry, stripping varnish or paint as necessary to allow the timber to breathe. If the material is very wet between the fibreglass tabs that bond it to the hull, these may also need to be removed and then replaced once the timber is dry.

In extreme cases, there will be visible damage to an area of the timber indicating it is beyond repair, either because the glue holding the laminates together has failed or because there's clear evidence of rot. If there is, all the damaged wood should be removed at the start of the drying stage.

Use a moisture meter to monitor the drying of the timber – once it is in the 15 to 20 per cent range, check the bulkhead for damage. Tapping with a light hammer will reveal areas of sound wood – these will produce a clear ring, while damaged areas will return a dull thud. Damaged areas can then be cut out and new timber scarphed in to replace it, ideally bonded in place using epoxy adhesive.

Scarph joints should have an 8:1 taper to provide plenty of surface area for the adhesive to bond securely. If this is not feasible, you can glue on a plywood backing pad of the same thickness as the bulkhead, but overlapping each side of the join by around 4in (10cm) – although this may not be such a neat solution.

Veneered bulkheads

Many bulkheads have decorative veneers, which can be a problem if new timber needs to be scarphed in. If it's possible to source new wood with the same veneer, this will reduce the visual impact. Alternatively, particularly on an older vessel, it may be acceptable to paint the bulkhead.

Although skilled boatbuilders can successfully apply a new veneer to a bulkhead, this is something even the most skilled DIY boat-owner is likely to struggle with. A better solution is to re-face it with a very thin marine plywood (about ⅛in [3mm]) that has a suitable decorative veneer.

Loose bulkheads

On fibreglass boats, bulkheads are normally bonded to the hull, but this bond can fail, usually as a result of impact damage or compression of the boat if it has been rafted up alongside several others when moored.

The easiest way to remove the fibreglass on a bulkhead is with a hot air gun and paint scraper, being very careful not to allow the heat to linger too long in one area. If it's of sound condition, the fibreglass on the hull side can be left in place, therefore avoiding the possibility of weakening the hull structure by accidentally removing too much. However, before new fibreglass can be laid up any paint on the hull side must be removed.

Bulkheads should not directly touch the hull or deck – this is to avoid hard spots where stress is concentrated. Instead, a small gap is left, so that loads are spread over the full area of the fibreglass that bonds the bulkhead to the hull and deck.

Repairing a damaged bulkhead

Using a hot air gun to strip the fibreglass bonding a damaged section of bulkhead to the hull. Care is needed not to scorch the wooden panel.

Using a jigsaw to cut away damaged timber in a bulkhead. Sound material will give a clear note when tapped with a light hammer.

A new section of bulkhead clamped in place while the epoxy adhesive cures. A bulkhead adds considerably to the rigidity of a GRP hull.

Bonding the new timber to the hull to replace the original structural strength. Make sure the fibreglass cloth is thoroughly 'wetted out'.

Re-bedding loose fittings

Fittings that have to cope with a great deal of strain or lateral movement, such as cleats or eyebolts, can sometimes work loose. This is most common in decks of sandwich construction, where repairs to the core material may be needed to prevent water ingress and make the fitting secure again.

If a deck fitting has become loose, it's often a sign of problems within the core of the vessel. It could be that the sealant around the bolts has broken down and that water has seeped into the core, which has made it spongy and caused the deck to lose some of its integrity. Alternatively it could be a lack of suitable backing plates, which means the cleat or bollard can be pulled upwards. If a fitting is loose, it's worth removing it for a full inspection. You may find that water drips out from the core when the bolts are removed, and this means you need to make a big repair to that area of deck.

Loose fittings are rare in un-cored decks but are usually due to excessive loading, which rips the fitting upwards and damages the fibreglass deck in the process.

Fittings that are going to take large loads should have very wide reinforcing plates underneath them. Although plywood is a good material,

Re-bedding techniques

1. If using studding for mounting the deck fitting, first cut each piece to the correct length.

2. Insert the studding into the fitting with a smear of sealant to lock each one in place and reduce inter-metal corrosion.

3. Mark and drill the holes for the fitting – unless it is to be refitted into the same position.

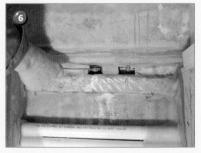

4. Apply a generous bead of sealant, which should ideally be polyurethane to ensure maximum sealing properties.

5. Place the fitting into position and make sure it is properly bedded down onto the sealant.

6. Moving inside, fit a backing plate or large washers then fit the nuts onto the studding and tighten them evenly in turn.

a pad of fibreglass, aluminium or even steel will make a much more solid base. Use wide washers beneath the bolts to spread the load.

Re-bedding fittings on a cored deck

Repairing a cored deck follows the same procedure as with a cored hull:

- Remove the offending fitting and check it over. Pay special attention to the bolts and backing plate.
- Check the deck itself for any core damage. A tell-tale sign will be water dripping out of the bolt holes, or a sponginess to the core material when probed. Check that the backing plate hasn't been pulled up into the deck.

Above **These fittings look secure enough, but the fastenings should be checked regularly to make sure they are tight.**

- Using a sharp, 90-degree implement, such as a dentist's probe, scoop out the damaged balsa wood or foam core as far as possible from any suspect holes. Vacuum out the scrapings.
- Seal up the lower hole with electrical tape, mix up some thickened epoxy resin and then pour it into the top of the hole until it is filled up completely. You may need to give it a second fill as the balsa wood may absorb some of the resin before it has cured.

TIP

Always over-engineer backing plates on deck fittings so as to spread the load more widely. Glassing the backing plates against the deckhead will also reduce the risk of movement.

- Carefully re-drill the bolt holes using the right drill for a tight fit. Smear sealant around the top of each hole before bedding the fitting down again. Consider enlarging the backing plate and using a more resistant material such as fibreglass, aluminium or steel.

Repairing teak-finished decks

Many fibreglass boats have teak planks laid on top of the GRP deck. In time the seams may open up and plugs may fall out, so some attention will be required to put things right.

How is a teak deck laid?

Strips of teak are bedded on top of the GRP deck using an adhesive. Some builders screw the strips down as well, and cap the screws with plugs. One side of each strip is rebated to half its depth, and the resultant grooves are filled with a flexible mastic.

What can go wrong?

If the owner repeatedly scrubs or pressure-washes the deck, this will remove the soft parts of the grain and the deck will become ridged. Teak decks should be cleaned with a soft brush or a kitchen scrubbing pad,

rubbed at right angles to the grain. The deck should be regularly doused in sea water to prevent it drying out.

Another problem is that the mastic can lose adhesion in the grooves, allowing water to penetrate the edges of the strips or even get underneath. Sometimes the wooden plugs over the screws become loose and fall out. This usually occurs because the strips are too thin in the first place or if the deck has been sanded, reducing its thickness and that of the plugs.

Below **A teak laid deck looks good but needs a lot of hard work and care to keep it in good condition.**

Above **Loose sealant should be replaced to prevent moisture getting underneath.**

Dealing with loose mastic in the seams

The loose mastic must be removed. How you do this depends on how much needs repairing. The aim is to remove the mastic without removing any wood. For small areas of loose material, it isn't worth making or buying a special tool just to rake out the mastic:

❂ Make a diagonal cut through the mastic a couple of inches (50mm) either side of the damaged area, using a very sharp hobby knife.

❂ Cut along the edge of the mastic with the hobby knife, taking care not to cut into the wood.

❂ Use a sharp chisel the same width as the groove. Hold it vertically, and drag it towards you to remove the old mastic.

For large areas of loose mastic, it will be worth making a raking tool or even buying an electric multi-function tool (the Fein MultiMaster Marine is expensive but versatile) with purpose-designed blades for cutting the mastic and raking out the grooves.

To make your own tool, bend a screwdriver blade at right-angles and sharpen the end. You can then pull it towards you to remove the mastic. You can do the same with a file tang, but in either case you will need to heat the tool with a blowlamp to be able to bend it.

Replacing wooden plugs

❂ Clean up the hole. An ordinary drill bit won't do, because the tip angle will prevent the bottom of the hole being cleaned. You'll need a 'spur point' bit to clean right to the bottom.

❂ As soon as possible after the hole has been cleaned, use acetone to degrease the surface.

❂ Use epoxy wood glue on the new plug, and push it into the hole. Align the plug's grain with that of the deck strip.

❂ When the epoxy is cured, trim to size and sand.

Replacing deck sealant

Make a diagonal cut across the seam at either end of the section to be replaced, and remove the old sealant.

Clean out the groove with a chisel, taking care not to damage the wood, and then clean up with acetone.

Slowly fill the groove with sealant, taking care not to create any air bubbles.

Smooth off with a palette knife and remove masking tape before sealant sets.

Leaking windows or hatches

Any hatch, window or vent in the superstructure of a boat has the potential to leak, but these leaks are usually quite easy to fix. Most commonly it is due simply to a failure of the rubber seal between the opening part of the aperture and the base it attaches to.

In 90 per cent of cases a leaking window or hatch simply needs new seals, and these are quite cheap to source. Of the remainder, there is sometimes a breakdown of sealant between the lower frame and the base and – very rarely – a gap will appear in the seal between the glazing and its supporting frame.

Some boats, especially river craft, are fitted with caravan-style sliding windows, and here multiple seals are used, including a soft, self-lubricating 'flocked' seal to allow the glass to slide. Some of these seals are similar to wiper blades on a car, and perform much the same function as the glass slides over them.

All watertight rubber seals will last for at least five years without any problems, but they can often be damaged by ultraviolet radiation, dirt and overcompression. Replacing a seal will usually cure the leak completely, and won't take long to do.

Replacing a seal on a window or hatch

✪ Identify where the water is finding its way in by dusting talcum powder all around the rubber seal, closing the hatch and

TIP

To prevent leaks in fixed windows that overlap an aperture, remove them and bed them down onto a strip of expanded neoprene. This is far more forgiving than sealant and allows for more distortion, as well as expansion and contraction. It may pay to source a better seal than the original if the hatch has been problematic for a while. A tubular seal with a void inside it can be compressed more readily.

Below **The foredeck hatch receives the most abuse, as not only does it catch the brunt of the waves, it is also stood on repeatedly by the foredeck crew.**

then spraying it with a hose. Mop up around the hatch to avoid a false result and then open it again. The leaking water will have left a track through the talcum powder.

❂ Before removing the seal, check with the window or hatch manufacturer that replacements are available. If not, specialist seal suppliers can often recommend a suitable alternative and can identify the right one from a sample.

❂ Hook the old seal out of the frame. If the seal is missing, or has broken down too far, either measure the recess with a vernier or make a cast using bits of Blu-Tack at strategic locations.

❂ Clean out the recess and then insert the new seal. No adhesive is necessary. Make sure the new seal won't be compressed beyond more than about 30 per cent of its depth, as it may not recover fully over a period of time.

❂ Hatches can sometimes become distorted, usually when a flat hatch has been screwed down too hard onto a curved surface, which makes any seal ineffective. Re-bed the entire hatch if this is the case (see page 58).

Replacing a hatch seal

Start by removing the old seal and cleaning up the frame. A sharp knife or chisel will get rid of most residue.

The new seal can then be laid in place. It should be a snug fit without having to be squeezed into place.

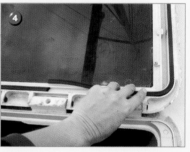

Make sure you have enough rubber to go around in one piece, to reduce the number of joins required.

Once the rubber is sitting snugly in the groove, cut the joint at the aft end of the hatch where it's less likely to leak.

A sharp knife is essential to achieve a neat joint – better to cut too long than too short!

The two parts should be a perfect fit, lying tight against each other. No adhesive is needed.

Replacing a hatch

Occasionally, replacing a hatch completely may be more cost effective than refurbishing it. This could be because the original design is just too dated, the catches have failed and are irreparable, or the frame is hopelessly twisted. Sourcing a similar-sized hatch will make replacement very straightforward.

Some older boats have unusual hatch sizes from long-defunct manufacturers, so before deciding to remove a hatch make sure a replacement is available. If you don't, you might find you have to change the size of the aperture.

However, you don't have to swap like for like. Buying a new hatch is a great opportunity to improve the looks and functionality of your boat. For example, you could opt for a low profile version, which would be less of a trip hazard – especially around the mast where you may need to

work the halyards. You can choose a hatch with a different colour of glass, acrylic or Perspex to reduce ultraviolet glare down below, or one strengthened with extra-large catches if venturing far offshore. Remember that you may need to do some structural modifications to your boat if significantly widening a hatch, or introducing one into a previously virgin area of cabin roof.

Finally, check how the hatch will open and what orientation you want. Most cruising folk favour a rearwards-opening hatch near the

foredeck, so that a breaking wave over the bow won't force it open. Some designs won't open flat onto the deck, which may cause a problem. Check the manufacturer's size chart carefully and remember the important measurement is the aperture size, not the frame size.

Below **Modern hatches add considerably to the look of a boat. Note how the main hatch opens aft, so a big wave slams it shut rather than filling up the forecabin.**

To replace a hatch

⊙ First, remove the retaining screws around the edge of the frame, and make a bridge out of old timber. Use a large G-cramp to hook under each corner of the frame in turn. If the frame won't budge, don't force it. Instead, slice into the sealant between the frame and the base with a thin, sharp blade, and then try again.

⊙ With the hatch removed, clean up the base. Remove the old sealant with a sharp blade and wash with solvent. Check the frame is still flat and build up again if necessary. Check the aperture is adequate for the new hatch, and use a jigsaw if it needs to be widened.

⊙ Dry fit the hatch using masking tape to denote the outer limits of the frame. Mark the masking tape and then trim the area inside the frame. The masking tape will catch the sealant when it is squeezed out. Apply sealant to the base of the frame, making sure you circle each screw hole.

⊙ Lower the hatch into position and then screw it down. To avoid distortion screw down gently and with diametrically opposed tension. Take care not to overtighten. When fully bedded down, peel back the masking tape to take the surplus wet sealant away.

TIP

Hatch surfaces can be slippery underfoot. There are a number of self-adhesive non-slip tapes that can be added to improve grip – including some transparent varieties.

Making a watertight seal

1 First check that the mounting surface is flat, otherwise the hatch frame will distort and leak when bolted down.

2 Remove the hatch from the frame for ease of fitting. Place the frame in position and drill the holes for the bolts. Check that the bolts fit the holes after drilling.

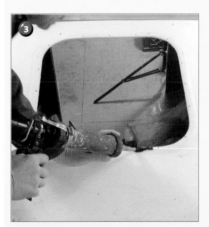

3 Remove the frame and clean the mounting area, then apply a generous bead of sealant. This may be either Silicone, polyurethane (such as Sikaflex) or non-setting mastic.

4 Fit the hatch frame and bolt it down. Clean off excess sealant using white spirit, methylated spirit or acetone. Fit the hatch back into the frame, and tap in the hinge pins.

Sheered or bent guardrails

Collisions with quaysides, other yachts or heavy crewmen pulling themselves up from the pontoon can easily damage or bend stanchion posts. If spare parts are available, though, repairs are relatively straightforward.

A lot is asked of stanchion posts, and the taller they are the more likely they are to get damaged. Most stanchions are made up of two components: a stanchion base, which is bolted to the deck, and the stanchion post, which drops into the base and is secured by a small grub screw. On small boats, the base and post may be a single unit welded together.

When a stanchion is bent, it's important to check how it has affected the base. A major knock may have bent the base over as well, and maybe even crazed the gel coat. In this case,

the base will need to be unbolted and the gel coat ground out and repaired. A new base can be bought if the original is too badly damaged.

If a stanchion post has been bent, it will usually occur near the base. A stainless steel tube bender can sometimes be used to straighten it. If that doesn't work, the damaged or kinked area can be cut off and a sleeve inserted. This ensures that the post is still the same height. Most chandlers, however, sell new stanchions and bases if repairs prove too difficult or costly.

TIP

Getting to the stanchion base nuts under the deck on some production boats can prove difficult due to bulkheads or furniture being in the way. It is therefore worth checking where all your bolts come through, and making an access panel in the furniture so you can access them.

Below **The taller the stanchions, the safer the crew will be – but this also makes the stanchions themselves more vulnerable.**

Above **Stanchions with a fixed base can be straightened by hammering the base back into shape on a hard surface.**

Right **This stanchion has been bent back but the base is intact, so the stanchion post can simply be removed and replaced.**

It pays to ensure the stanchion bases have a wide and thick backing plate to minimise the effects of lateral forces. Some owners also beef up the bases by adding an extra foot at 90 degrees to the deck to brace against sideways force.

Checking your stanchion bases

Stanchion bases are prone to leaks as the abuse they get can weakens the sealant between them and the deck. It is therefore important to regularly check the condition of your stanchion bases. To do this:

⊕ Remove the guard wires and undo the retaining screw at the base of the stanchion to withdraw the post from its base. Carefully check the base for damage, as well as the surrounding gel coat for signs of stress crazing.

⊕ The base itself can be removed by accessing the bolts under the deck. This is a good chance to review the size of the backing plate.

⊕ Stanchions on ferro-cement or steel boats may be substantial enough to be forced back into shape with a sledgehammer. Put a steel tube, such as part of a scaffold pole, over the post and either use it as a lever or strike it a few blows with a hammer.

⊕ Stanchion bases attached to a toe rail are trickier to repair because a whole section of toe rail may need replacing at the same time. If stainless steel bolts were used to secure an aluminium base to the toe rail, you might find the whole thing has welded itself together as a result of galvanic action (see page 62).

Above **This yacht has been smashed against a quayside, damaging the hull, the toe rail and the stanchion.**

Above **After repair. The toe rail and stanchion base had to be replaced, but the stanchion post was reused.**

Upgrading aluminium fittings

Many production boats were originally fitted with aluminium deck furniture such as cleats and bow rollers. Unfortunately, they are usually attached to the boat with stainless steel bolts or screws, and consequently suffer from corrosion over the years.

Aluminium fittings are lighter and cheaper than stainless steel ones, and often match the rest of the fittings and deck furniture such as spars, hatch frames and toe rails. They look very smart when new but, over time, galvanic action between the stainless steel bolts and the aluminium fittings will take place, causing corrosion and eventually locking the two metals together. As this happens, you will notice a white powder oxide around

the join of the dissimilar metals. The aluminium itself will also begin to pit and discolour, making it look tired. In extreme cases, the corrosion can lead to failure under load.

Although proper marine-grade 316 stainless steel is expensive, it will retain its good looks indefinitely. It is also harder wearing and, of course, fully compatible with marine-grade stainless steel bolts, so will not suffer from corrosion.

TIP

If you lightly coat the threads of stainless steel bolts with a non-metallic grease or zinc chromate paste, it will make them easier to undo at a later stage. It will also act as a barrier and help limit the effects of corrosion, especially if you are still using some aluminium fittings on deck.

Right **Cheaper production boats often have basic aluminium fittings. This one is being replaced with a much more functional, and striking, stainless steel bollard.**

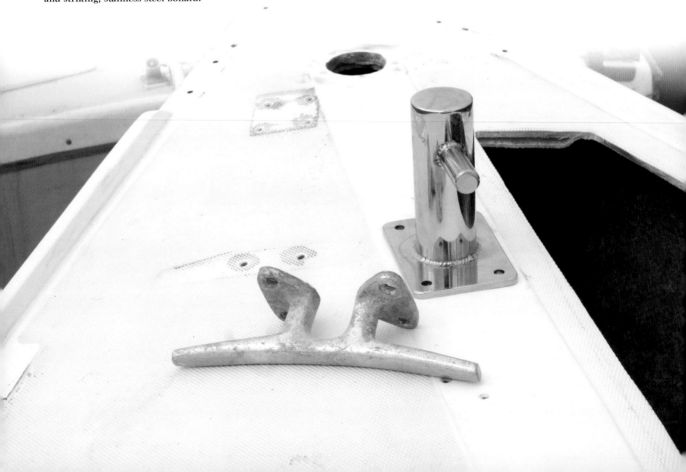

Above **A plywood backing plate. Note how the edges have been rounded off to allow for GRP reinforcement to be added.**

Left **The new cleat position is lightly marked with a drill, dead centre of the boltholes, prior to drilling through.**

During a refit, or at the same time as doing a repair, it is a good idea to swap old aluminium fittings for new stainless steel ones. Removing the fittings should be straightforward, although you might find the bolts have corroded firmly onto the body of the fitting. This can make removing them tricky, but if the nuts themselves come undone it shouldn't be too much of a problem as the whole assembly will pull vertically out of the deck. If not, the bolts may have to be cut off.

Replacing old fittings

✪ Remove the old fitting, allowing for the fact that the bolts may come away too. If the fitting is not too badly corroded, it may still have some value on the second-hand market, so it is worth trying to remove the bolts at a later stage.

✪ Reappraise the fitting's position, and consider replacing it with a more substantial fitting in stainless steel, especially if the yacht is to be used for long-distance cruising.

✪ Clean up the area and re-bed the fitting on polyurethane sealant, taking care to circle each bolt hole.

✪ Select a wide backing pad, either in wood, fibreglass or mild steel. Nyloc nuts, which have a nylon collar insert in them to increase friction between the screw and the nut threads, will prevent the fitting from vibrating loose if it is near an engine bay.

Right **To fill old screw holes, use a countersink drill to widen the screw holes, and then apply some epoxy filler. Stick some electrical tape on the other side to prevent the epoxy falling through.**

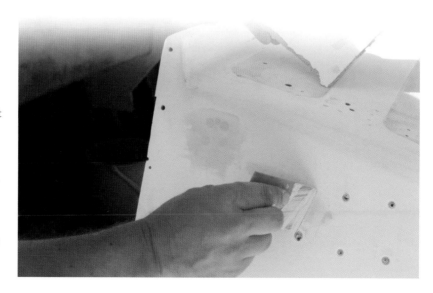

Refurbishing old fittings

Deciding to have a replacement metal fitting cast instead of fabricated is often a trade-off between several factors, namely weight, strength, shape and the number of items to be produced.

If you decide to have a new fitting cast, the process begins with making a pattern. You can use the existing metal fitting as a pattern although, if you do this, the new casting will be slightly smaller due to the shrinkage of the metal as it cools in the mould. However, this shouldn't be a problem for stand-alone items that do not have to conform to a strict set of dimensions. To turn an existing metal fitting into a pattern, simply fill the screw holes and eliminate any imperfections before applying a coat of pattern paint. This will ensure it can be easily released from the sand at the foundry.

If a new pattern has to be produced, it can be made from virtually anything, as Classic Marine's Moray MacPhail explains: 'A wide selection of materials can be used including wood, metal, plastic, MDF and even cardboard.' On completion, the pattern is sent to the foundry for casting.

When the new metal fitting is delivered, it will have a rough external appearance that is referred to 'as cast'. Although there is no practical reason to prevent it being used like this, most fittings are polished up using 80 to 240 grit on a belt polisher, followed by a further three 'cuts' on a mop polisher. This will give the fitting a mirror-like finish.

Above **New metal fittings are cast using patterns like the one on the left.**

Re-galvanising

Re-galvanising steelwork is a straightforward process and involves a specialist removing the original layer of galvanising by sand- or shotblasting it, before hot-dip galvanising it by dunking it in a bath of molten zinc. Unfortunately, the process can be more troublesome when dealing with old galvanised castings. Some parts of the casting

Below **A belt polisher is used to remove the rough 'as cast' finish of a bronze fitting.**

Right **Pattern paint is applied to the wooden pattern to ease its release from the sand at the foundry.**

may be semi-porous, which will make it virtually impossible to completely remove the original layer of galvanising. Failure to remove any part of the previous coating will undermine the new layer's ability to bond properly to the metal fitting and compromise the end result. Galvanising new castings is an entirely different matter, however, and can be carried out very successfully.

Making a wooden pattern

Cutting out the central opening with a bandsaw – watch out for your fingers!

A table mounted router is used to round off the pattern's inner edge.

The lower section of the wooden pattern is cut to the required depth.

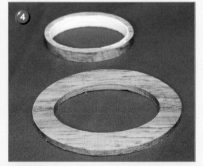

The upper and lower sections of the wooden pattern.

Re-chroming

Re-chroming can be an expensive process due to the amount of preparation required in between removing the original layer of chrome and applying a fresh coat. It is therefore worth checking how much a replacement fitting would cost before starting work. If re-chroming proves to be more viable, or the only option, then the metal fitting will need to be sent away to a specialist electroplating company for the original chrome to be removed. This is done using either an acid dip or reverse electrolysis. On its return, the fitting will have to undergo abrasive finishing work to remove any pitting or corrosion before it can be sent off to be re-chromed.

Replacing anodes

Strangely, the anode is the one thing on a boat that you do want to have to replace on a regular basis. Its gradual degradation means that it is working properly and protecting your expensive stern gear from electrolytic and galvanic action and corrosion.

Anodes are usually made from pure zinc, and are designed to attract the stray electrical currents created by dissimilar metals in salt water. Rather than your costly bronze propeller, aluminium stern drive or stainless steel propeller shaft dissolving away, the 'sacrificial' anode takes the hit instead. As zinc is further down the galvanic scale than nearly all other metals, your stern gear and other metalwork below the waterline will avoid any damage if your anodes are doing their job.

Ideally, anodes should be checked and, if necessary, replaced every year. However, if your anodes are not showing any signs of being eaten away, you should be concerned, as it means that something is probably wrong. It could be that the anodes themselves are not made from the right metal, or that they are not properly earthed to the keel inside. If the anodes still look brand new, they may not be close enough to the metals they are trying to protect.

Anodes aren't just located on the outside of the hull either – they are also found on propeller shafts, on outdrives, inside engine heat exchangers, and on the cavitation plates of outboards.

Above **Anodes should be replaced when they are 50 per cent wasted, as above. This has taken an entire season, which is about right.**

Replacing anodes

On many boats, the anodes attach to a pair of steel studs that protrude through the hull. If an anode isn't replaced for several seasons, these studs can corrode, which can make it very difficult to remove the anode when it needs to be renewed. If the studs have corroded, the whole bolt could turn without undoing. The only solution is to locate the nut inside the boat, drill a hole through the nut to split it open, and then drive the entire stud out with a drift. Unfortunately, these anode studs are sometimes hidden away under engines or other inaccessible areas.

Anodes and skin fittings (eg seacocks) are often bonded together with wire to form a 'circuit' of protection. The propeller shaft can also be protected with a bonding attachment, rather like the bush on an electric motor. Check these connections occasionally as they can corrode in a salty bilge.

Above **Corroded studs from a large anode that wasn't replaced when due, and had almost completely dissolved away.**

Left **Some anodes are not easy to find, such as this one hidden under the transom bracket of an outboard. Make sure you know the location of all your anodes.**

Right **New, large anodes, placed very close to the expensive bronze stern gear they are protecting.**

Below **A ring anode on an outdrive should protect the propeller, but this one won't. It is almost completely gone and needs changing as soon as possible.**

Pencil anodes protect the inside of an engine but can occasionally fracture, leaving part of the anode trapped inside. The only way to remove it is to carefully insert thin pliers and use a hooked piece of wire or a rod with a blob of quick-drying glue on the end to pull the anode out.

Outdrives and even the smallest outboards have anodes bolted onto the casing. These anodes are sometimes quite hard to spot and can often be overlooked. Check them occasionally, and replace when they are 50 per cent dissolved. The ring anodes on a stern drive can be replaced when the props are taken off at the end of the season.

TIP

After removing an anode, smear the threads with a little non-metallic grease. This will help removal of the new anode at a later date. Don't use copper grease, though, as it will react with the studs and anodes. Always make sure your anodes are from a reliable source as some cheaper makes may not contain the right amount of pure zinc.

Left **Replacing anodes is a regular but necessary expense, and will save you money in the long run. Here, failed anodes have allowed galvanic corrosion to eat into the propeller shaft, requiring a costly repair.**

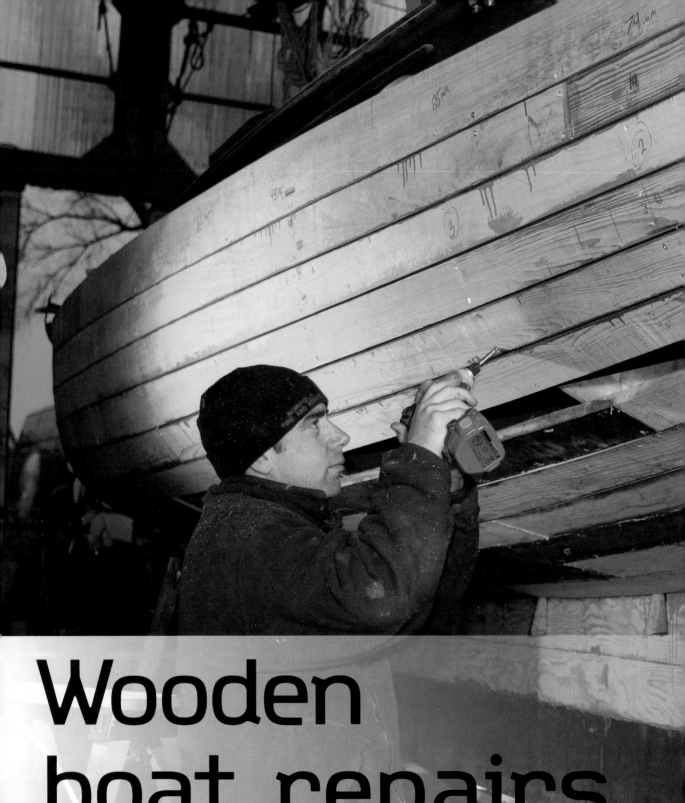

Wooden boat repairs

Woodworking skills

The ability to use a basic selection of hand tools will enable a boatowner to carry out most of the woodworking repairs needed to keep their vessel shipshape.

Sharp edges

Working with sharp edges requires constant attention to achieve the best results and avoid any unnecessary injury. It is always better to sharpen a blade before it becomes blunt, so aim to sharpen your tools at regular intervals. If you have time, a tool should be sharpened before it's put away so that it can be used immediately when it's needed again. If you don't maintain a sharp edge, you'll find that more effort is required to drive the tool through the wood, which in turn will undermine the quality of

the final result, as well as increasing the risk of an injury caused by the tool slipping.

When it comes to sharpening a blade, there are a variety of methods and sharpening materials available, including diamond, oil and water stones. Deciding which method to use will probably be determined by personal preference because they are all effective – although keep away from cheap stones as they are invariably too soft, they wear quickly and unevenly, and are generally a poor investment.

Above **For final trimming work use the chisel with the flat edge down.**

Using a chisel

To achieve the best results with a chisel it should be 'driven' whenever possible by a mallet, rather than 'pushed' by hand, as it's less likely to slip. If there is a lot of material to be removed, use the chisel with the bevel edge down, because this will lift the material away from the surface. Use the chisel with the flat edge down to carry out the final trimming work; this will produce a flatter surface. Once you have finished using the chisel, protect the tip with either a plastic guard or by putting it in a canvas tool roll.

Below **When using a plane, 'follow through' by keeping the plane flat and level until the end of the stroke to avoid leaving a rounded surface.**

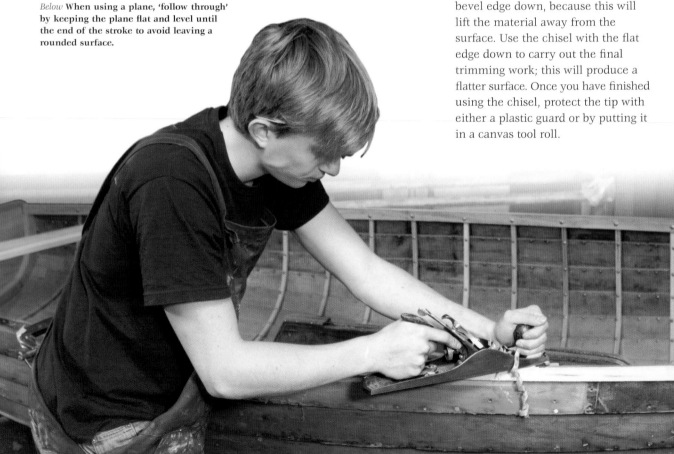

Using a plane

Before a plane can be used, it must be set up correctly. Having checked the blade is sharp, make sure it's parallel to the base of the plane, using the lever to adjust its angle. If this is not done properly, the plane will leave 'tramlines' (lines with raised edges) on the planed timber surface. Once the blade is parallel, set the depth by which the blade projects below the plane's base.

Depending on the type of wood you're working on, a plane's blade will start to cut when it projects below the base by 1/32in to 1/16in (½-2mm). You should therefore begin with the blade projecting almost flush with the base and gradually increase its depth until it cuts. If you want a smooth finish, it's always better to take off lots of fine shavings than a few coarse ones.

Your posture is also important. Stand comfortably; do not overstretch, and ensure your weight is over the top of the tool. Try to 'follow through' by keeping the plane flat and level until the end of the stroke to avoid leaving a rounded surface. When the plane is not in use it should always be placed on its side to protect the base.

Using a spokeshave

The spokeshave should be set up along the same lines as a plane – although the adjustment mechanism for the blade tends to be more basic. When it comes to holding a spokeshave, do so lightly with the thumb and first finger of each hand, while wrapping the remaining fingers around the handles. It's important not to grasp the spokeshave too tightly and to simply direct it with your hands. Best results can usually be achieved by using a spokeshave at a slight angle to its direction of cut.

Above **A Japanese back saw gives a clean cut, though the teeth are more vulnerable.**

Saws

The majority of cutting tasks can be carried out successfully using one of the two main types of saw. A tenon saw is ideally suited for finer work, whereas a panel (or 'hand') saw should be used to cut larger pieces of timber when a coarse cut is acceptable. As we will see on page 78, a Japanese back saw gives a nice clean cut; however, the teeth can not be resharpened and are very vulnerable to hidden nails and screws.

Above **For a smooth finish it is always better to take off several fine shavings.**

Above **Hold a spokeshave lightly and guide it with your hands. Try not to force it.**

Dealing with minor hull leaks

Any hull leak is a cause for concern and should be thoroughly investigated without delay. Despite the initial alarm triggered by the discovery of a leak, the remedy may be relatively simple and inexpensive to carry out.

Once you have identified the possible location of the leak on the inside of the hull, it is important to put the boat on a hard to dry out or take it out of the water for a thorough inspection. Check for cracks along the seams, putty that has gone hard, failed fastenings, and loose splines (thin strips of wood glued in the seams as an alternative to putty). All can be symptoms of a leaking hull.

Hardened putty

Over time, the putty that is used to cover the cotton or oakum during the caulking process (see page 86) will go hard and no longer flex in sympathy with the natural movement of the hull planking, therefore allowing water to penetrate the seam. If a small length of putty has gone too hard, it can be replaced without resorting to full scale recaulking.

Simply rake out the affected part of the seam and, if the cotton or oakum is sound, harden it back in the seam using caulking irons. If necessary, add a single run of cotton over the top. Alternatively, if the cotton is damp or rotten, remove it, dry out the seam, replace the cotton or oakum and apply a

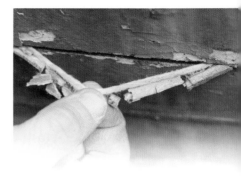

Above **When the putty becomes too hard, it no longer flexes in sympathy with the adjacent planking and can cause leaks.**

coat of primer along the repaired section of the seam.

Lastly, apply an appropriate stopping compound to fill the seam. Avoid mixing different types of stopping compound whenever possible. Some boatbuilders use modern polyurethane mastics, such as Sikaflex, squeezed straight from the tube, but these should only be

Below **Use a raking tool to remove the old caulking from the affected seam.**

TIP

To ensure a stronger bond, apply the putty along the seam over the primed cotton when the paint has reached the 'tacky' stage, rather than allowing it to cure completely.
Peter Graham, International Boatbuilding Training College.

Minor recaulking

Use a making iron and mallet to force the cotton into the seam.

The hardening iron leaves little nibs in the cotton's outer profile to create a strong bond for the stopping material.

Primer is applied to the cotton, as well as the surrounding wood.

Red lead putty is applied with a putty or palette knife.

used if the seam has been dried out properly. Alternatively, a traditional stopping compound such as red lead putty or black pudding mix can be applied with a palette knife.

Black pudding mix was devised by Scottish fishermen as a stopping material for their workboats, and comprises cement and tar. The main benefits are that it is cheap, easy to fair and totally waterproof. The outer surface will go hard whereas the mixture between the planks remains soft and pliable, so it moves in sympathy with the wood.

Red lead putty consists of red lead, linseed oil and putty. Once the putty has warmed up, it becomes very pliable and easy to use. Either warm the putty in your hands (plastic gloves are recommended) or put the tub in a bucket of hot water for about 20 minutes before use.

Loose splines

If a spline is loose, pull it out, and clean out the seam. The seam must be completely dry before any remedial work can begin and, if necessary, should be dried out using a hot air gun. Once a new spline has been made or the existing one has been cleaned up for re-use, it should

be glued in position with either resorcinol resin glue or epoxy – epoxy may prove to be a better choice due to its gap-filling qualities.

Once the spline has been glued in place, it will naturally try to slip out of the seam before the glue has cured. Hold it in place by stapling thin offcuts of plywood over it. Once the glue has cured, remove the strips and fill the indentations left by the staples with putty or thickened epoxy prior to repainting.

Above **Loose splines should be removed and replaced or refitted.**

Repairing a damaged deck

Replacing a section of plank in a laid deck due to localised rot is a fairly straightforward task. Use a router or a chisel to cut out the area that needs to be removed.

The amount of deck you need to replace will be determined by the condition of the sub-deck, and the location of the adjacent joints in the deck planks. Whenever possible, follow the original pattern of the joints to achieve the most aesthetically pleasing result.

Routering out the planks

✪ Use a router with a straight cutter and attach a batten to an adjacent seam to provide a guide. Use either screws or nails to ensure no marks are left on the planking.

✪ To avoid changing the position of the batten for each cut, tape a suitably sized wooden block to the base of the router, increasing the size of the block with each cut until the whole plank is routered out.

✪ Establish the thickness of the planking. For planks more than 8mm thick, it's better to make several passes rather than attempt to cut all the wood out in one go.

This reduces the risk of the router jarring and/or the blades getting damaged.

✪ Once the router's depth has been set, start at one end and work steadily along the section to be removed.

Patching a plywood sub-deck

Once the plank has been routered out, inspect the plywood sub-deck underneath for signs of damage. If a small amount of rot is found, it might be possible to remove the affected wood and fit a graving piece. To do this:

✪ Cut out the damaged wood with a chisel and make a square or rectangular hole.

✪ Mark out a 3in (8cm) perimeter around the hole, and plane or chisel the marked area to a feather edge, so as to create one half of a scarph joint.

✪ Cut out the graving piece, feathering the edges to form the other half of the joint.

✪ Glue the patch in position using epoxy.

Laying the replacement planks

If the ply sub-deck has been repaired, seal the new wood using the same method that was originally used to seal the rest of the sub-deck, before laying the new plank(s).

✪ Once the new planks have been machined to the correct size, use a bedding compound such as mastic or glue to attach them to the sub-deck. The planks should be held in place by penny washers or small wooden blocks temporarily screwed into the deck seams, until the glue or bedding compound has cured.

Preparations

Smooth the surface with either a plane or an electric sander.

Attach a batten to guide the router, locating the nails in the seams.

Use a router with a straight cutter to remove the damaged plank.

For planks more than 8mm thick, make several passes to remove the wood.

Above **Once the router depth has been set, start at one end and work steadily along the section to be removed.**

✪ Once the glue or bedding compound has cured, remove the penny washers or wooden blocks, clean up the planks and fair them off before recaulking the seams with cotton and paying with a black polysulphide rubber caulking compound (see page 54).

Above **Finishing off a caulking seam with a rebate plane on a new deck plank.**

Above **Whenever possible follow the original pattern of the planks.**

Doubling up fastenings

Fastenings on a wooden boat often begin to fail at the end of the planks or along the garboard planks, and it is here that small leaks may start to develop. Fortunately, this can be resolved cheaply by adding new fastenings.

The forward ends of the planks (known as the 'hood ends') and the garboard planks take the most punishment when a boat ploughs through a wave. If moisture finds its way to the fastenings, they will start to corrode and eventually fail as the wracking forces sustained by these parts of the hull take their toll. Obvious signs that the fastenings have failed include cracks in the paintwork and minor leaks along nearby seams, unusually big gaps between the frames and the planking and, in extreme cases, a sprung plank.

Occasionally, it may be possible to remove the old fastening and reuse the same holes. However, it is usually quicker to add a new fastening either side of the old one.

Doubling up the fastenings
If the plank has sprung enough to reveal the rabbet in the stem or sternpost, it is worth springing out the plank a bit more to remove the old hardened putty. A fresh layer of mastic can then be applied along the back of the plank and the rabbet, before the plank is offered up to the hull, and secured in place with G-cramps or wooden cleats. It can then be refastened.

Below **Adding new fastenings is an economic solution for minor leaks caused by the failure of old fastenings.**

If a plank requires additional fastenings, the procedure is as follows:

✪ If the red lead putty in the adjacent seams has gone very hard, this should be removed to make it easier to work the plank.

✪ Mark out the positions of the new fastenings on either side of the old ones. The number of additional fastenings required will be determined by the width of the plank. Silicon bronze fastenings are the best option.

✪ Drill a pilot hole to ensure the frame behind the plank is sound enough to screw into. If the wood is sound, drill the size of hole required for the fastening. If possible, counterbore the hole so that the screwhead lies below the outer profile of the plank. It can be plugged with a softwood dowel afterwards. For thinner planks, countersink the hole so that the screwhead is just below the surface of the plank. The head can then be skimmed over with putty.

✪ Screw the fastenings into position.

✪ To complete the repair, the seams should be recaulked and stopped up with putty.

Fitting new fastenings

Mark out the positions for the new fastenings, avoiding any weak spots.

Drill the hole, using a drill bit which matches the size of the screw shank.

Counterbore the hole, so that the screw head lies well below the surface.

Screw the new fastenings in tight – but not so tight they can't ever be removed.

Left **The best way to protect the screw head is to counterbore the hole and plug it with a dowel.**

Replacing damaged or rotten planks

If you discover rot in your boat's hull, or it has suffered from localised impact damage, you may need to replace a section of the planking. It's a major job but, with a little care, it can be undertaken by a skilled boatowner.

The first job when repairing a section of carvel planking is to remove the damaged or rotten plank from the frames.

If the hull is copper-clenched and the interior has been stripped, begin by taking out the dowel or putty to expose the head of the copper nail on the outside of the plank. Use an angle grinder to cut off the copper rove (or washer) on the inside of the hull, and drive the nail back through the plank with a centre punch. The protruding nail can then be extracted with a claw hammer. Repeat the process for all the remaining fastenings to release the plank from the frames.

Alternatively, if the plank has been fastened to the frames with nails or screws or the inside of a copper-clenched hull is inaccessible, start by drilling off the screw or nail heads. Use a jigsaw or pad-saw to cut out the rotten or damaged section of plank, before pulling it off the headless nails.

Once the plank has been removed, trim the protruding nails with an angle grinder. The remnants of the old fastenings can be left in the plank, providing the new fastenings are made from the same type of metal.

Scarphing a plank

If you are replacing a section of planking, the usual way of joining the new and old planks is using a single-lipped scarph. The scarph should have a ratio of at least 4:1, so that the length of the scarph is four times that of its width (Lloyd's Rules specify this as a minimum for planking). To provide additional strength, the scarph should be placed over a frame or timber, so that the 'feather' edge of the inboard half is supported. This is because the ends of the joints are usually glued, being too thin to rely on conventional fastenings. If it is supported by the frames or timbers, then it will eliminate the possibility of any movement in the joint when the boat is under way.

To create a scarph

- Once the adjoining plank has been trimmed to ensure the joint is over a timber or frame, spring out enough of the plank to provide plenty of access to mark up and cut the scarph. To ensure the plank does not move while this work is carried out, insert a wedge behind the 'liberated' section of plank.
- Use a set square to mark out the inboard half of the scarph.
- A smoothing plane can then be used to remove the majority of the wood to form the scarph joint more swiftly.
- To avoid a 'feather' edge on the outboard half of the scarph joint, use a tenon or a Japanese back saw to cut a straight edge and create a firm lip. The 'lip' of the scarph should be one third of the thickness of the planking.
- A shoulder plane can then be used to fine tune the shape of the inboard part of the joint.
- Use a metal ruler to ensure a uniform level is achieved across the length and width of the joint.

Left **Attaching a spiling board to the frames. Any size board can be used as long as it fits in the space comfortably.**

Fitting the plank

Once the plank has been cut and planed to the required dimensions, cut the scarph joints at each end.

Following any final adjustments to the fit of the plank and the scarph joints, the plank should then be secured firmly to the frames, using either nails, screws or copper nails and roves.

SPILING THE NEW PLANK:

If the old plank cannot be used as a template, you will need to work out the required shape of the new plank using a rough template, or spiling board, and a short strip of wood known as a dummy stick.

HOW TO SPILE:

✪ Attach the spiling board to the timbers with tacks or clamps. Each frame should be numbered, before their positions are recorded on the spiling board.

✪ Place the outer edge of the dummy stick up against the adjoining planks, and mark the inner edge of the dummy stick on the spiling board. Repeat at each frame.

✪ Remove the spiling board and place it on top of the wood for the new plank. The inboard edge of the dummy stick should then be placed on one of the lines on the spiling board and a pencil run along the outer edge to plot the shape of the replacement plank. Repeat for each position.

Above **Place the outer edge of the dummy stick up against the adjoining plank and mark along the lower edge to record the required shape on the spiling board.**

Cutting a scarph

Trim the adjoining plank to ensure the scarph joint will be above a timber.

Ease the plank out enough to mark the scarph.

Use a smoothing plane to remove the majority of the wood to form the scarph more swiftly.

To avoid a feather edge use a tenon or Japanese back saw to create a firm lip.

Replacing a sawn frame

Choosing how to deal with a damaged frame will be dictated by a combination of the available materials, position of the damaged frame and the cause of the problem.

A thorough inspection of a boat's frames should be carried out at regular intervals and in any case after impact or the discovery of a leak. Look for clues in the paintwork to discover potential fractures. If in doubt, use a paint scraper to remove any suspicious paintwork that may be concealing a bigger problem. Cracks can sometimes be difficult to locate because they may only open and close when the boat is under way.

Doubler or sister frames

If the fractured frame is free of rot, a doubler, or sister frame, can be fitted alongside, and side-bolted to the damaged frame. Not surprisingly, the process of making the doubler follows the same sequence of steps as outlined below for a new frame. This option will provide the same level of strength as replacing it, while minimising the overall disturbance of the hull's structure.

However, if the fractured frame is in a prominent position, a doubler might not be aesthetically pleasing, so you may need to consider replacing the frame. Likewise, if the damaged frame contains any sign of rot, it must be replaced.

Making a pattern

Once the damaged or rotten frame has been removed, you will need to make a pattern for its replacement:

- Cut a plywood pattern roughly to shape, and clamp it to the adjacent frame. Use a dummy stick and a pencil to spile out the shape of the planking (see page 78).
- To work out the bevel required to fit the frame snugly against the planking, make a series of marks every 2½–5in (6–13cm) on both the planking and the pattern.
- Place a bevel gauge against the pattern and measure the angle of the planking at each station.
- Mark these angles off on a straight-edged board.
- Number each angle in accordance with the station numbers.

Left **When choosing a suitable crook, place the pattern on top of the wood to ensure it has a nice sweep and a clear grain that is free of knots and sap.**

Fitting a new futtock

Clamp the new futtock in position, making sure it lines up with the old screw holes.

Drill the holes for the through bolts. A 90-degree drill will help access awkward places.

Bolt the futtocks together. Galvanised steel or bronze bolts are usually used.

Searching for a suitable crook

Sawn frames usually consist of at least two pieces of wood, known as futtocks, due to the difficulties of obtaining a grown crook of the right shape that is long enough to stretch from the keel to the deck. Good quality grown crooks are becoming increasingly hard to find.

Historically, boatbuilders sourced their grown crooks from a local timber yard, but now, chances are you will have to contact saw mills further afield. Ideally, you should select the wood in person by

Right **Use a bevel gauge to record the angle between the pattern and the planking to determine the required bevel for the frame's outboard face.**

placing the pattern on top of a crook to ensure it follows the required shape as closely as possible, and has a nice sweep with a clear grain that is free of knots and sap. If the piece of wood is located further away, it may be necessary to send drawings of the pattern to the saw mill and rely on their judgment.

Cutting and shaping the frame

- ✿ Place the pattern over the selected crook and mark out the desired profile, including an allowance for the maximum degree of bevel needed on the outboard face.
- ✿ Cut the wood to shape on a band-saw (or ask your friendly sawyer to do it for you!).
- ✿ Ensure the frame is correctly orientated before transferring the angles from the bevel board to the appropriate station numbers on the frame.
- ✿ Trim the frame's outboard face to the required bevel with either an electric planer, a drawknife and/or a spokeshave.

Fitting the frames

Once the frame conforms to the required shape, apply primer to the inside face of the planking, and the outboard face and sides of the frame. When the primer has dried, place the bottom part of the frame into the mortice in the keel and fasten the top part to the beamshelf, before fastening the planking to the frame from the outside.

Above **Use a dummy stick and pencil to spile out the shape of the planking.**

Making a laminated deck beam

Lamination is an effective method of creating a strong deck beam (or frame) without having to hack at massive lumps of timber with a chainsaw.

A laminated deck beam essentially consists of several thin layers of wood, which are glued together and held on a jig until the glue has 'set' to form the desired shape. To make the jig, first cut a piece of 16mm plywood or MDF to create the base. The shape of the new beam then has to be transferred onto the base. If you've been able to extract the old beam in one piece, you can use this as the pattern for the new one – otherwise you'll have to use a dummy stick (see page 78). Once the required shape has been marked out, screw a series of wooden blocks along the outer edge of the curve. These blocks should be no more than 3in (75mm) apart and must be firmly screwed in position as they will have to counter the natural resistance of

the timber when it is pulled in to create the desired shape. The jig should be covered in packaging tape and/or plastic sheeting to prevent the beam sticking to it while the glue cures.

Cutting the laminates

To determine the thickness of the laminates, work backwards from the size of beam you require; for example, a 4in (100mm) beam might consist of ten 10mm thick laminates. To ensure the selected thickness will bend to the required shape without too much effort, cut the first laminate and try bending it on the jig. If it's too thick, plane it down until you reach the right thickness, and adjust your calculations accordingly to determine the final number of layers.

Above **Use a serrated spreader to ensure an even layer of glue between the laminates.**

Below **Laminated beams consist of several thin layers that have been glued together.**

Making the jig

Wooden blocks are screwed to the jig along the desired curve for the new beam.

The laminates will be clamped to these wooden blocks while the glue cures.

The blocks are covered with packaging tape to stop the laminates sticking to them.

Gluing the laminates together

- ✿ Resorcinol resin glue, epoxy or a polyurethane glue can be used to bond the laminates together.
- ✿ Depending on the manufacturer's instructions, apply glue to both surfaces to create the strongest bond between the laminates. Although a brush can be used to apply the glue, it is easier to achieve an even layer by using a serrated spreader.
- ✿ Time is of the essence, so stack the laminates as soon as the glue has been applied to the mating surfaces. Once all of the laminates have been glued together, place the beam on the jig and start clamping it in position.

Clamping the beam to the jig

- ✿ To avoid distorting the beam while clamping it, start from the middle and work progressively outwards.
- ✿ Do not over-tighten the clamps as this will distort the shape of the beam.
- ✿ If you're using a temperature-sensitive glue such as resorcinol in a cold workshop, it may be necessary to erect a small tent over your work while the glue cures. Any available plastic sheeting can be used, such as bubble wrap or tarpaulin, and the heat should be provided by an electric, oil-filled radiator to avoid the risk of burning down the workshop.
- ✿ Once the glue has cured, clean off the excess glue with a belt sander and plane, before fitting the beam.

Right **The laminates must be clamped at regular intervals to ensure a good, even bond. You can't have too many clamps!**

Making & fitting a graving piece

Finding an area of rot on the hull of a wooden boat is always bad news. Rather than replace a whole plank, however, it may be possible to simply insert a graving piece into the affected area.

Finding rotten wood

A sure-fire give-away is blistering, crazing or flaking paint. Initially this may be due just to moisture under the paint, but do nothing and rot can follow. Tap lightly with a plastic-faced hammer, and you will hear a different sound when you hit soft wood. A sharp-pointed tool can be used to gently probe further for soft spots. Rot is possible both inside and outside the hull planking. Inside, anywhere that allows water to collect is a likely candidate.

Removing an area of rotten planking

It is tempting to remove as little as possible, but old hands would always renew the complete plank. However, if the area of rot is genuinely small and not the complete thickness of the plank, it is permissible to 'let in' a patch, or graving piece. If you need a lot of graving pieces, then renewing the

Below **If the area of rotten wood is only small, a graving piece may be inserted rather than replacing the whole plank.**

plank may be the best option. If the rot is around any fastenings, it may have penetrated deeper than you would like and a graving piece may not make a suitable repair.

- ❂ Probe the area to find the extent of the rot.
- ❂ Mark out the maximum extent of the rot using a soft pencil or a marker pen.
- ❂ Remove all the rotten wood with a chisel.

Right **A graving piece has been let in to replace a section of rotten wood. In time, the whole plank may need to be replaced.**

Making the graving piece

- ✿ Measure the depth of the hole you have cut in the hull.
- ✿ Plane a suitable piece of wood so that it is slightly thicker than the depth of the hole.
- ✿ Cut a shape which is slightly bigger than the area of rotten wood removed, and ensure the sides are straight and at right angles to the surface. Graving pieces are traditionally diamond-shaped, but a simple square will work just as well.

Fitting the graving piece

- ✿ Offer the graving piece up to the hull and scribe its outline onto the hull using a sharp knife, ensuring it covers the area of removed wood fully.
- ✿ Remove the wood from the enclosed area with a chisel, ensuring the sides of the hole are at right angles to the hull and that the hole is of equal depth over the whole area.
- ✿ Drive a couple of screws into the outside of the graving piece to act as handles.
- ✿ Offer up the graving piece, trim the recess/graving piece to size if necessary and then remove the screws.
- ✿ Apply waterproof glue or epoxy to the hole and tap the graving piece into place. Excess glue can escape through the screw holes.

Finishing off

Once the glue has fully set, the graving piece can be faired into the hull using a suitably sized plane.

Fitting a graving piece

Cut a piece of wood to cover the rotten area. Straight sides make it easier to fit.

Chisel out the rotten wood over an area to exactly match the graving piece.

Glue the graving piece in place, tapping it to ensure it's well bedded in.

Once the glue has set, finish it flush using a smoothing plane.

Caulking & paying methods

The planks of a carvel-built hull are not glued in any way, and the only thing that keeps the hull waterproof is the flexible sealing between the planks. In time this will need to be replaced.

How do you know a seam needs to be re-caulked?

If the seam is either opening up or cracking, it needs to be investigated, because it will allow water into the joint and may start the process of rot. If it is opening up, the seam should be re-caulked, rather than just refilled with stopping.

Removing the failed caulking

Great care should be taken not to damage the wooden planking; improvised tools are more likely to cause damage than a purpose-made one. A proper raking tool has long handles and can be driven with a hammer. The aim is to remove only the caulking, not damage the wood and not drive it all the way through to the inside of the hull. Rake out only as much seam as you can re-caulk in one session. Open seams will dry out rapidly, which means that the wood will shrink, and this will cause trouble later when it swells against the new caulking.

Above **A professional will have several caulking hammers and irons, each used for a specific part of the caulking process.**

Below **Getting into a good, even rhythm is essential for successful caulking.**

Re-caulking the seam

Either cotton or oakum is used for caulking, oakum being more suitable for wider seams. Slightly different techniques are used in different parts of the world, and amateurs may find some things helpful that the pros wouldn't use. The method described below is suitable for amateurs and professionals alike.

- ✹ Separate the cotton into strands thick enough to fill the seam.
- ✹ Twist together the strands you are going to use. You can use a hand drill or a low-speed electric drill to do this – just tie the strands to the chuck of the drill and run the engine at low speed.
- ✹ Make sure the cotton stays clean by keeping it in a box.
- ✹ Paint the seam with an oil-based primer.
- ✹ Loop the cotton into the seam and then drive it in with a caulking iron and mallet.
- ✹ Use a hardening iron, which has a groove in its working face, to drive the caulking deep into the seam, rocking the iron as you go.

- ✹ You need to fill the seam to about half its depth, so you may need a second layer of cotton.
- ✹ Again, paint the seam with oil-based primer.
- ✹ Before the primer is fully dry, fill the seam with red lead putty using

Above **The cotton is unravelled from the ball and spun together to create a strand thick enough to fill the seam.**

a putty knife. Some boatbuilders recommend thinning the putty with linseed oil and adding a little grease, to make it easier to squeeze into the narrow seams.
- ✹ Wet the knife with linseed oil and run it along the seam to polish it.

Relaunching the boat

Once the seams have been re-caulked, the planks will continue to dry out and shrink, so repainting the hull and getting the boat back into the water should not be delayed for too long.

Re-caulking a seam

Once some cotton has been hammered in, gather some more up in a loop using the iron and push it into the seam.

Hammer the cotton into the seam using the caulking iron. Use a hardening iron to 'harden up' the seam.

Refurbishing solid teak decks

General wear and tear, especially that caused by over-enthusiastic cleaning, will dictate whether a boat's deck planking needs sanding down to preserve its looks and even to prevent water penetration.

When is sanding necessary?

If a deck is scrubbed hard and along the grain (rather than gently, and in circles or figures-of-eight), softer parts of the timber get worn away, leaving ridges. This is particularly true of teak. When the ridges become too deep, the deck will have to be sanded to restore its finish.

General wear of the wood will also leave the flexible caulking standing proud, and this may cause separation between the caulking material and the wood. If the adhesion between the caulking and the wood has failed, re-caulking will be necessary to ensure a waterproof deck.

Below **A variety of tools can be used to remove the old caulking and clean up the seams, including mallet and chisel.**

CAULKING WITH TAR OR PITCH

Because the deck is more or less horizontal, tar or pitch can be used to seal the deck joint above traditional oakum/cotton caulking, rather than the red lead putty that is used in hull seams. Jeffrey's Marine Glue is almost pure pitch and may be more easily obtainable than tar.

Sanding the deck

Remove as many deck fittings as possible. A belt sander removes wood rapidly, so it needs to be used with care to ensure that no more wood is removed than is absolutely necessary. You will have better control using a floor sander, but it's probable that it will be too big for the space available. If any underlying screw heads are revealed, stop sanding until the screws have been removed.

Removing the screws

If any screws need to be removed:

- Mark the centre of the dowel with a centre punch.
- Drill out the old dowel with a 'spur point' drill bit.
- Stop as soon as you feel the drill bit touch the screw.
- Clean the screw slot and remove the screw with a correctly fitting screwdriver, so that the counter-sinking can be deepened. If necessary use a shorter replacement screw.

Right **A belt sander is an effective tool for cleaning up a deck — but use it with care.**

Deepening the rebates

The easiest way to deepen the rebates is to use a palm router. You may be able to use the remains of the adjacent rebate as a guide, though you may have to devise a tool to do this yourself according to the circumstances. The rebate should be 0.25in (5-6mm) deep.

Re-caulking the planks

If the grooves have been completely removed by sanding, the joints between planks will be revealed and so the traditional caulking between planks may need to be replaced. How to do this is shown on pages 86 and 87.

Re-sealing deck seams

Remove the old sealant. A craft knife is being used here, but a hammer and chisel or bent-over screwdriver can also be used.

A palm router can be used to deepen the rebates. Here, a guide is being used to keep the rebate even.

Having primed the rebate, breaker tape is inserted into the base to stop the sealant sticking to the bottom of the seam.

The rebate is filled with new sealant using a caulking gun. Once cured, any excess will be removed with a belt sander.

Filling the rebates

❂ Polysulphide is the best, most expensive type of sealant. It takes a long time to cure properly.

❂ Most manufacturers recommend using bond breaker tape to prevent the sealant sticking to the bottom of the rebate.

❂ Apply breaker tape to the bottom of the rebate and then fill the rebate with polysulphide or polyurethane sealant to about 0.04in (1mm) above the plank.

❂ Glue dowels into any screw holes, using epoxy.

❂ Ensure that you observe the manufacturer's curing times prior to sanding or even walking on the deck. When the compound has fully cured, sand the sealant and dowels to the same level as the rest of the deck.

Resurfacing a leaking coachroof

As the canvas covering on a coachroof nears the end of its working life, it will begin to crack and allow water to collect underneath. This can result in leaks and, ultimately, rot. Although the canvas can be renewed, many boatowners opt for a modern, longer lasting alternative, such as epoxy sheathing the coachroof.

Preparing the coachroof

If the bond between the canvas and the coachroof is still generally sound, use a Stanley knife to cut the canvas into thin strips. Each piece of canvas should be removed in a steady, yet gentle, manner to minimise the number of wooden shards that are pulled away with the canvas. Thoroughly inspect the coachroof. Any damp patches can be dried out carefully over a couple of days using a hot air gun, while any rot must be cut out and the timber replaced.

Adding a layer of plywood

Minor imperfections in the upper surface of the coachroof must be filled with epoxy before the plywood is sanded flush. A fresh layer of plywood is then added to increase the strength of the entire coachroof. The thickness of this layer will be dictated by the thickness of the original wood, the extent of the coachroof, and whether it has to support the weight of people standing on it.

TIP

The real secret is being able to get the glass cloth down as smoothly as possible, because the more ripples you have, the longer it takes to achieve a smooth finish, which in turn increases the risk of stretching the cloth in the wrong places. Equally, you must ensure there is enough resin on the plywood, otherwise you will have to force more resin through the cloth, which generates additional ripples. *Roger Hodds, ANH Yachting.*

Below **Use a spreader to 'work' the cloth from the centre of the coachroof to eliminate any ripples in the glass cloth.**

Above **Plastic sheeting is applied immediately below the working area to protect the varnished cabin sides.**

Epoxy sheathing the coachroof

❂ Apply a generous coat of resin to the plywood.

❂ Carefully lower the glass cloth into position.

❂ Apply resin on top of the glass cloth.

❂ Eliminate any ripples by using a spreader to 'work' the cloth from the centre of the coachroof outwards.

❂ Once the sheathing has cured, cover it with a thin layer of filler to conceal the weave of the cloth.

❂ Sand the filler, before applying a two-pack paint with a durable finish to complete the job.

Fitting the new plywood

❂ Cut the plywood to shape.

❂ Apply epoxy to the mating surfaces.

❂ Lower the new plywood into position.

❂ Screw the new plywood firmly in position with neat rows of screws no more than 6in (150mm) apart.

❂ Leave overnight before filling the screw heads and any imperfections. Failure to do this will cause problems later on when the glass cloth is laid, because air pockets will form between the plywood and the glass cloth.

❂ The leading edge of the plywood should be rounded, so create a bevel using epoxy mixed with a low density filler.

Fitting a second layer of plywood

Once the epoxy has been applied, lower the new plywood into position.

Screw the plywood firmly in position. The screw heads should be filled with epoxy.

Roll out the glass cloth and cut to length before applying the resin.

Apply a generous layer of thickened epoxy to the plywood.

Dropping keel bolts

Owners of wooden yachts should inspect their keel bolts on a regular basis as part of their long-term maintenance programme. The interval between inspections will be determined by the type of keel bolt. For example, mild steel bolts will require checking every four to five years, while bronze ones can be left for at least eight years.

When slipping a boat to drop the keel bolts, make sure the supporting blocks do not prevent access to the bolts, and that there is enough space under the boat to remove them. You can achieve greater clearance by either raising the boat on blocks or by digging a pit under each bolt.

Dropping the bolt

Expose the head of the bolt under the boat by chiselling out the cement or filler that was used to cover it. Two people will be required to drop and fit the keel bolt. To do this:

- ✪ Unscrew and remove the nut on the inside of the boat.
- ✪ Use a sledge hammer to drive the bolt down through the keel with a drift. To minimise the risk of injury, a second person should hold the drift with either a piece of wood with a hole drilled in it or a piece of metal rod with an 'eye' bent in one end. Either device will keep hands clear of the danger zone.
- ✪ Once the bolt begins to descend, pause for a moment and check it's emerging underneath. If it is, then carry on. If not, the bolt may have corroded to a fine point and have been compacted by the force you applied with the sledge hammer. One way of getting around this is to weld a T-shaped piece of metal to the head of the bolt to enable the lower half to be drawn out from below. A punch can then be used to drive the top half back up the hole so that it can be withdrawn from inside the boat.

TIP

It's worth putting some diesel or penetrating fluid on the nut inside the boat about a week before dropping the keel bolt, as this will make removing it easier.
Peter Graham, International Boatbuilding Training College.

Fitting the keel bolt

The keel bolt should be thoroughly examined for any signs of damage. If it was easily drawn out, and there are no signs of corrosion, it can be reused. If the keel bolt has some very minor surface corrosion, it may be possible to reuse it for another season if the boat has to be relaunched before a new bolt can be fabricated. When replacing the keel bolt:

- ✪ Apply a protective coat of metal primer, epoxy or black tar varnish. The number of coats will be determined by the tightness of the hole. There's no point applying several coats if they are going to be knocked off when the bolt is fitted. Conversely, if there is a little slack in the hole, an extra coat could be beneficial.
- ✪ Grease the thread at the top of the bolt to prevent it becoming clogged up with debris, and grease it along its length to help it slide back into position.

Below **Use a sledge hammer to drive the bolt down through the keel with a drift.**

Above **Dig a pit under each bolt to ensure there is enough clearance to physically remove/fit the keel bolt.**

- ❂ Apply a ring of mastic around the head and wind two turns of caulking cotton around it to form a grommet.
- ❂ A second person should be inside the boat to report on the bolt's progress as it is knocked back into place with a sledge hammer.
- ❂ Once the bolt is in position, secure it firmly in place with a nut and washer.
- ❂ If the bolt head is recessed into the bottom of the keel, cover it with a softwood dowel, some cement or an appropriate filler.

Fitting a new keelbolt

Grease the thread of the bolt – preferably using waterproof grease.

Apply a ring of your favourite mastic around the head.

Wind two turns of caulking cotton over the mastic to form a grommet.

Apply grease along the bolt to help it slide into position.

Repainting after a repair

If the majority of the hull's paintwork is sound, you can save valuable time after replacing a plank by blending in the new paint with the existing surface.

Preparations

Once the repair has been completed, sand the new wood and the adjacent painted surfaces with a random orbital sander to ensure there are no lumps and bumps. The key to blending in the new and old paintwork is being able to feather in the paintwork successfully. This in turn requires a uniform surface. Run your hand along the area to be painted: if it is fair, it should feel like one continuous surface. A change in texture from the paint to the bare wood should be the only detectable difference.

❂ Fair the area to be painted with a random orbital sander. Start with 80-grit sandpaper, followed by 120-grit and possibly 240-grit, especially along the edge of the original paintwork where you want it to blend in perfectly. The paintwork along a sharp edge is always more susceptible to cracking and chipping, which could ultimately lead to the paint lifting. Carefully hand sand any sharp edges, such as the corner of the transom, using a piece of 120-grit sandpaper.

If any of the new wood is to be varnished, the grain must be sealed with two coats of varnish before you start painting the rest of the woodwork. This will prevent any splashed paint penetrating the wood and ensures that any stray specks can be easily removed. To create a crisp line between two coatings, such as paint and varnish, use masking tape. Varnished areas can 'overlap' painted areas before painting, to ensure the wood is continuously sealed – but not vice versa!

Blending in the paintwork

❂ Apply primer to the bare wood. If the primer is quite thick, add thinners to make it flow more smoothly and improve penetration.
❂ Apply two further coats of unthinned primer. Sand very lightly by hand between layers to ensure no ridges build up, and remove the dust with a dedicated dusting brush before applying the next layer.
❂ Apply two coats of undercoat. Sand by hand between coats and remove the dust with a brush or tack rag.

Below **Use a random orbital sander to fair the area to be painted.**

✪ Once the undercoat has been applied, it is time to assess the overall standard of the paint finish, and look for any imperfections that might be highlighted by the top coat. Depending on the extent of these imperfections, it might be worth using a product such as International's Interfill 200 to fill any defects. It can be applied as a thin coat and sanded down to leave a smooth finish.

✪ Apply a final layer of undercoat.

Right **The quality of the finish will be determined by a combination of preparation, brush quality and personal skill.**

Priming

Sand carefully by hand along the leading edge of the existing paint.

Start by applying primer to the bare wood.

Sand by hand in-between coats of primer and remove dust with a brush or tack rag.

Use masking tape to create a crisp line between finishes, eg paint/varnish.

Before applying the top coat, assess the overall dust conditions of your working environment. Even though dust should be kept to a minimum during the application of the previous layers, it will now become a critical factor. Use a tack rag to remove the dust created by sanding the final layer of undercoat. The quality of the finish will be determined by a combination of how well you have prepped the surfaces, the quality of the brush, and your personal skill. Ideally, a soft brush with no loose hairs should be used. The paint should be applied with vertical strokes initially before switching to horizontal strokes along the grain to finish off.

Steel & ferro-cement repairs

Metalworking skills

The core skills for cutting and welding metals are relatively easy to learn. However, it's important to ensure any work carried out is done safely.

There are a number of possible methods for cutting metals. The old-fashioned hacksaw can be used for small jobs, although it can be a laborious process even with a power hacksaw. Angle grinders are considerably faster – especially those fitted with 9in (23cm) cutting disks – although cutting an accurate line requires a good eye and a steady hand. Other disadvantages are that time is needed afterwards to clean up the edges of the cut, and using an angle grinder for an extended length of time is an unpleasant, noisy and dusty task.

Below **An angle grinder is useful for cutting small amounts of metal, but becomes tiring, noisy and dusty for larger jobs.**

Plasma cutting

For large projects, a plasma cutter is a better option. These electrically powered devices blow an inert gas out of a cutting torch at high speed, using an electrical arc to turn the gas into a focused plasma stream, which melts the metal. It's a quiet and dust-free method that requires minimal cleaning up afterwards.

Another advantage of plasma cutters is that a plywood template can be clamped directly to the work, enabling complex shapes to be cut easily. Oxyacetylene cutting has some of the benefits of plasma cutting, but does not give such a clean cut, and cannot be used with templates in the same manner.

Above **Plasma cutters are ideal for cutting large amounts of metal – hand-held models are available for use on site and are cleaner and faster to use than grinders.**

Welding

Welding uses heat to melt the edge of each item being joined, so that the two fuse together in a structural join. It is important to ensure that each element is heated right through to the correct temperature. An easy mistake when welding two thick sheets of metal is for the weld to fail to penetrate the full thickness of the material, thereby weakening the join. However, turning the heat up too high risks burning a hole in the metal, a problem that's accentuated when welding thin materials. It's therefore worth practising on scrap material first to get the right settings, before starting work. In any case, steel panels used in the construction of boats should be welded on both sides of the join, to ensure full penetration.

Arc welding is one of the most common welding techniques and is ideal for many marine applications.

An electrical supply is used to generate the heat required via a welding rod. These rods act as an electrode and provide additional molten material for the joint. Oxygen must be kept away from the weld to prevent it oxidising and losing significant strength when red hot, so welding rods are typically covered with a flux that produces carbon dioxide during the welding process.

Welding thin materials

MIG (metal inert gas) welding is more suitable for thin materials of under 0.08in (2mm) thickness. The electrode is a spool of wire that is automatically fed into the weld, providing the filler material, while an inert gas is fed from a compressed bottle over the weld to prevent oxidisation. Another option for thin metals, especially aluminium and stainless steel, is TIG (tungsten inert gas) welding. This, however, is a more skilled process than MIG or arc welding – the tungsten electrode provides the arc and new metal (aluminium or stainless steel, depending on which you are welding) is fed into the join.

Above **Welding encompasses a variety of techniques for creating strong structural joints.**

Below left **Thick sheets of metal are joined by welding from top and bottom to achieve a structural bond. The welding rod melts part of the substrate, as well as filling the gap between the two sheets.**

Below right **A fillet weld joining two plates held at 90 degrees to each other.**

SAFETY

Working with metal inevitably carries a large potential for personal injury. It's vital, therefore, to adhere to safe working practices and wear good protection, including heavy-duty leather gloves, ear defenders and safety glasses. In addition, when welding or using a plasma cutter, a decent welding mask is essential – viewing the arc directly will burn a hole in your retina.

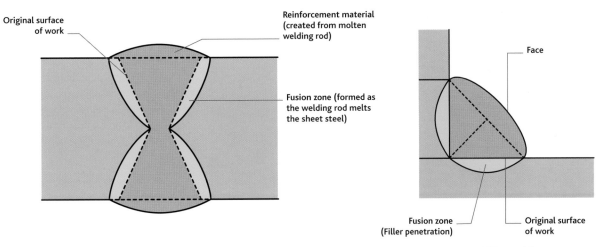

Original surface of work

Reinforcement material (created from molten welding rod)

Fusion zone (formed as the welding rod melts the sheet steel)

Face

Fusion zone (Filler penetration)

Original surface of work

Welding a thick sheet from both sides

Fillet weld

Welding new panels

Steel hulls are almost infinitely repairable – but there are no shortcuts. If the repair is to last, every stage of the process must be completed to a meticulous standard.

Any steel hull that requires new panels is likely to have experienced significant rusting. All oxidised material should be removed before new steel plate is welded in place. Many steel boats are able to cope with what may at first sight appear to be chronic rusting – each 0.04in (1mm) thickness of metal will create a 0.4in (10mm) thickness of rust.

Many hulls have 0.25in to 0.4in (6–10mm) thick bottom plates and 0.16in to 0.25in (4–6mm) thick topsides, and so a large amount of material can therefore be chipped and ground away before the structure is weakened. However, owners of older boats must not be complacent – a significant amount of material may have been lost in previous ownerships. The only way to reliably determine the thickness of the remaining steel is through an ultrasound survey.

The lightest steel yachts are built with only 0.12in (3mm) steel on the topsides, deck and superstructure. This has no margin for corrosion, so the thickness of the metal must remain intact throughout the life of the vessel.

Removing rust

To remove localised areas of loose and flaking rust, use a chipping hammer. This will make quick work of the job, without creating large amounts of airborne dust. More stubborn corrosion, including the layer of surface rust, can be removed with an angle grinder. If possible, try to achieve a bright finish, as this will help to keep future rust at bay. Larger areas of corrosion are better treated with shotblasting (see page 102 for more on this).

Although it's tempting to simply weld a new patch over an area of rust, this is a short-sighted solution as the rust will continue to form at an alarming rate around the edges of the weld. Any weakened material must be removed using an angle grinder, plasma cutter or oxyacetylene torch. A new panel, cut to match the hole precisely, can then be welded in place.

Left **All existing rust must be removed before new material is welded in place.**

Above **Use a chipping hammer to remove loose rust. The remaining corrosion can then be removed by shot blasting or with an angle grinder.**

Welding

The heat generated in welding is sufficient to warp sheet metals. A new piece should initially be tacked in place at a number of points around its perimeter. Start with locating each corner, follow with a tack midway along each side, and then use further tacks until the maximum distance between each one is no more than around 8in (20cm). Once the panel has been secured in place in this fashion, a continuous seam can be welded between the tacks.

Before starting work, make sure any combustible materials inside the boat, including hull or deck linings, are moved well away from the areas that are to be welded.

Electric arc welding

Start with short tacks that will hold the metal in place...

... this prevents distortion from the heat generated when welding a longer seam.

The completed weld, before chipping off the slag of oxidised by-products...

... and after chipping away the slag, showing a neat, but visible, seam.

The raised seam can be ground flat using a small angle grinder...

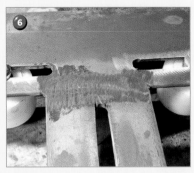

... to produce a neat flush finish that retains the joint's structural strength.

Shot blasting & painting

Modern paints, especially epoxy primers, have greatly reduced the amount of maintenance that steel boats need. Thorough preparation, however, is essential and a large number of coats are needed to achieve an impregnable finish.

Before painting a steel boat, it is vitally important that the metal is absolutely clean and rust-free. If not, the paint will not adhere properly and rust will form beneath it. Small areas of damage, such as scratches caused by a minor collision, can be prepared by hand. If the damage has not reached down to the surface of the metal, it can be treated as any other touch-up job – sand to feather the edges of the damaged paint, and touch up each coat, using the same primers, undercoats and top coats as the original system.

However, if bare metal is showing any rust or surface scale, it will need to be removed. An angle grinder with a coarse (18–24 grit) sanding disk will achieve this for small areas, but the only realistic way to achieve this over large areas is to shot blast the metal to a clean, shiny surface. Although this is not a DIY procedure, it's an investment that will pay off many times over, as it will speed up progress and ensure that the repaint is carried out to the highest standards possible. Shot blasting should leave a bright surface, and this must be primed as soon as possible, because the surface of the metal will start to oxidise immediately after blasting.

Above **It's essential to have the best possible protection against corrosion, including in all the hidden corners below deck.**

Left **There are no short cuts when painting a metal boat. Attention to detail is needed for a long-lasting result.**

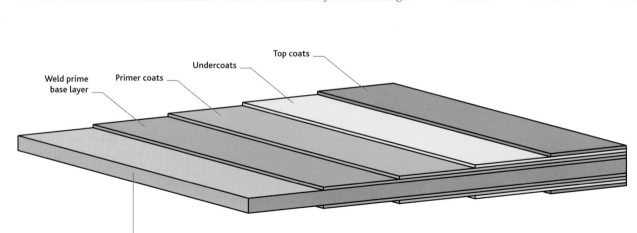

Weld prime base layer

Primer coats

Undercoats

Top coats

Base steel

Above **Components of an effective paint system for steel boats – several coats are needed at each stage.**

Right **A well-maintained steel hull will give decades, if not centuries, of service, as this immaculate Dutch barge proves.**

Painting steel

Steel boats can be painted with high-performance two-pack polyurethane, epoxy or conventional single-pack polyurethane paints. Two-pack paints are harder and more scratch resistant than single-pack types, so epoxy and two-pack polyurethanes score on both counts. However, they are more expensive, more difficult to apply and should only be used when wearing a decent filter mask, because the isocyanates contained in polyurethane paints are toxic. Epoxy primers are ideal for protecting steel, but should be overcoated with polyurethane paint as bare epoxy degrades in sunlight.

Never skimp on the thickness of application – most manufacturers specify the thickness of paint needed to create an effective system. It's likely that between eight and ten coats will be needed, at least, with a minimum of five coats of primer, two of undercoat and two top coats, although an even thicker paint system will always help to provide peace of mind.

After priming coats have been applied, it's important to decide how fair you want the final finish to appear. It will save a lot of work if you're happy for minor distortions to show through a low-gloss top coat, as providing a perfectly fair finish with a mirror-gloss top coat will require a huge amount of fairing with epoxy filler.

Left **A considerable amount of filling and fairing is needed to prevent high-gloss top coats showing multiple imperfections.**

TIP

The finish on the outer skin of the hull and deck is likely to be uppermost in your mind, but the unseen parts of the boat's interior demand an equally rigorous treatment. Rust will form in any remote corners that are skimped on – the very areas which are most difficult to treat.

Replacing deck fittings

Fittings can be welded directly to the deck of steel boats, or through-bolted in a conventional fashion. Most boats employ both methods for different applications.

There are a number of advantages to welding fittings to the deck of a metal boat. It can be an enormously strong arrangement and, because the deck is not pierced by bolt holes, the potential for deck leaks is minimised. In addition, fittings can be fabricated from mild steel, which is considerably cheaper than the stainless varieties typically used for marine deck gear.

However, there are also some drawbacks. In particular, any paint on mild steel will tend to be worn away by ropes and other gear, requiring frequent repainting. Painted mild steel, however, can still be good for deadeyes, cleats and mooring bollards, and is a good, low-cost option. Modern rope technology means that there's an increasing trend for blocks to be attached with a lashing rather than a shackle, which can reduce the damage to paintwork over time.

Below **Steel boats can make use of mild steel fittings that are significantly cheaper than their stainless steel counterparts.**

Above **Welding stainless steel fittings to the deck prevents the possibility of deck leaks around bolt holes, but is a skilled job.**

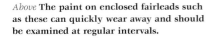

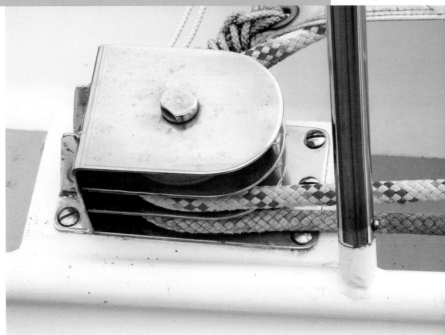

Above **The paint on enclosed fairleads such as these can quickly wear away and should be examined at regular intervals.**

Right **These stainless steel genoa sheet blocks are bolted to a mild steel plinth welded to the bulwark, making servicing the blocks easy.**

Although welding deck gear in place on a new build is relatively straightforward, retro-fitting deck gear using this method is more involved. The new items must be cleaned and shot blasted before fitting, paint must be stripped around the location of the fitting, and then the paint system reinstated.

As a result, most additional gear fitted to steel boats after manufacture is bolted through the deck.

Removing welded fittings

Fittings that have been welded in place can be removed relatively easily with the right tools. A plasma cutter is ideal for this, and an oxyacetylene torch is also quite good, although inevitably not as neat.

An angle grinder can be used for this purpose, but be prepared for the mess – small bits of mild steel swarf and dust will embed themselves into paintwork, sails and anything else around. These are very difficult to remove and will soon start to rust, creating ugly stains, so effective masking off of the work area is vital. In any case, if a fitting is not being

replaced with one of an identical size, the angle grinder is likely to be needed to smooth down the welds.

Bolt-ons

Through-bolted fittings are much easier to replace if they become damaged, or when modernising equipment and layouts. They also offer a wider choice of off-the-shelf fittings and the possibility of moving items more easily if their original location is not ideal. This also allows galvanised fittings to be used – these cannot be welded to the deck because the heat of welding will melt the zinc coating around the weld.

Above **A mooring cleat made from the same mild steel bar as the bulwark capping is inexpensive, but needs regular painting.**

Repairing ferro-cement hulls

Water ingress is one of the biggest enemies of ferro-cement boats; if water penetrates the concrete, it can cause the internal steel framework to rust. Repairs can be tricky, but are relatively inexpensive to carry out.

Ferro-cement boats were extremely popular in the 1970s and 1980s, particularly in the UK, France, Australia and New Zealand. The reinforced concrete hulls allowed large boats to be built comparatively cheaply, and because a well-made hull is fairly strong, many ferro boats are still around today. Be warned, though, there are also many poorly constructed, amateur-built hulls in existence.

A ferro-cement hull is essentially a steel armature that is encased in concrete. The shape of the hull is created using a framework of galvanised steel rods, with chicken wire tied to it to reinforce the wet cement as it dries. Several different methods of plastering the hull can be used, but all involve allowing the cement to penetrate the mesh,

before slowly curing into a single, solid skin. Concrete hulls never set completely smooth, and you can usually spot them from their dimpled appearance. Consequently, perfectionists will often finish the hulls with a thin plaster top coat or a layer of epoxy filler.

Concrete cures within a few days, but will continue to harden for the next 60 years, so older boats are particularly tough. If you can prevent water from reaching the wire mesh, the hull should last for a long time. In fact, one of the oldest ferro-cement boats still in existence is an experimental fishing boat from the late 19th century.

Below **Tell-tale rust streaks in this ferro-cement yacht indicate water has reached the steel armature and has started corrosion.**

Signs of water ingress

The tell-tale sign that all is not well is the appearance of rust streaks on the hull's surface. This indicates that water has penetrated the concrete and is corroding the steel framework. The only way to inspect a ferro hull below the waterline is to slurry blast (a wet shot blast) the antifouling to reveal the concrete underneath. Care needs to be taken here, as some older hulls were originally coated with a

Above **Slurry blasting will quickly remove the antifouling and expose the concrete.**

Right **The concrete over a corroded area can be cut back with an angle grinder fitted with a carbide 'marble levelling' disc.**

chlorinated rubber compound, which slurry blasting can remove unevenly. A more laborious method is to strip the antifouling chemically and tackle the primer with an angle grinder fitted with a 40-grit disk.

Using heat on the hull should be avoided, as it can cause expansion and contraction within, which could separate the cement from the armature.

Exposing the steel mesh

If rust streaks have been identified, further investigation may be necessary. To do this:

✪ Use a grinder to remove the concrete above the rusting area and expose the mesh. Allow it to dry out, and then paint the area with a rust inhibitor, and allow to dry.
✪ Refill the hole with epoxy cement. Specialised epoxy cement is readily available from DIY stores, and is ideal for large repairs.

Filling holes

1

This hole was made by air trapped under the fresh cement when the boat was built.

2

It is broken open, and then filled with a mix of epoxy resin and cement.

✪ Occasionally air may become caught under the fresh cement, and these pockets will sound hollow when tapped. To avoid replastering, inject activated epoxy into the pockets. Alternatively, for small holes, break them open and fill with epoxy cement.

✪ Damaged areas such as on the trailing edge of the skeg, or impact damage to the keel or bow, can be filled with epoxy cement, and a mould used to remake the shape. Larger damaged areas should be cleaned out, the mesh exposed and the area primed before it is refilled.

Working with ferro-cement

Ferro-cement can be challenging to work with if it needs to be modified or painted. It can be very hard to drill through, and the alkaline content of the lime in the cement can also cause some paint systems to blister within a few weeks of application.

Ferro-cement boats often have ferro-cement decks, which have distinct advantages over wooden ones: they are far more resistant to the elements, much stronger, and require less maintenance.

When it comes to upgrading, repairing or relocating deck fittings, removing the old bolts should be straightforward. Metal backing plates are often used for the bolts, so a little easing oil is normally all that is required if the bolt is stubborn.

Below **There are many neglected old ferro boats that need good homes. They are relatively cheap to buy and will provide a big hull that needs little maintenance.**

Drilling into concrete, however, can be tricky, and will require an SDS (Special Direct System) hammer drill, with a hardened masonry bit. SDS drills have a slightly different pneumatic action to a standard DIY hammer drill, and make neat holes in concrete without shattering the underside as the bit emerges. Avoid leaving freshly drilled holes exposed for too long, as moisture can get in and start corroding the steel framework. If a hole has to be left, run some epoxy primer around the exposed armature first to provide some protection.

Cutting apertures for windows requires an angle grinder with a diamond cutting disk, as the grinder will have to cut through the steel mesh in the hull. When making holes for skin fittings, a diamond hole borer is recommended. This equipment is readily available from DIY outlets, or can be hired from a tool shop.

Right **To make holes in concrete, use an SDS drill. These have a far more efficient hammer action than conventional DIY masonry drills, and won't shatter the cement.**

Painting a ferro-cement hull

❂ If the original paintwork on your ferro-cement hull is still intact and in good condition, simply rub it down to 'key' the surface, apply the undercoat and once dry roll on the top coat. 'Keying' the surface is very important as ferro hulls are usually painted with a tough two-pack polyurethane, which gives a very hard gloss surface. Unless this is properly abraded first, new paint may not adhere well. Ideally, if the original paintwork is blistering, it should be completely removed with a slurry blast.

❂ The surface of a bare concrete hull should be washed with an acid solution initially to neutralise the alkaline in the cement. The easiest method is to use brick acid, which is usually a 5 per cent solution of nitric acid, and is available in 5 litre containers. Take care to protect yourself from splashes, so apply the acid with a large brush, allow it to work for about ten minutes, and then wash it off with plenty of fresh water.

❂ After acid washing, the best treatment for bare concrete is to coat it in a special ferro-friendly epoxy (there are several available on the market). On a warm, dry day, apply the epoxy to the manufacturer's recommendations using a roller, followed by a brush to remove any bubbles or streaks.

The epoxy will soak into the cement and form a tough, watertight priming layer, on which to build up successive layers of paint.

Below left **Ferro decks are often quite thick. Here an old deck fitting is being removed for upgrading. Note the size of the mild steel backing plate.**

Below right **After removing paint from ferro-cement, it pays to wash the decks with acid to neutralise the alkaline in the lime. This will prevent blistering of the new paint.**

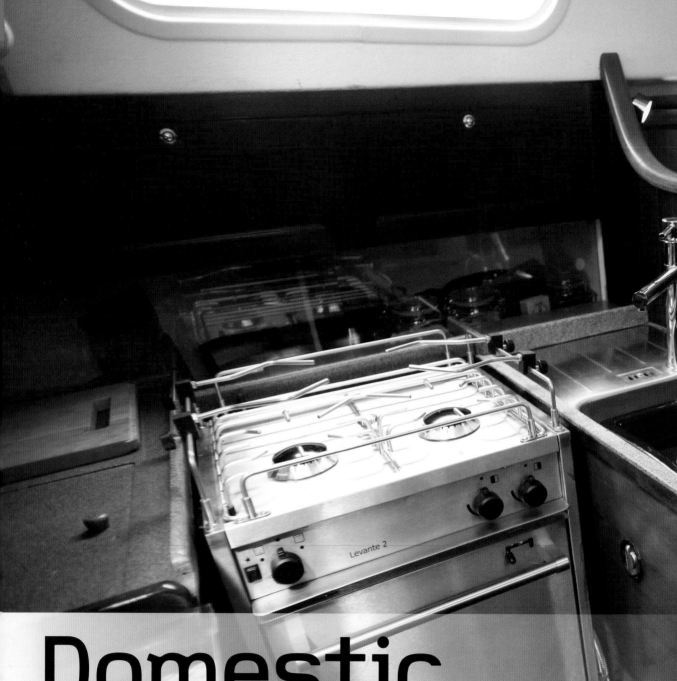

Domestic repairs

Repairing upholstery

Over time, upholstery can become tired, frayed and misshapen. However, you don't always have to replace it at great expense – quick repairs can do much to revive it.

There are two distinct types of material used in boat upholstery: waterproof vinyl, which is usually used for cockpit cushions, and a softer, polyester-type fabric that is used for interior bunk cushions. Some older boats may have vinyl seat covers down below, too.

Waterlogged foam

A common problem with vinyl cockpit upholstery is that the foam can become saturated when water finds its way in through the stitching. In most cases the cover can be removed, and the foam squeezed out so it can dry naturally, or be replaced. A waterproofing agent should then be applied to the cover's stitching to seal up the holes and reduce further water ingress.

Un-seizing corroded zips

Seized zips as a result of corrosion are more difficult to repair, because the evaporated salt water leaves behind hard carbonates, and may also have eaten away the metal parts of the zip mechanism. Use very hot water, or even steam from a kettle, to dissolve the hard deposits and un-seize the zip. Acetic acid (vinegar)

TIP

If a zip is so badly damaged that it needs replacing, specify a large tooth plastic replacement zip, as this will give fewer problems with salt water corrosion in the future. Make sure it is smeared with plenty of silicone lubricant after it has been fitted.

or lemon juice can also be effective. Use an old toothbrush to work the fluids into the zip, and with a bit of effort it should free up, although it may take some time. Once the zip is running again, smear the teeth with a silicone lubricant, and work the zip a few times so that all the parts are well covered.

Repairing vinyl seat covers

If a vinyl seat becomes stained or torn, or cracked due to ultraviolet radiation, use a vinyl repair kit, which can be colour-matched to your existing upholstery. Entire seats can be painted with a specialised, hard-wearing paint system to extend the life of your vinyl. To make a repair:

- Thoroughly clean the area with warm water and detergent.
- Allow the area to dry, before gently abrading it to remove the shine.
- Glue a vinyl patch over the damage, and paint it for a complete colour match.

Left **Boat upholstery will last many years, but suffers from the effects of salt water and mildew in the harsh marine environment.**

Right **Stretching stockinette over the foam of a cushion will help the foam keep its shape and make it easier to fit the covers.**

Bolstering your cushion foam

It is usually not cost effective to replace the foam in a cushion, as it is unlikely that it will fill out the cover properly again. Over the years both the foam and the fabric stretch, taking on a different shape. The ultimate solution is to invest in a new set of cushions, so that both the cushion and the foam are an exact match.

However, a temporary solution, which can be very effective, is to use an additional piece of polyester matting to bolster the old foam.

❂ Remove the cushion cover and then cut a layer of polyester wadding to fit over the top of the existing foam. This material is readily available from most fabric shops, and is inexpensive.

❂ Cut some stockinette material to the length of the bunk. Pull the stockinette over the foam and the polyester to hold the two parts together.

❂ Reinsert the foam back into the cover. With a little manipulation, you will find the new layer will fill out the cover again and give a bit more spring to the cushion.

Making cushion filling

A layer of polyester material is pulled over the foam cushion and cut to length.

The surface of the foam is sprayed with a spray tack adhesive.

The polyester is pressed onto the adhesive and patted all over for a complete bond.

The excess is then trimmed to shape, before being covered in stockinette.

Relaminating interior surfaces

Laminated surfaces on boats can be found on galley worktops, bulkheads and even floorboards. If these laminations start to lift, there are two courses of action: stick them back down again, or strip them off completely.

Repairing a delaminated surface can be fairly easy if the problem is at the edge and isn't too advanced – although a complete strip down will give you an opportunity to upgrade the décor.

Below **Laminates are used extensively in boat interiors, such as the formica on the chart table of this 1960s yacht.**

Delaminated floorboards and washboards

Delamination of floorboards and washboards is usually caused by water finding its way into the interface between the layers of wood. This type of delamination can be stabilised by using a urethane glue, designed to soak into the wood fibres and then react with the moisture.

Such a repair involves cleaning and drying the affected area, teasing it open to gain access, and then introducing the first stage of a specialised epoxy. This usually comprises two components, and will use the moisture in the timber to aid the reaction. Once the epoxy has been introduced, cramp the laminates together and allow them to cure.

Where laminates are exposed to damp or the weather, a good preventative measure is to run some urethane glue into the exposed end grain. This will soak in and form an adhesive seal, which can then be either varnished or painted over. This technique works particularly well on dinghy floorboards, which are regularly flexed and occasionally immersed in water.

Repairing delaminated bulkheads

If the laminate has parted from the substrate (the core layer) in the middle of a bulkhead, or it has wrinkled or distorted, then it's a good idea to remove it completely and start again.

Removing a laminate requires care and precision. A useful tool for this kind of work is the electric chisel. (This tool is also very good at removing old deck coverings.) Sharp hand chisels can be used to achieve the same result.

Right **Formica is surprisingly hard wearing. This chart table surface is more likely to be changed for aesthetic reasons than because of wear and tear.**

Even with careful removal, you may still have some raised areas where the glue has been particularly effective, and these will need to be flatted off with either a belt or random orbital sander. Once the old laminate has been removed:

✪ Cut the new laminate to size, using the old veneer as a pattern, allowing a small amount of overlap on the exposed edges.

✪ Key both surfaces that are to be glued, and wipe them down to remove any dust. Then apply the glue. Contact adhesive should be spread onto both sides and allowed to go almost dry before the two surfaces are aligned and pressed together. Accurate positioning is vital as contact adhesive lives up to its name and sticks firmly on contact.

✪ Once the laminate is glued in place, use a router fitted with a 'flush trim' blade to cut off the overlap on the exposed edges. This will ensure a neat and accurate finish. Use a suitable solvent to wipe off any surplus glue.

Regluing lifting laminate

Use the side of a chisel as a scraper to remove old adhesive under the laminate.

A thixotropic contact adhesive is ideal for regluing most types of laminates.

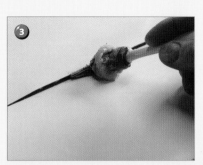

Use a brush or stripper knife to squeeze adhesive under the laminate.

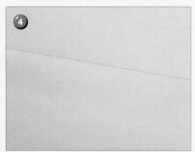

Wait for the adhesive to become tacky and press the laminate back into place.

Repairing interior linings

Foam-backed decorative vinyl is often used to line the interior of boats, and over time the backing of these linings can break down, causing the material to droop. Replacing the vinyl is usually the most cost-effective option.

The cabinsides and under-deck areas of most production boats invariably have large expanses of foam-backed vinyl that is glued directly to the fibreglass. The headlining, however, is usually made up of vinyl-covered plywood boards, which are detachable to access wiring runs and the bolts securing deck fittings. Steel boats tend to have wooden panelling throughout, which is often painted or vinyl covered, with foam or Rockwool insulation behind. All these decorative materials have a finite life, if only in terms of their styling. What looked trendy in 1980, for example, may make you wince now.

When interior linings do start to droop or show signs of wear, they can make your boat look scruffy. It is sometimes caused by water ingress through leaky deck fittings, but it is usually just the foam becoming brittle through sheer old age. Occasionally, the lining may have been glued incorrectly when new, or a subsequent re-sticking has failed.

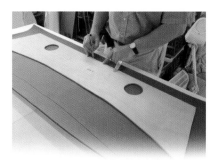

Above **Headlinings are usually made of foam-backed material glued to a sheet of plywood, commonly 0.25in (6mm) thick.**

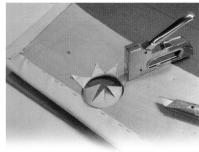

Above **Making holes involves cutting the vinyl into a star shape, removing the foam, and then stapling each 'finger' in turn.**

To replace the lining:
- Firstly, strip the old lining out, taking care to remove it as intact as possible so that you can use it as a pattern for an accurate replacement. It is also worth marking which way it was orientated before removing it, and then transferring these marks to the hidden side of the new lining to aid fitting. Where the material is trapped behind windows, you'll need to remove the interior frames.

- When the lining has been removed, clean as much of the old foam and glue off the GRP cabinsides as possible. The best tools to attack this with are an angle grinder or an electric drill fitted with a wire brush.
- Choose a replacement vinyl. A foam-backed covering is more forgiving over uneven surfaces, and will also provide some additional insulation. Use the patterns to cut the replacement sections, and then apply contact adhesive to both the foam and the cabinsides. Allow it to go tacky – usually around five minutes on a warm day.

Left **Headlining droop, a common problem on older boats. The backing foam or adhesive has failed, and gravity has done the rest.**

✿ Now carefully attach the new vinyl. You need to be bold, and accurate, as the adhesive will grab and hold immediately. On big areas, the trick is to have an alignment mark, and to start in the middle, carefully sweeping outwards from the starting point with both hands. Avoid attaching individual points around the panel first and then joining them up. Instead, have a continuous leading edge, as this will avoid wrinkles and air pockets.

✿ Tidying up involves trimming the vinyl around the windows, and reattaching the interior frames. Use a sharp craft knife to trim any edges, which can then be tucked up under the frames. Wooden trims can also be used to hide joins. If there is any glue on the decorative surface, remove it using white spirit. Don't use acetone, however, as it will remove the colour.

Repairing headlinings follows much the same procedure, except that the vinyl is curled around the back of the plywood (usually 0.25in [6mm] ply) and fixed with stainless steel staples. Non-flammable PVA glue is recommended for headlinings.

Replacing a lining

Remove the old lining as intact as possible to use as a pattern.

Using a wire brush, clean off as much of the old foam and glue as you can.

Having cut new panels, paint contact adhesive onto the hull.

Spray contact adhesive onto the foam of each marked panel.

Apply from a fixed start point with a gentle sweep of the hand.

Replace trims and clean up any glue spills with white spirit.

Fixing domestic water pumps

Fresh water pumps are one of the most important items on a vessel, and one of the most inconvenient to have malfunction. Fortunately, most models, whether manual or electric, are relatively easy to strip down and repair.

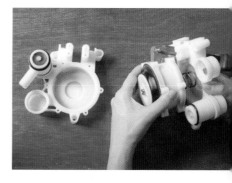

Above **Manual pumps are easy to dismantle and reassemble. This is a double-action foot-operated fresh water pump.**

If water ceases to flow, don't automatically assume the problem is with the water pumps – like any other troubleshooting task this must be approached in a logical fashion. Start by confirming there is water in the tank, and no leaks, blockages or other restrictions (see page 120).

Manual pumps

Manual fresh water pumps are generally simple and long lasting, with little that can go wrong. However, the rubber valves and diaphragms don't have an infinite lifespan. Service kits containing these items and any necessary seals are available for most pumps. To replace the rubber valves and diaphragms:

✿ Drain the water tank(s) or turn off the isolating valve (if fitted).
✿ Remove the inlet and outlet pipes from the pump, and unbolt the pump from its mountings.
✿ Remove the bolts or screws that hold the two parts of the pump body together, and carefully prise out the diaphragm and valves, replacing them with new components.
✿ Reassemble the pump, ensuring any seals are replaced.
✿ Before refitting, test that the pump will suck air, by placing a finger over the inlet and activating the pump handle.

Electric pumps

These generally suffer similar problems to manual pumps, with valves and diaphragms being the

---

TIP

Would an electrical failure make it impossible to get water out of your tanks? If you don't have a manual pump in the system, it could be worth installing one, or at least carrying an easily accessible container of fresh water for emergency use.

Below **We can take inboard conveniences for granted, so it's important to be able to rebuild a pump when necessary.**

most likely components to need attention. However, before stripping the pump down, it's worth checking problems are not caused by electrical faults. If the pump fails to operate, first check the fuse or circuit breaker, then use a meter to confirm power is reaching the unit.

The switchgear for most pumps is usually reasonably easily accessible – use a meter to check that this operates correctly. If not, a replacement switch can be soldered in place (see page 156), although this may need to be sourced from a specialist electrical retailer, rather than as a spare part from the pump manufacturer.

Electric pumps are more complex than their manual counterparts, so as well as a service kit, it's vital to obtain a parts diagram for your specific pump that shows how everything fits together, before you strip the unit down. When stripping an electric pump:

⊙ Start by draining the water tank or closing the isolating valve.
⊙ Then, label the wires to the unit so they can be refitted on the correct terminals. Remove them and the inlet/outlet pipes.

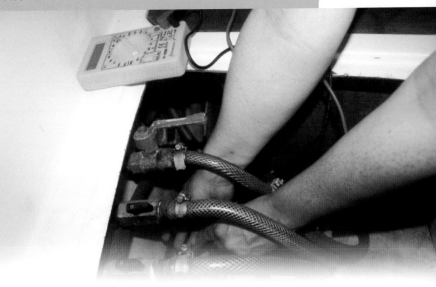

⊙ With the pump on a workbench or table, remove the screws holding the valves and diaphragm assembly in place – these will normally be at the opposite end of the pump body to the electric motor. Remove the valves and slide the diaphragm away from the pump body.
⊙ Refit the new valves and diaphragm, together with any new seals or other parts in the service kit, and reassemble the pump. If you have access to a 12-volt supply the pump can be tested before refitting the unit in the boat.

Above **Most problems with electric pumps stem from the power supply. Check this out thoroughly before stripping the pump.**

Extending pump life

The life of electric diaphragm pumps will be extended if the water is turned off at the tank, and the pump depressurised when the boat is left for extended periods.

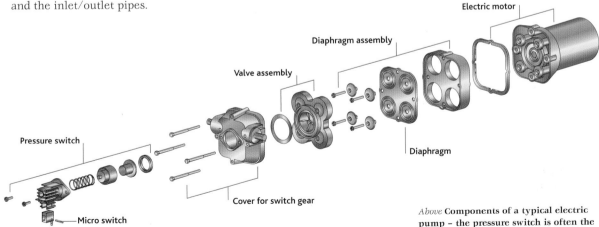

Above **Components of a typical electric pump – the pressure switch is often the part that gives most trouble.**

Tracing & fixing water leaks

We tend to assume the complex water systems on modern yachts are completely reliable. There are, however, a number of possible failure points to look out for.

Leaks are most likely to be found at the many pipework connections, so these should be examined with the system pressurised to check for problems. Small drips can be very hard to identify, but a piece of kitchen towel held around the joint will highlight small amounts of water escaping. Similarly, talcum powder sprinkled below the joint will identify the tiniest of leaks.

Below **A leak on the suction side of a pump is difficult to diagnose – air is sucked into the system rather than water spraying out.**

Difficult problems to diagnose

Air leaks on the suction side of water pumps can be really confusing to diagnose – when the pump is running they will tend to suck air into the pipework, rather than expelling water. If there's a problem that otherwise can't be explained, check for seepage on all the connections between the pump and the tank, with the pump turned off.

Leaky joints should be dismantled, cleaned and reassembled. Ideally, any hose clips used with flexible pipes should be replaced at the same time. If the leak is still in evidence, the compression-type fittings used with rigid and semi-rigid pipes should be replaced, remembering not to overtighten the nuts, as excess force can cause the pipes to distort.

Inadequately supported flexible pipes can also cause problems, especially on the suction side of the pump – if the pipe becomes kinked it can block the flow, just as with a kinked hosepipe. Some systems have a filter before the water pump, and this should be changed at the intervals specified by the manufacturer. It should also be checked if there is an otherwise unexplained blockage in the system.

Leaking tanks

Problems may also be associated with water tanks. Flexible tanks tend to chafe as they age, to the point at which they eventually wear through, with the leak becoming progressively faster over time. Solid-walled tanks, whether made from plastic, fibreglass or stainless steel, also have the potential to sprout leaks, and these often manifest as pinholes.

If the leak cannot be found, a pressure test will confirm the diagnosis. Drain the tank, seal any exits, including the vent pipe, then pump air in using a dinghy pump to a pressure of around 0.3 bar. If the pressure is not maintained for at least ten minutes, the tank is leaking.

A mix of detergent and water can be used to determine the location of

Above **A collapsed and kinked flexible pipe on the suction side of the pump will significantly restrict the water flow...**

Above **... the solution to this is to support the pipe in its proper position – in this case a cable tie was sufficient to do this.**

the leak – escaping air will cause the soap to bubble – although it may not be possible to gain access to all sides of the tank until it's removed from

the boat. Once the source of the problem has been isolated, most tanks can be repaired by metal or plastic welding.

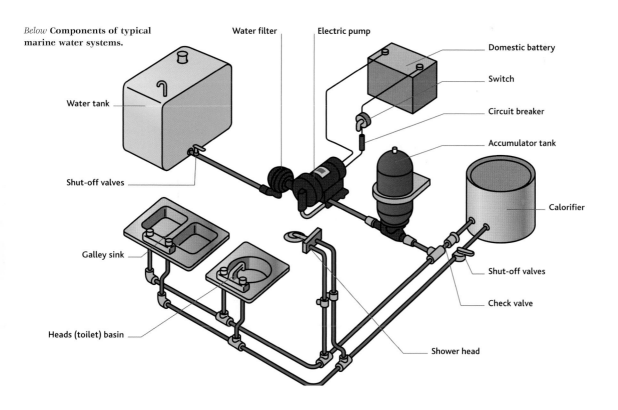

Below **Components of typical marine water systems.**

Water filter

Electric pump

Domestic battery

Switch

Circuit breaker

Accumulator tank

Water tank

Calorifier

Shut-off valves

Shut-off valves

Check valve

Galley sink

Heads (toilet) basin

Shower head

Tracing & fixing gas leaks

Gas leaks on boats are, fortunately, very rare, but many of the system's components have a finite lifespan and therefore must be inspected and replaced at regular intervals.

LPG is heavily scented and can usually be detected by smell at around one-tenth of an explosive concentration. However, don't be led into a false sense of security: our noses are generally far from the bilge, where the highest concentration of leaked gas can be found. A gas alarm will detect a much lower level of gas than a human nose, and its sensor can be located low down in the vessel. In the event of a leak, the supply should be turned off at the bottle, the interior of the boat ventilated and the bilge pumped with a manual pump to remove the gas.

Component lifespan

Flexible pipes should be kept as short as possible (under 3ft 3in [1m] in length) and must be led so that chafe is minimised. They are date stamped and should be replaced every three to five years. In addition, they must be regularly inspected for damage. Regulators contain rubber components that will eventually start

Left **Any hint of a gas leak has the potential to be devastatingly dangerous and should be investigated immediately.**

Above **Checking for a leak by applying soapy water to joins in the pipework – bubbles indicate gas escaping.**

to degrade, and these should be replaced every ten years.

Solid copper pipes can have an almost indefinite lifespan, provided they are well supported throughout their entire length. However, not all installations on older boats are to such a high standard, and if the pipe is able to move, this will result in fatigue and an early failure. Such pipes should be replaced as a matter of urgency.

Testing joints

If a leak is suspected, the best method to check for this is with a mix of detergent and water applied to each joint. Once applied, get someone to turn on the gas at the bottle, then watch for the detergent to start bubbling at the leaking joint. Apply more of the mix if necessary to ensure all joints are fully wetted.

Replacing a flexible gas pipe

Flexible pipes have a limited lifespan and should be replaced regularly.

The new pipe can be cut to the correct length with a sharp knife.

Apply suitable 'gas tight' paste before fitting the new pipe.

After fitting, secure with a new hose clip and check for leaks before use.

TIP

Whether working with compression fittings on copper pipes, or hose clips on flexible gas pipes, it's vital to resist the temptation to overtighten connections. If you do so, you risk creating problems: hose clips can cut into flexible pipes, while compression joints can be distorted through excess force.

Right **Gas alarms are a sensible precaution and will provide a warning of a leak if the sensor (inset) is placed low in the bilge.**

Replacing gas piping & fittings

Gas installations need to be carefully examined at least once a year for leaks, and any worn or chafed component must be replaced. Flexible gas piping and some fittings have a finite life and need to be changed on a regular basis for safety reasons.

Rigid copper tubing

Some authorities require that all gas pipes are rigid copper tube, with flexible pipe used only at the gas bottle and at a gimballed cooker. Rigid copper tubing should be run in continuous lengths, with no joins except at each component. Where the tubing passes through a bulkhead, either a specialised bulkhead fitting should be used, or a grommet fitted to prevent chafe. The tubing must be supported regularly along its length; the spacing of the supports may be specified by national regulations. Some regulations require that the pipe can be visually inspected for its whole length.

Flexible piping

Flexible piping must be specified by the manufacturer as suitable to be used with LPG, and the date of manufacture should be printed on the cover. It may be connected to the barbed connector of a fitting or directly to the correct size of copper tube. In both cases, it must be secured with pipe clamps. It is also available in specific lengths with special end fittings to suit particular applications, such as direct fitting to a gas bottle.

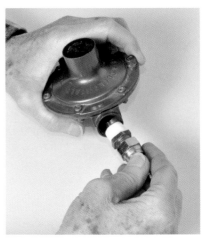

Above **Screwed fittings are best sealed using PTFE tape.**

Below **The gas supply pipes must be supported regularly, and an isolation valve fitted close to any appliance.**

Armoured flexible pipes

These come in specific lengths and have several different types of end fitting. They are used where chafe may occur, such as when connected to a gimballed cooker.

Pipe connections

Apart from where flexible pipes are attached to the system, all pipe connections must be compression fittings. These comprise a nut and an 'olive' that (when compressed by tightening of the nut) is forced to make a gas-tight seal between the tube and the fitting. Once compressed, the olive cannot be removed from the tube, but the joint can be separated from the fitting.

Making a joint

Use a pipe cutter to cut the tube to length (don't use a saw, or you will make a ragged edge that will not seal properly), and then de-burr the cut using a fine file or a deburring tool such as a reamer. Clean the tube with wire wool to remove tarnishing and dirt, then slide the nut onto the tube with the screwed end towards the join. Slide the olive onto the tube, push the tube fully into the fitting and tighten the nut.

No sealing compound is required when first making a joint, but if one is made and then undone, a small amount of LPG-compatible sealant may be used when the joint is remade. All joints should be leak-tested when made. The joint should not be over-tightened or the olive may be deformed and cause a leak; however, insufficient force will leave the olive loose on the tube.

Making a joint

Compression joints in copper tubing must be carefully made to avoid leaks. The beauty of this method is that the joints can be undone and rejoined as required.

Cut the tube to length using a pipe cutter, not a saw which will leave rough ends.

Use a reamer to tidy the end of the pipe, which will have been squashed by the cutter.

Slide first the nut and then the olive over the end of the pipe.

Do not apply too much joint sealant; this is all that is required.

Push the tube into the fitting. The olive should be flush, leaving no gap.

Tighten the nut onto the fitting with a spanner, but do not tighten too hard.

Troubleshooting diesel heaters

Diesel-fuelled central heating systems either blow warm air around the vessel, or pump hot water through radiators. Problems tend to be associated with poor installation, lack of maintenance and dirty fuel.

There's no denying the convenience of thermostat-controlled automatic heating systems on board a boat, but these are not fit and forget items – regular maintenance is required to keep them operating effectively. These systems rely on electric power to pump the water or warm air around the vessel, and to fire up the unit from cold. This is done using a glow plug, in a similar manner to most diesel engines. Most models also have an electric fuel pump. A good supply of electrical power is therefore essential, especially on start up, when the glow plug will draw up to 20 amps from

Below **Diesel central heating provides near-instant heat but you should know how to fix the system when it breaks down.**

12-volt systems. Many start up problems are therefore caused by a battery that's either low on charge or overdue for replacement.

Fuel problems

Dirty fuel is the second most common problem encountered with diesel heaters. This can quickly foul the burner, so a filter is fitted in the fuel line between the tank and the heater. A clogged filter will result in the unit running unevenly and eventually failing to fire up.

A metal gauze in the burner helps the fuel/air mix to atomise – this is essential for clean combustion. Carbon deposits form on the gauze, and this will eventually reduce its effectiveness. White smoke on

start-up is an indication that an excess of carbon is preventing proper combustion of the fuel. As a temporary measure, cleaning the gauze with solvent will help get a broken-down heater functioning again. Both gauze and fuel filter should ideally be replaced during an annual service.

> **TIP**
>
> Exhaust gases contain carbon monoxide, so all types of heater, whether solid fuel or diesel stoves (drip or carburettor-fed, bulkhead-mounted or free-standing) must have an efficient chimney to take fumes outside the boat. Even then it's possible for such heaters to emit carbon dioxide into the confines of the boat's cabin, so a carbon monoxide alarm is a must.

Air requirements

There's a strong flow of air into the intake for combustion when the unit is operating, and this must not be obstructed, although leaves or even plastic wrappers can get sucked into the opening, reducing flow. Forced-air types of heater have ducting of 4in (100mm) diameter around the boat, and if this is restricted the flow of warm air will be reduced, and, in extremis, the unit will shut down to prevent overheating.

Many models have a system of flash codes (which vary between manufacturers and models) to indicate the status of a fault. This means it's essential to have a copy of the unit's documentation on board, so that faults can be identified and rectified easily.

Above left **Dirty fuel can foul the burner of warm air or water diesel fired central heating type systems.**

Above right **A carbon monoxide alarm is a must for any heater that relies on using air from the cabin for combustion.**

Below **A typical hot water type diesel heater installation on a large motor yacht.**

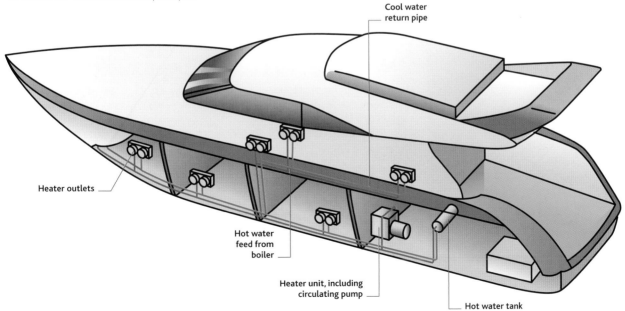

Cool water return pipe

Heater outlets

Hot water feed from boiler

Heater unit, including circulating pump

Hot water tank

Troubleshooting for manual heads

Most problems with marine toilets stem from lack of maintenance. As well as issues with pump valves and seals, the gradual build-up of limescale will eventually narrow the outlet pipes severely.

Dealing with blockages

There are a number of possible reasons for a heads failing to pump out, so don't jump to conclusions without checking the basics. First, check the valves at the skin fittings are turned on and that the lever on top of the pump (if fitted) is set to the flush position. If the boat is in a drying tidal berth, also check she is afloat.

If these are okay, the likelihood is that there is a blockage. The first reaction of many at this stage is to start stripping the pump immediately. A little patience, however, may pay dividends. While it's important not to force the pump, which could result in a breakage and terminal damage, if it's possible to move it a little, then do so, waiting for a few minutes between each mini-stroke if necessary. If progress is made, carry on – often a blockage will be removed gradually this way.

If the pump is stuck hard, the

Above **If a hose is difficult to fit, heating it in very hot water will make it expand slightly and become more supple.**

pump will need to be dismantled to reach the blockage. For most units, this is done by unscrewing the six bolts at the top of the pump, followed by the six at the bottom of the pump chamber – although the manufacturer's instructions should be consulted whenever possible.

If water starts leaking from around the pump handle, this type of leak is usually on the fresh-water side of the pump, so it doesn't demand instant attention. However, this can be a precursor to further problems – such as it becoming possible to move the pump handle up and down without pumping liquid in or out of the bowl – so don't delay too long before taking

action. The solution is to dismantle the pump as described above and replace the seals and valves.

Beating limescale

Limescale forms on all surfaces in the pump and outlet pipework, making it one of the biggest enemies of marine toilet systems. A thin layer will reduce the performance of the seals and valves in the pump, effectively reducing the pump capacity and making the unit more prone to blockages. Therefore,

Left **Stout rubber gloves offer some degree of protection when working on sanitation systems.**

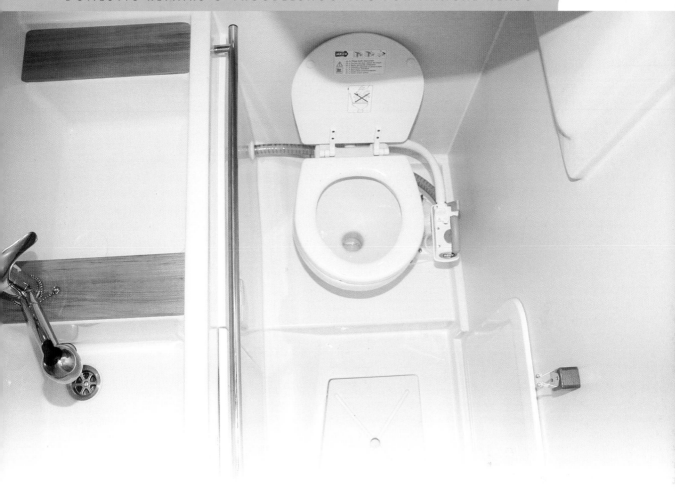

an annual inspection, with replacement of any affected parts (spares can be bought as a service kit) is a sensible precaution.

On a well-used boat, it's worth changing the pipework at least every ten years. Proper marine-grade sanitation hose must be used for this, because otherwise the material will absorb odours from the effluent, spreading them to the rest of the boat. New pipework can be difficult to fit, but if you soften each end in a bucket of hot water, it will slip over the fittings easily.

Above **Manual heads are easy to fix when they go wrong, but it can be an unpleasant job. Regular maintenance is more palatable than occasional repair.**

Left **An outlet valve housing severely restricted by limescale. If a replacement is not available, it can be removed with a scraper.**

TIP

This is one area in which preventative maintenance is much less unpleasant than dealing with a breakdown. Even then, before starting work, it's worth flushing the system through with disinfectant – and make sure you have a supply of stout rubber gloves.

Troubleshooting for electric heads

Electric toilets can succumb to many of the problems of manual models, but may also develop problems with the power supply, motor, switchgear and macerator pump.

The simplest electric marine toilets are manual models with an electric pump in place of the standard unit. If space is available, some models allow both manual and electric pumps to be fitted, allowing the toilet to continue to function in the event of power failure. Dedicated electric heads benefit from a more streamlined design that's easier to clean, a quieter operation, and often a reduced amount of water is needed to flush – an important consideration for a boat fitted with holding tanks.

Dealing with blockages

Both types of electric heads tend to be more susceptible to pump blockages caused by foreign objects than manual models. The macerator pump of most models has an impeller similar to those used for marine diesel engine water pumps (see page 181). The impeller relies on water for lubrication, so if the pump is repeatedly run for long periods (more than about 30 seconds) with the bowl dry, the impeller will eventually burn out.

Some models have an access point that allows a blockage to be reached without dismantling the pump; otherwise the pump will need to be stripped to clear the problem.

The pump draws a significant current – up to 16 amps on a 12-volt system – so many electrical supply problems relate to corroded connections or a weak battery, resulting in a significant voltage drop. A long run of cables is often needed from the battery or switch panel to the heads, so relatively heavy wiring – 0.013 sq in (0.8 sq mm) cross section (approximately 0.12in [3mm] diameter) wire – should be used if it has to be run over a distance of more than 16ft (5m).

If the toilet bowl is installed below the (static or heeled) waterline, a solenoid valve should be fitted on the vented loop to prevent too much air being sucked in for the pump to prime. If the pump appears to run as normal, but the toilet doesn't flush, this is one of the most likely problems.

Slow or noisy evacuation is a sure sign the pump needs servicing, and

Below **Electric heads are a convenient for the user, but are more complex to fix than manual models when they go wrong.**

the valves and impeller replacing. In any case, this should be carried out at least every two years, or annually on heavily used systems.

Laying-up and recommissioning

Water should be pumped out of the bowl by turning the valve at the inlet skin fitting off, and operating the pump for a few seconds to drain the bowl. If the unit has not been used for some time, the pump and components can dry out, so add around one litre of water to the bowl before use.

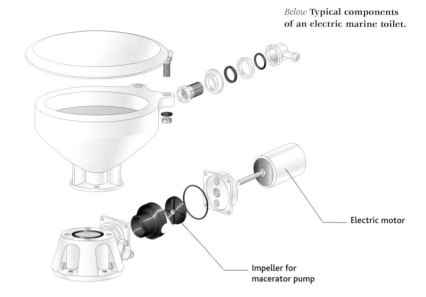

Below **Typical components of an electric marine toilet.**

Electric motor

Impeller for macerator pump

Replacing a damaged impeller

① Start by draining the bowl, then unscrew the electric pump...

② ... and withdraw this from the base of the toilet.

Above **Some systems are very similar to a manual heads, but with the pump replaced by an electric motor.**

③ The impeller can now be removed, together with any broken vanes.

④ Reassembly is a straightforward reversal of the dismantling process.

General
mechanics

Mechanical skills

Using the correct techniques for each job will reduce the time the task takes to complete, minimise the risk of unnecessary damage to your boat, and significantly cut down the possibility of injury.

A good quality spanner should fit a nut or bolthead to perfection, allowing the maximum force to be used without the tool slipping off. When a tool slips, it rounds the corners of the nut, making its removal even harder. Adjustable spanners and wrenches are often expensive, and are rarely a perfect fit. They should, therefore, only be used for applications where little tightness is required – if at all.

Despite the initial appeal of these multi-purpose tools, in most cases, the money is better invested in a proper set of spanners and sockets. Even then, a spanner should be gripped with an open hand, so that if it does slip your knuckles will be spared injury.

The same principle applies to screwdrivers – if these don't fit the screwhead exactly, there's a risk of slippage and the screwhead being damaged. After low-grade tools, this is perhaps the biggest mistake made. It's wrong to think of the correct screwdriver as simply being one that's small enough to get into the slot; the screwdriver and slot should be an exact match.

Below **Don't skimp on tools. Good quality tools, of the right size for each job, will earn their initial cost many times over.**

Above **Lateral thinking can work wonders. Here, detergent is used to ease the installation of a water pump impeller.**

Left **As with spanners and sockets, screwdrivers should be a precise fit in the head of the screw.**

Far left **Avoid damaging your knuckles by holding spanners and other tools with an open grip.**

Stubborn fastenings

We've all experienced nuts and bolts that won't come apart. In the marine environment, this can be exacerbated by corrosion and a build-up of salt crystals. The first step is to dissolve any encrusted salt with warm water, allow the item to dry, and then treat it with penetrating oil. This may free the fastening enough to allow it to move, but if not, providing there are no plastic, rubber or other components that would be adversely affected, heat can be used to help free the fastening.

This technique works on the principle that heating the nut with a blowtorch will cause it to expand faster than the bolt, therefore relinquishing some of its grip. Patience may be required at this stage – if the nut moves only a fraction, allow it to cool, and then repeat the process. Once you know it will move, you can be confident it will come apart eventually. It's important to apply heat as evenly as possible around a casting, as uneven heating may cause it to crack. An impact driver can also help at

this stage. The traditional mechanical type works by turning a screwdriver bit a few degrees when hit with a hammer. The hammer blow helps to ensure that the bit remains in contact with the head of the screw, while simultaneously turning the bit. This principle has been incorporated into a device of a similar shape to an electric drill, that speeds up the process by repeating it several times a second.

Freeing seized fittings

When you discover that screws, bolts or entire fittings have locked into position, a job that should take a few minutes can last for hours. Galvanic corrosion can bond dissimilar metals together, but all can be freed up with the careful application of heat, pressure and/or chemicals.

It is tempting to use brute force when faced with a seized or rusted fitting, but this doesn't always work. In fact, the situation can often be made worse, with the fitting breaking off. Rust and corrosion are the two main enemies of metal-to-metal fittings, especially where dissimilar metals are used. Ideally, these fittings should be assembled with a smear of anti-corrosion lubricant, and low-quality fastenings, such as mild steel screws, should be avoided.

However, all is not lost, as many seized fittings can be freed using the following methods.

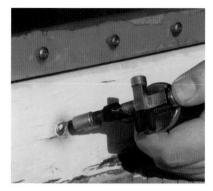

Above **Using a blowtorch on a stubborn screw is remarkably effective – but a soldering iron will do less damage.**

Below **A rusted nut on an old engine bed is drilled prior to splitting open with a cold chisel. Drilling and cutting are last resorts.**

Heat

Heat causes different metals to expand at different rates, so it can help break one metal free from another. Boiling water, a small blowtorch, a hot-air gun, or even a soldering iron can all be used, but always take care that heat sources are kept away from plastic components or pooled oil or diesel.

The most common type of metal corrosion is between aluminium and steel, where the creation of aluminium oxide locks the metals together. Directly heating the aluminium will cause expansion, helping to break the seal. Once the metal contracts on cooling, pressure can be applied to move it. The same technique can be used with nuts on engine bolts, but take care not to apply too much heat to the bolt.

Heat is particularly effective on seized woodscrews, and the best tool is a soldering iron. Hold it against the screwhead until the screw is very hot, and then leave it to cool completely. The shaft will have expanded and effectively widened its screwhole, so it will be easier to remove when it contracts again.

Right **An impact driver can loosen a stubborn screw by applying a short, sharp burst of torque. It sometimes helps to alternate between tightening and loosening.**

Below right **Penetrating oil should be applied liberally and left for several days to work.**

Torque

It is easy to apply too much pressure to a seized nut, especially when using a long lever arm, and this could lead to you snapping off the nut. One trick is to tighten the nut first, and then unwind it. Wind it back again slightly, and then wipe the threads with a cloth. This will prevent the displaced rust from being compacted towards the end of the bolt.

For machine screws or woodscrews, use an impact driver. Striking the driver results in a hard, twisting motion at the tool end, which can snatch the fitting free.

Chemical assistance

If it is feasible, soak the fitting in a basin of penetrating or easing oil. The small molecules in the oil gradually percolate between the two metals, and if left to soak for a few days, greatly assists separation. The careful use of some heavily diluted acids can have a similar effect, but you need to ensure they don't eat into the metal itself.

Drilling/cutting

If all else fails, then you need to drill out the screw or split open the nut. Using a small drill bit, drill a hole in the seized nut and then widen it using a bigger drill bit. A cold chisel can then be used to split open the nut. Alternatively, cut off the nut very close to the threads using a hacksaw.

Screws can also be drilled out, but take care that the drill doesn't slip. If possible, use a pillar drill, with the fitting secured to a jig, as hand drills can skid off hard stainless steel, scoring the surrounding aluminium.

With any seized fastening, it usually involves a combination of methods to unseize them, although the application of heat will often do the trick. Drilling and cutting should be considered last resorts.

Right **To avoid damaging equipment when striking it, use a soft striking plate, such as a block of wood.**

Freeing seized seacocks

Skin fittings that have been allowed to languish without care may well seize in position – either open or closed. The exact course of action to take depends on the type of fitting.

Traditional cone-type Blakes seacocks are the easiest to free once seized. Start by loosening the two nuts holding the top plate in position by one or two turns – this will loosen the force pressing the (rotating) cone into the fitting. It may now be possible to move the handle by hand, otherwise try tapping it gently with a small rubber mallet. If not, the next stage is to resort to heat, but take care not to apply it anywhere other than on the skin fitting itself.

This process can be carried out with the boat afloat; however, unless the fitting is dismantled, cleaned, regreased and reassembled, it will only be a temporary fix. It's also worth regrinding the faces of the seacock, so that they are a perfect, watertight fit.

This is done using the valve grinding paste that's sold by automotive parts retailers for grinding the valves of engines. Simply smear a little paste onto the faces of the cone, rotate it in the fitting and keep turning for a few minutes. A few applications may be needed, but eventually any pitting should disappear and both sides should be matched perfectly. Before regreasing the unit, it's essential that all traces of the grinding paste are removed.

> **TIP**
>
> Gate valves – the type with a rotating wheel as a handle – are unsuitable for marine use, as it's impossible to tell whether the valve is open or shut. Once removed from the thread on the through-hull part of the fitting, it should be replaced with a marine-quality ball valve.

Above **Most modern boats are fitted with ball valves. These can seize in one position if they are not regularly opened and closed.**

Freeing seized skin fittings

① Loosening these two bolts may be all that's needed to free the tapered cone...

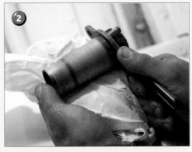

② ... but it should still be removed and cleaned up – as should the housing.

③ If badly pitted, the valve can be reground using car valve grinding paste.

④ Before refitting, coat the valve with a thin layer of waterproof grease.

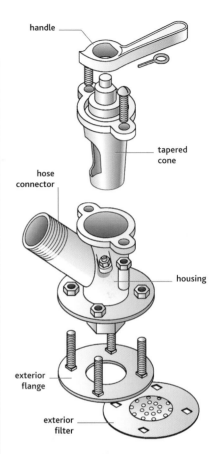

Above **Components of a traditional tapered seacock. These can easily be reconditioned and have an almost indefinite lifespan.**

Labels: handle, tapered cone, hose connector, housing, exterior flange, exterior filter

Ball valves

If a ball valve is stuck in position, the judicious application of heat may help to free it. However, be aware that the handles of these are less substantial than those on the Blakes's valves, and may not withstand taps with a mallet. If heat doesn't free the valve, it will need to be unscrewed and removed, with the boat laid-up ashore. Easing oil can then be applied – or it can be soaked in a paraffin bath. Another application of heat (this time you can afford to be more brutal) should free it. Before replacing the fitting, lubricate it with a light oil.

If ball valves start to become stiff, when the vessel is next laid-up they can be lubricated from above and below. This should restore their normal function with only a few minutes' work. If they are then opened and closed on a regular basis – rather than left permanently in one position – they should continue to function for their normal operating life.

Above **Cutaway of a ball valve, showing the central, 'business' part of most skin fittings specified for modern boats.**

Replacing through-hull fittings

A leaking through-hull fitting needs to be attended to without delay, as it may indicate an underlying problem such as corrosion. This could lead to rapid and catastrophic failure of the fitting and cause serious flooding.

Types of through-hull fittings

Traditionally, through-hull fittings have been made from bronze – a copper/tin alloy that can suffer from degradation when immersed in sea water. They therefore need to be checked annually. A reddish colour indicates there is electrolytic or galvanic corrosion, and that the device needs to be changed.

Below **Check the through-hull fittings every time your boat is taken out of the water. It will save heartache later.**

Glass-reinforced polymer resin through-hull fittings are available, and these do not suffer from corrosion. They are fully approved for use below the waterline. Unreinforced plastic through-hull fittings should never be used below or close to the waterline because of their lack of strength and durability.

Leaking through-hull fittings

A through-hull fitting may be leaking due to deterioration of the external seal or because of corrosion. The

only satisfactory cure is to remove the fitting, replacing it if necessary, and then resealing it to the hull.

Removing through-hull fittings

Unless a through-hull fitting is mounted well above the waterline, the boat must be lifted out of the water before it can be removed.

Generally, plastic through-hull fittings above the waterline will have no seacock, so only the hose attached to its barb needs to be removed. Unscrew the plastic

backing nut, try to break the sealant with a sharp knife, and push the fitting out from the hull. If the fitting needs to be knocked out it will probably be damaged in the process, and will have to be replaced.

If mounted below the waterline, bronze through-hull fittings will have a seacock attached to them, so the hose and seacock will have to be removed first. Access is often difficult. The fitting's backing nut will have to be removed, and this may have been covered in sealant. There is also likely to be a wooden backing plate glassed to the hull to make a flat, solid surface. Some through-hull fittings are bolted through the hull and backing plate.

Because the fitting will have been screwed down hard, it may well be difficult to break the sealant, and with limited access it may be impossible to drive out. In this case, the outside head of the fitting will need to be ground away with an angle grinder, so that the unit can be driven into the boat from outside.

Marelon through-hull fittings may have a backing nut or be bolted through the hull and backing plate. However, corrosion won't be a factor, so removal of the seacock and backing nut should present no problem.

Re-bedding a through-hull fitting

Clean the hull thoroughly, both inside and out, and use a high quality underwater sealant to re-bed the fitting. Be sure to use the recommended torque on any fastenings.

Removing a through-hull fitting

You will probably need a grinder to cut grooves in the outside of the fitting. Take extra care if you take the guard off.

Use a cold chisel to cut between the grooves and remove the outside flange.

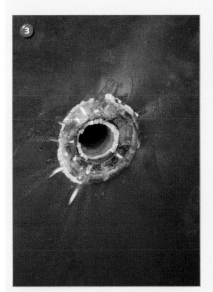

With the outside flange removed, the fitting can now be driven into the inside of the hull.

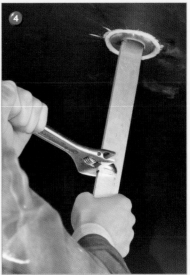

The new fitting has lugs on the inside, so you can use a flat bar to hold it still while fitting the inside nut.

Split fuel & water tanks

Water and fuel tanks may be made from a variety of materials, all of which can succumb to problems in the long term. However, in most cases, long-lasting repairs are feasible.

The best water and fuel tanks are made from stainless steel, or in a few cases Monel, a very corrosion-resistant alloy of nickel and copper. Tanks made from these materials are generally long lasting, although problems may arise due to poorly welded joints, or pinholes that develop over time. Problems with welds can be solved by re-welding the seam; however, pinholes may need more investigation. The best solution is to cut material out from around the hole, until sound material is reached beyond the damaged area, then weld in a patch. As stainless steel is both expensive and difficult to work, many boatbuilders use less expensive materials for tanks. Mild steel has only a finite life, even when used for a diesel tank, and once rust has got a grip the tank will need to be replaced. If, however, remedial action is taken at an early stage, by restoring the paint system (see page 102), then its lifespan can be extended considerably. Similarly, galvanised tanks that are starting to show surface rust can be shotblasted and taken to a specialist regalvanising facility – this will restore them effectively to as-new condition.

(see page 102)

TIP

Water tanks and pumps can both be damaged in a harsh winter due to the expansion of water when it freezes. It's therefore always worth draining the freshwater system when the boat is laid up.

Below **Stainless steel tanks are strong and reliable, but they are certainly not immune to problems.**

Left **This large inspection hatch enables internal baffles to be checked and cleaned.**

Below **A tank with evidence of corrosion – the cause of this should be eliminated.**

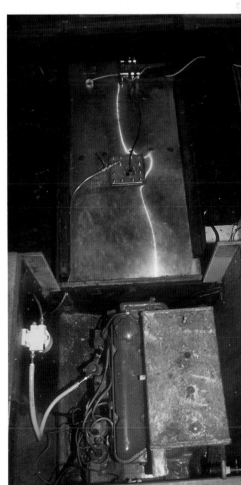

Plastic tanks

These can be made in a number of ways. Some are one-piece mouldings, which can be very tough, with any problems generally arising from chafe. This can be remedied by plastic welding – an analogous process to welding metals, in that the material on each side of the join is softened, and a plastic filler introduced to bridge the gap and form a structural bond.

The key disadvantage of moulded plastic tanks is that they must be mass-produced, so they are only available in a very limited variety of sizes and shapes. For this reason, many boats have custom-made polythene or polypropylene tanks made from sheet material welded together to fit the available space precisely. One disadvantage of these is that the seams have the potential to split, although this is a rare occurrence. Repair is, again, through plastic welding.

Fibreglass is another commonly used material – tanks can be made in one piece, or directly incorporated into the shape of the hull or keel. They can be repaired using the same procedure as general fibreglass repairs (see page 26).

Flexible tanks

These are an attractive option in many ways, as they are relatively cheap, easy to install and can be made to fit into awkward spaces. However, the downside is that they tend to chafe every time the boat moves on a wave, so their lifespan is relatively short compared to other materials. Flexible tanks can be patched, but this tends to give them a temporary reprieve, rather than being a long-term solution.

Right **A stainless steel fuel tank fitted in the bilge of a yacht. Its location means it's impossible to check the condition of the underside.**

Stripping a seized manual windlass

Of all the equipment and machinery on board a boat, it is the windlass that is the most exposed and vulnerable. Fitted to the foredeck, it is frequently exposed to salt water spray, and in some cases is completely immersed in water.

A neglected windlass that is gummed up, or even completely seized, can often be brought back to life if it's stripped down, cleaned and reassembled. Both horizontal and vertical axis units operate in a similar manner, and there are numerous similarities between many windlasses and winches. The most common causes of failure are generally connected with lack of use – even if you rarely anchor, operating the windlass a few turns every couple of weeks will keep all the parts moving, and highlight any developing problems at an early stage.

Dismantling a windlass

Before stripping a windlass apart, it's important to find a copy of the service manual for that model, and to understand what holds the gypsy on its shaft. There may, for example, be a screw that needs to be removed first, or the clutch may need to be unscrewed.

The biggest problems likely to be encountered when stripping the windlass are damaging the case, or breaking a stainless steel screw that has become corroded in aluminium. There may also be a lot of corrosion between the gypsy and the shaft. If possible, flush the area with hot water to remove encrusted salt, allow it to dry, then spray thoroughly with penetrating oil 24 hours before starting work.

Once removed, seized assemblies can be bathed in paraffin (kerosene) to help free them. Once parts have been thoroughly cleaned, inspect carefully for damage. Parts for many older units may no longer be available; however, a skilled welder can often repair a component that is cracked.

When the unit is reassembled, components should be covered in a waterproof grease, taking care not to over-grease them. Remember to smear zinc or barium chromate paste on the

screws and other stainless steel components that are in direct contact with aluminium, as this will help reduce corrosion between the two.

Electric windlasses

Electric models often develop problems with the wiring. All connections should be kept as dry as possible, and electric motors in exposed on-deck locations should be removed periodically to ensure

Below **Even the most idyllic location can turn nasty if the yacht's windlass seizes and the anchor can't be raised.**

Vertical-axis windlass

Clutch nut

Chain gypsy

Plain bush

Pawl and spring

Pawl assembly

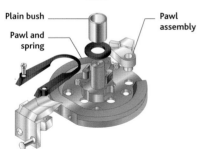

Above and above right **Elements of vertical-axis and horizontal-axis windlasses. They are similar to winches, but more complex.**

Horizontal-axis windlass

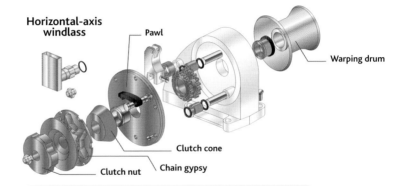

Pawl

Warping drum

Clutch cone

Clutch nut

Chain gypsy

Stripping a manual windlass

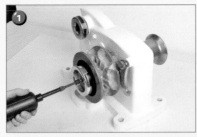

The gypsy's clutch is lubricated through the shaft nipple with waterproof grease.

Loosen the clutch ring by rotating it counter-clockwise.

Ensure that the gypsy can be slid sideways to release the clutch cone.

Undo the retaining bolt securing the warping drum.

Slide off the warping drum, ensuring the key doesn't fall out and get lost.

Remove the key, clean the key-way groove and regrease. Reassemble the components.

water has not penetrated the casing. If an electric windlass stops working, the fault is most commonly with the electrics. First, check the circuit breaker; then check whether power is reaching the motor. Only start dismantling the mechanical part of the unit once you are certain there are no electrical faults.

Leaking hydraulics

Many powered craft of all sizes, as well as larger sailing yachts, depend on hydraulic systems for high-load applications, ranging from trim tab actuators to backstay tensioners.

Hydraulic systems are ideal for many yachting applications as they are capable of converting a relatively small input into a considerable force applied at a remote location, as with the braking and power steering systems of road vehicles. However, with improvements in rope and deck hardware technology, hydraulics are increasingly being replaced by cascade block-and-tackle systems on sailing yachts.

There are three key elements to any hydraulic system:

✪ A manual or electric pump.
✪ An actuator that moves the item controlled by the system.
✪ Pipework, to join these two elements together.

There will also be a reservoir for hydraulic fluid, and usually filters to keep impurities out of the fluid. On sailing boats, the pumps tend to be manually operated, such as with a hydraulic backstay or kicking strap. However, some larger lifting-keel yachts have an electric pump that drives a hydraulic mechanism

MODERN ALTERNATIVES

Over the past 10 years, improvements in rope technology and in blocks and pulley systems mean that hydraulics are gradually being replaced by cascade block and tackle systems on new yachts. Before replacing a hydraulic backstay it's worth considering whether a modern rope pulley system would be a better option.

for lifting the keel. Motorboats of all sizes are more likely to use electric pumps, whether for steering, trim tabs or outboard/outdrive tilt mechanisms.

Below and right **Motor and sailing yachts use hydraulic systems for a variety of purposes, including backstay tensioners and trim tab actuators.**

Above **The hydraulic fluid reservoir must be kept topped up when bleeding air out of the system.**

Left **Unscrewing a hydraulic pipe connection – note that even old systems should be kept as clean as possible.**

A clean environment

When working on hydraulic systems, it's vital to maintain an absolutely clean environment – the biggest enemy by far is any dirt or grit that enters the system. Other than this, the most common problems include air in the system and fluid leaks. On older systems, the rubber seals may also lose their effectiveness, and allow fluid to move past the actuating piston. Some manufacturers sell the seals as low-cost spares; otherwise the only remedy for this is to replace the actuator.

Cracked or perished pipework can also create problems that, if left unchecked, will ultimately result in complete failure of the system. However, replacement is a straightforward process:

✿ Drain the fluid.
✿ Remove the offending element and replace it.
✿ Then, refill the reservoir with hydraulic fluid and bleed the system.
✿ The screw fittings at each end of the pipes are almost universally standard metric or imperial sizes, so these can be sourced easily.

Bleeding the system

If air is drawn into the hydraulic system, this will be compressed, rather than the hydraulic fluid being compressed and operating the piston of the actuator. Removing air is relatively straightforward – there should be a bleed screw at the end of the system. Loosen this a turn while operating the pump. If air bubbles out, along with hydraulic fluid, continue pumping until no more air is seen, then close the bleed screw. Remember to keep the reservoir topped up during this process, especially following work that required the system to be drained of fluid.

Below **Hydraulic backstay and mainsail outhaul controls for a 45ft yacht. Loads in the backstay can reach several tonnes.**

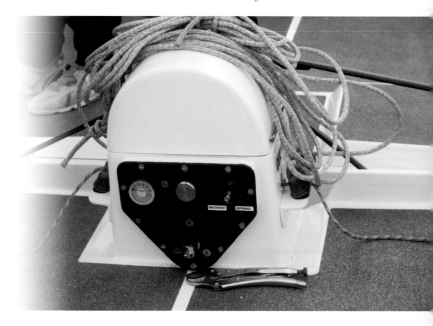

Repairing wind vane self-steering

Wind vane self-steering systems are popular with long-distance sailors because they are not a drain on electrical power, and are generally very robust. However, they are not infallible.

Most wind vane systems work on broadly similar principles, transferring the (small) movements of the vane to the tiller or wheel via a submerged blade that swings to one side when activated by the vane. The force that originates from the movement of the vane is amplified

TIP

If a wind vane steering system fails in heavy weather, many skippers feel compelled to rectify the problem immediately. However, given plenty of sea room, it's often more prudent to heave-to until conditions have moderated, as this doesn't require input from the self-steering.

by the pressure of the water moving past this blade, and it is this that creates enough energy to move the wheel or tiller.

Although many wind vane systems have the appearance of being very robust, even agricultural, they are a piece of precision engineering, and any unnecessary friction will impair their performance, especially sailing downwind in light airs. It's important, therefore, to ensure friction is minimised, especially in the control lines that link the tiller or wheel to the unit, and that bearings and bushes are in good working order.

Each model of self-steering gear is designed with a weak link – in effect a fuse – that protects the unit from damage if loads exceed the design criteria, such as an impact with floating debris. It's therefore crucial to be aware of how this weak link works on your system, the procedure for replacing it, and to carry spares. In some cases, the weak link is a short sacrificial length

Left **Wind vane self-steering has a reputation for being solid and reliable, but it's important to be prepared for problems.**

of tube above the system's rudder blade; in others it's a pin, or a weak section in one of the control lines.

As part of your general preparations before setting off on a long passage, it's worth checking the steering gear thoroughly. This should include wear in the bushes and bearings, chafe in the lines, and the security of each element, particularly the rudder. It's also worth carrying spares for all these items – most manufacturers sell a kit of the items most likely to be needed.

More catastrophic types of failure are unlikely; however, even then, with a little ingenuity jury-rigged repairs are possible. These are more likely to be successful if sail is reduced a little in boisterous conditions to avoid overloading the repair.

Above **Wind vanes are a product of precision engineering. Any jury-rigged repairs must ensure friction is kept to a minimum.**

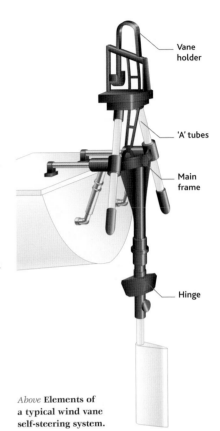

Above **Elements of a typical wind vane self-steering system.**

- Vane holder
- 'A' tubes
- Main frame
- Hinge

Refurbishing wind vanes

Badly neglected steering systems can often be refurbished relatively easily – many of the first commercially available models are still in operation. However, although the basic design of many models has changed little over the years, a process of gradual improvement has increased efficiency dramatically and reduced friction.

Left **Examine every element of the wind vane unit for wear before undertaking a long passage.**

Right **Check for play in the bearings by gripping the blade top and bottom and twisting it from side to side.**

Electrical
repairs

7

Electrical skills

To many boatowners, marine electrics are something of a black art, but the fundamentals of fault-finding and repairs are governed by only a few basic principles.

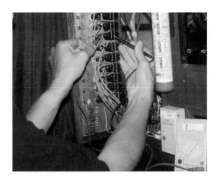

Above **A digital multimeter is a key diagnostic tool used in electrical repairs.**

Multimeters are the key tool used for diagnosing electrical problems – the resistance settings of a meter can be used to check the integrity of electrical equipment, from fuses and bulbs to complex items such as water pumps and heaters.

Battery state

The simplest way to check the state of charge of the batteries is by using a meter to test the battery's voltage – digital models are ideal for this, as they give a resolution better than 0.1V. It can take several hours for the voltage of a battery bank to stabilise after charging, or using power, so the

longer you can wait before taking voltage readings the better. However, most of the change in voltage occurs in the first 30 minutes.

When fully charged, a battery with a nominal 12V will, in theory, provide 13.2V, although 12.9V is a more realistic maximum. When this figure has reduced to 12.2V, only 50 per cent of the battery's capacity is remaining, and it should be recharged to maintain its lifespan. At 11.9V the battery will be around 90 per cent discharged. Some larger boats have a 24V electrical system, in which case the values above should be doubled.

Using a voltmeter can lead to a false sense of security with batteries that are near the end of their life, because the meter won't show

whether the battery's capacity to accept charge has declined dramatically. However, if navigation lights are turned on during the test, a change in the reading will give an indication of the battery's condition. Ideally, only a small voltage drop will be noticed for a battery that's in good condition. If a large voltage drop is experienced – ie over 0.3V – then the battery is suspect.

Below **Using a digital meter to check the voltage at a battery. At 12.21V, this one is holding about 50 per cent of its full charge.**

Installing a deck gland

Loosen the top ring, and drill a hole a little smaller than each wire through the rubber part of the gland using a sharp drill bit.

Pull the wires through the rubber part of the seal. Soapy water can be used for lubrication if necessary.

A water-tight seal is created when the top part of the gland is screwed down tightly, compressing the rubber.

Wiring diameter

When electricity passes along a wire, some energy is lost as heat. The smaller the wire for a given current, the greater the heat. To minimise energy loss in a long cable run, use a wire one or two sizes larger than the recommended minimum, especially for high-load items such as anchor windlasses and bow thrusters. The dangers of using wires that are too small cannot be overemphasized: a wire that becomes too hot will catch fire. If fuses rather than circuit breakers are used to protect circuits and equipment, it's important to use the correct size fuse for each circuit. To work this out, find out what each device or circuit draws, and then select a fuse which is the next size up.

If you know the voltage of your boat's electrical system and the power rating of the device in watts, simply divide the number of watts by volts to get the current the device will draw.

For example, an interior lighting circuit with eight 10W bulbs will draw 80W, so:

$$\text{Current drawn} = \frac{50}{12} = 6.67\text{A}$$

Therefore, an 8A fuse is needed.

If a fuse blows repeatedly, don't be tempted to replace it with a larger size – fuses are designed to protect wiring from overheating. Instead, identify the fault and rectify it.

Waterproofing

Although most boats' 12V and 24V DC electrical systems don't present the dangers inherent in mains voltage systems, water ingress can cause significant damage. Any cable passing through the deck should therefore be led through a deck gland to ensure water is kept out of the wiring.

Never leave the waterproofing of connections to chance – join the cables within a waterproof junction box or use waterproof wire connectors. Standard electrical connections should not be used, as they will not keep the water out.

Right **Water ingress is a common problem. Corroded contacts should be cleaned with fine emery paper.**

Replacing damaged wiring

Many older boats have poor quality wiring, with the system often extended in a piecemeal fashion to accommodate additional electronics and other equipment. Rewiring is, therefore, usually a sensible project.

Most problems encountered with wiring on boats involve connections and joints in the wiring. Water ingress leading to corrosion is perhaps the biggest issue; however, if the wires at the connection are able to move, this will lead to fatigue of the wiring – every time the boat rocks, the joint will move. If both problems exist, you can be sure of endless trouble with your electrics.

If not led through conduit, cables should be supported every 11–19in (30–50cm), with further support to prevent movement at each end. It's important to prevent chafe of the wire and its insulation at bulkheads and, ideally, wires should pass through rubber grommets.

Types of wire
Although many boats were built using standard household or automotive flexible wiring, this should be avoided at all costs and only properly tinned marine-quality wiring should be used. If wire is not tinned, the copper quickly oxidises in a marine environment, increasing energy lost due to resistance and increasing the possibility of failure. A proper tinned wire, however, will last for decades.

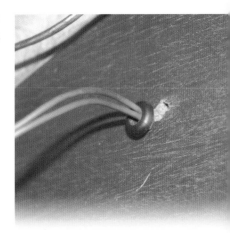

Above **Ideally all wires should be protected by rubber grommets where they pass through bulkheads.**

Below **Many older boats will need to be rewired to achieve a modern standard of electrical installation and to run up-to-date systems.**

Right **Stripping out old wiring at the beginning of a rewiring project can be a time consuming job.**

Most modern boats have wires run through conduit, with mousing lines supplied so a new wire can be tied to one of these and pulled through the conduit. However, don't forget to tie on a new length of mousing line – a lightweight whipping twine will do – otherwise next time it will be a harder task to lead a new wire through it.

Although not many older boats are fitted with conduit, if rewiring, it's worth installing some to make future modifications and repairs easier. In this case, household electrical conduit, or plastic ½in (15mm) waterpipe is adequate. It should be supported at 11in (30cm) intervals by gluing to the hull, deck or bulkheads with a waterproof gap-filling adhesive.

If your boat lacks conduit, there's a very good chance that headlining panels will need to be removed to access any wiring. If so, it's well worth relocating any wiring junctions clear of the headlining, and then installing conduit for the new wiring.

See page 156 for details on how to make reliable wiring connections.

Full rewiring

If a large part of the boat's electrical system needs to be rewired, it's usually worth making the effort to upgrade the entire system. In particular, the wiring from the battery to the positive and negative bus bars may benefit from being replaced with a larger diameter cable to match the increased loads of modern systems.

It's also a good idea to update the switch panel to one with plenty of space for more circuit breakers for additional equipment that may be added in the future. The same also applies to the bus bars, if they are running short of connections.

Left **Feeding a wire into conduit hidden behind headlining. It's often necessary to remove the headlining panels to do this.**

Soldering & replacing connectors

Most electrical connections never see the light of day, yet the integrity of these connections is essential for the reliable operation of the boat's various electrical systems. Vibration, rough handling and corrosion due to the marine environment all contribute to a gradual deterioration of connections, which may result in equipment failing to operate.

TIP

Practise soldering on some spare wire before you start the actual job.

Avoiding connector strain

Four types of electrical connector are commonly found on boats – soldered, crimped, screwed and clamped – all of which are examined individually below. However, connectors of any type must never be placed or left under mechanical strain, otherwise they may fail. Therefore it's essential that the wiring on either side of a connector is fully supported.

Soldered connections

Soldered connections have excellent mechanical strength and, if the soldering work is carried out properly, have almost zero electrical resistance, even if the surface is corroded. The correct way to make soldered connections is as follows:

✪ Strip the insulation to expose just sufficient wire core.
✪ Clean the tip of the hot soldering iron and melt a small quantity of flux-cored solder onto it – 'tinning' the iron.
✪ 'Tin' each wire/connector by heating it with the hot soldering iron and applying the flux-cored solder to the wire (not the iron).
✪ Place the two components together and apply the iron to them to heat up the components so that the solder melts and combines.
✪ Remove the iron, holding the components absolutely still until the solder hardens.

Wires that are to be joined can be first twisted together to increase mechanical strength – but be aware that this makes subsequent disassembly more difficult. When joining two wires, you should insulate the join. If you intend to use sleeves or 'heat shrink' tubing to do this, remember to thread them onto the wire prior to soldering.

Crimped connections

The connector is mechanically squeezed onto the wire using a crimping tool. Mechanical strength is good provided sufficient compression is applied by the tool. Ratchet tools supply much more compression. Electrical conductivity is good, given sufficient compression, but corrosion can occur between the connector and the wire over time. The correct method of making these connections is:

Soldering connections

Strip off the end of the plastic sheathing using a wire stripper.

'Tin' (ie apply solder to) each component separately.

Bring the wires into contact and apply heat with the soldering iron. This will melt the solder so that the components join without any need for additional solder.

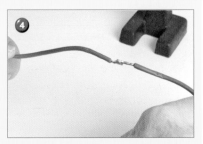

The two components are now joined. The joint should be protected using electrical tape or plastic sleeves.

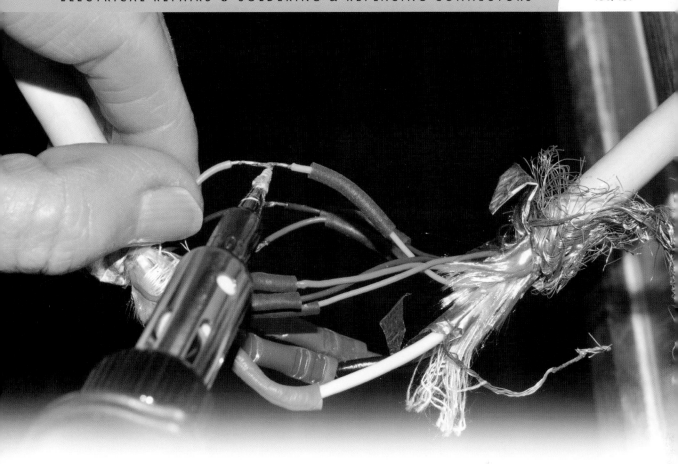

❂ Use the correct (colour coded) size of connector for the wire diameter.
❂ Strip just sufficient insulation from the wire to enter the connector sleeve.
❂ Insert the wire into the connector.
❂ Match the crimping tool anvil to the connector size by its colour.
❂ Use the ratchet crimping tool to squeeze the connector to its full extent.

Screwed connections

Screwed connectors allow easy dismantling of the joint. However, they don't inhibit corrosion, so should be liberally smeared with silicone sealant. The correct method is:

❂ Strip the insulation to expose just sufficient wire core.
❂ Insert the wire into the connector.
❂ Tighten the clamping screw securely.
❂ If the connector is exposed to corrosion, coat it with silicone sealant.

Clamped connections

Instead of using a screw, security is achieved by a lever clamp. These are neater and often smaller than screw clamps, and can be soldered to a circuit board.

Above **Soldering is best done with a gas soldering iron. Ensure that each joint is insulated from the others using a sheath.**

Below **A heavy-duty crimping tool can be used with a hammer or in a vice.**

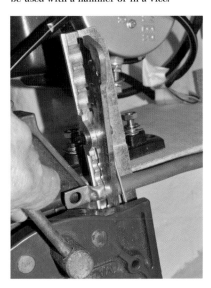

Tracing connection problems

If your boat has poor quality wiring, then chances are you'll have problems with your electrics at some stage or another.

As always, the most likely place a boat's wiring will fail is at the connections, where water ingress, fatigue or shoddy workmanship can lead to problems. When tracing faults, it's important not to rely on there being a continuous run of wire from the switch panel to the device. An obvious example of this is a navigation light circuit, in which a single switch powers port and

Below **Using a voltmeter to check the voltage drop at a terminal of an engine start battery.**

starboard lights, as well as the stern light. Although it would be possible to lead all three circuits to the main switch, it's usually more convenient for the cables to split elsewhere.

If an item stops running, the first step is to check the power supply is still working. Switch the device on, and use a meter to check whether there is 12V (or 24V) at its input. If not, check the fuses, remembering that many items are protected by an additional fuse or circuit breaker to the one on the main switch panel, which protects the wiring in the circuit. Next, the wire will need to be traced back towards the switch panel, checking any joints in the circuit.

Resistance testing

The multimeter can also be used to check the electrical integrity of your equipment, from bulbs to water pumps and electronics. At the simplest level, testing whether or not there is measurable resistance may suffice for fault-finding. Infinite resistance confirms that current is not able to flow through the device, while zero resistance indicates a short circuit.

A more detailed analysis can be made with some simple maths, using this formula:

$$\text{Resistance} = \frac{\text{Voltage}}{\text{Current}}$$

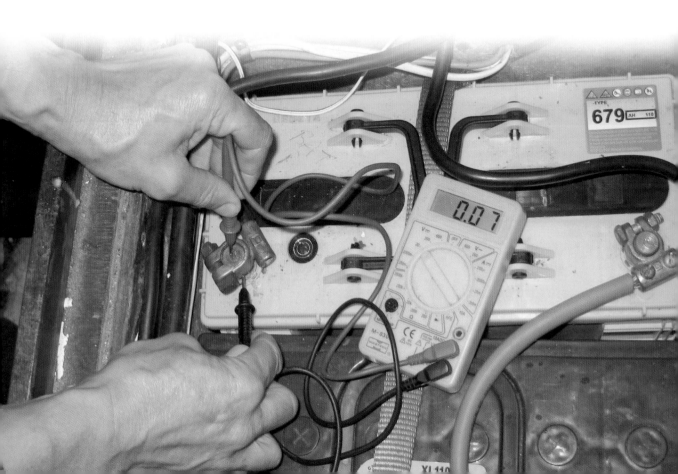

Right **Resistance testing a bulb using a multimeter. This is a quick method of fault-finding electrical equipment.**

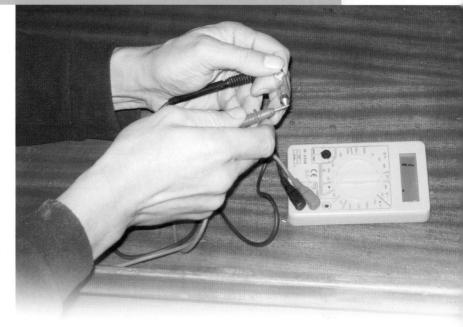

So, in a 12V system, a 10-watt bulb that draws a current of 0.8A will produce a resistance of:

$$\frac{12}{0.8} = 15 \text{ ohms}$$

Resistance testing is always done with the power supply isolated – a low voltage is supplied by the meter itself – and can also be used to check that switches, circuit breakers and fuses are functioning correctly.

Voltage drop testing

This test is used to identify and isolate faults with wire connections in high-load circuits; for example, those used for starter motors, anchor windlasses and bow thrusters:

✪ Set the meter to the 0–2V DC scale.

✪ Put the negative probe on the battery post, and the positive one on the adjacent battery terminal.

✪ Operate the bow thruster/ windlass/starter motor for a few seconds, noting the meter reading.

Repeat for all connections between the battery and the device.

✪ If any connection shows a voltage greater than 0.2V, or if there is a sum of more than 0.6V in the circuit, the contacts should be dismantled, dried, cleaned thoroughly with emery paper and reassembled. Smearing the connection with petroleum jelly will help to prevent the problem recurring in future.

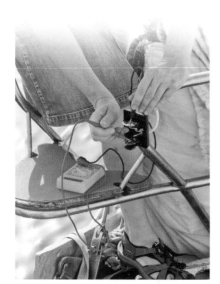

Above **Checking that the 12V supply is reaching a navigation light on the bow that is not functioning.**

Above **Be prepared to find joins in wiring in unlikely places. This junction box is behind a waste holding tank.**

Earth leaks

Stray current has the potential to corrode rapidly any metallic fittings that are under water, including skin fittings, propeller and shaft, P-bracket and outdrives. With conventionally built wooden boats, the fastenings are also at risk.

There are three interconnected sources of electrical current at play when it comes to corrosion of underwater fittings. These are the DC supply from your boat's 12V or 24V electrical system, AC from the shore power system, and the galvanic potential between dissimilar metals immersed in sea water.

LIGHTNING

Lightning has the potential to inflict serious damage on a boat, so it makes sense to give the electricity an easy route to earth. On a sailing boat, a heavy gauge wire from one of the chain plates to a keelbolt is an easy way to achieve this. Alternatively, some grounding plates are also designed for use in lightning protection.

When two or more dissimilar metals are immersed in sea water an electric circuit is set up, in which the least noble metal on the galvanic chart is gradually eaten away. This results in brass or bronze items on board your boat (eg the propeller and skin fittings, and fastenings on a wooden boat) suffering, unless sacrificial anodes are fitted so that these are eroded instead of your boat's fittings (see page 66). It is also possible for galvanic corrosion to arise from sources external to the boat, such as steel pilings.

Stray current corrosion

This can be a much bigger problem than galvanic corrosion, because it is driven by much higher voltages – the potential difference in galvanic corrosion is rarely much more than 0.2V. Bilge pump wiring is often the biggest culprit, although any wiring junctions in the bilge can be an issue if immersed in salt water, as can wires with damaged insulation. If possible, it pays to reroute any wiring out of

Left **Effective grounding against lightning strikes is vital, either via a keelbolt or a suitable grounding plate.**

Above **This heavy-duty grounding wire links a chain plate to a keel bolt as protection against a lightning strike.**

the bilge. Failing that, its condition should be checked regularly and any problems rectified immediately.

AC shore power supplies are normally earthed to a common ground point on the boat's engine, which is also shared by the negative wiring from the boat's batteries. This enables current to flow from the shore to the boat through the earth

wire, then back to the shore via the engine, prop shaft/propeller and sea water. The solution is to fit a galvanic isolator, which is fitted between the shore power earth and the engine ground. This blocks destructive low-voltage currents, but maintains the shore power system's earth connection by allowing high voltage AC current to pass.

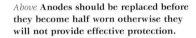

Above **Anodes should be replaced before they become half worn otherwise they will not provide effective protection.**

Grounding communications antennae

The antennae of communications equipment (eg SSB long-range radio transceivers) need to be grounded through an effective connection to salt water. On a fibreglass boat, the best way to do this is to fit a pair of grounding plates. These are designed to provide a large, effective surface area relative to their area, and are bolted to the bottom of the hull in a place where they will remain immersed when the boat is heeled or on the plane.

Left **When fitting a new shaft anode ensure self-locking nuts are used so that it cannot vibrate itself free.**

Navigation instruments

Navigation instruments are one of the more expensive parts of a boat's inventory, yet they are frequently ignored during annual maintenance, and only get looked at when they stop working.

Above **In-hull (left) and through hull (right) depth sounder transducers. Only the in-hull transducer is in use here.**

Many manufacturers stock spare parts for navigation instruments and are happy to give advice, so if you have problems with your instruments it's worth contacting them.

As with many other on-board items, water ingress is the biggest enemy. Despite the harsh conditions that may be experienced at sea, most instruments only have relatively lightweight water seals – witness the number of displays with condensation behind the glass.

If fresh water has entered the instrument, taking quick action to dry the unit should prevent lasting damage. In dry weather, simply leaving it switched on may suffice;

otherwise you might have to dismantle the case and place it on a heater. Salt water, however, is a much more corrosive enemy, and it is harder to rescue a unit that has been dropped in the sea. The starting point, though, is to rinse it with fresh water and then dry it thoroughly.

Broken display glass

The instrument's location on many craft is a compromise, which may leave them vulnerable to being broken. If the display glass does get broken, a piece of 2mm polycarbonate sheet should suffice as a replacement. When removing the old glass, make sure the case

is cleaned up thoroughly to allow the adhesive to form a strong, waterproof seal.

Degradation from ultraviolet light is another common problem with the displays on older instruments, which can leave them cloudy and difficult to see. However, in most cases, this is easily solved using a cutting/polishing paste such as T-Cut. This can also restore the appearance of faded outer casings.

Replacing instruments and displays

Instrumentation can vary from a simple speed and depth unit to complex interconnected systems in which every item needs to talk to each other. Before replacing any item, it's therefore worth assessing what your future requirements are likely to be, and ensuring replacement units will interface with the existing and future systems.

Left **Examining the circuit board of a non-functioning navigation instrument for problems.**

WATERPROOFING RATINGS

A product's International Protection Rating classifies the protection it has against intrusion of water:

IPX0 No protection.

IPX1 Protected from vertically falling water.

IPX2 Protected from water falling at an angle of up to 15 degrees from vertical.

IPX3 Protected from water falling at an angle of up to 60 degrees from vertical.

IPX4 Limited ingress of water sprayed from any direction.

IPX5 Limited ingress of water when sprayed by low-pressure water jets.

IPX6 Limited ingress of water when sprayed by strong water jets.

IPX7 Protected against immersion to a depth of 6-40in (15-100cm), for up to 30 minutes.

IPX8 Protected against longer periods of immersion, at greater depths.

Above **The waterproofing seal of instruments must be in perfect condition to prevent water ingress.**

Below **The appearance of faded instruments and cloudy displays can be restored with car body polish.**

Most displays are of the industry-standard 4.5in x 4.5in (113 x 113mm) size, which makes replacement relatively straightforward. Some items, notably chartplotters, may be significantly larger than previous equipment, but this need not pose a problem. They should be supplied with a template that shows the size of the cut-out needed, which can be created using a jigsaw for the straight lines and a large drill bit for any rounded corners. The best templates are self-adhesive – this helps prevent the gel coat being chipped by the saw blade. If you have to use paper templates, masking tape placed along the lines of the saw cuts will have a similar effect.

Autopilot repairs

Electric autopilots are complex items that deal with large loads. Although generally very reliable, there are a number of problems that may be experienced.

SAIL TRIM

Sail trim has a major influence on the steering characteristics of any yacht; however, when sailing under autopilot it's easy to become distanced from the feel of the helm, with the result that the vessel becomes difficult to steer. It's often instinctive to blame the autopilot when this happens, but time and again the crew is at fault. If the sails are reefed to the optimum size for the prevailing conditions and accurately trimmed, it will be much easier for the pilot to steer an accurate course. In addition, the boat will sail faster and provide a more comfortable ride.

Autopilots experience considerable loads – even on the smallest of boats, a tiller pilot operates only 18in (45cm) ahead of the rudder. This means that mountings must be strong and secure. It's normal to set the mounting, and any screws used, in epoxy for maximum strength. Any play in the mountings will mean the unit is unable to respond to small changes of course, and the play rapidly increase in a rough sea.

Tiller pilots

These are a significant challenge to waterproof, due to the changes in internal pressure as the tiller arm moves in and out of the unit. An O-ring around the tiller shaft is the main barrier against water penetration – this should be checked periodically to ensure it is in good condition, and replaced as necessary. To reduce wear on the O-ring, lightly oil the shaft occasionally, as this will help maximise its life.

Autopilot problems

There are a huge number of possible reasons for autopilot failure, depending on the complexity of the model. Start by checking the electrical supply to the unit, ensuring all contacts are watertight and that the supply voltage remains at or above 11.8V when the motor is activated. After this:

Below **Electrical autopilots are subjected to large cyclical loads and require a power supply that is beyond reproach.**

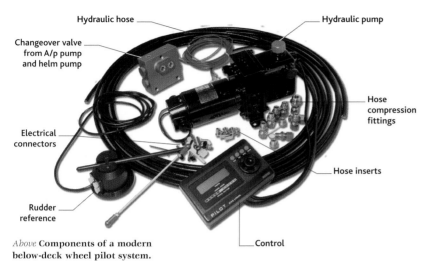

Hydraulic hose

Changeover valve
from A/p pump
and helm pump

Hydraulic pump

Hose
compression
fittings

Electrical
connectors

Hose inserts

Rudder
reference

Control

Above **Components of a modern
below-deck wheel pilot system.**

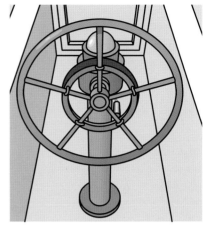

Above Wheelpilots driven via a rim
attached to the spokes of the wheel
have an internal belt that should
be replaced every 400 hours.

✪ Consult the autopilot's manual
to see whether there's a fuse that
might have blown in the powerhead,
or elsewhere within the unit.

✪ Examine the unit for water ingress,
looking for corroded or broken
soldered connections – see page
156 for more on repairing these.

✪ On a well-used system, the
brushes that supply power to the
electric motor can wear out after
a few years. These are designed to
be replaced easily – again, see the
autopilot's manual for details of
how to do this.

Larger boats with hydraulic pilots,
rather than those driven solely by
electric motors, may also encounter
further problems. See page 146 for
more information.

Replacing a below-deck auto pilot

The actuating unit must be securely
mounted to a structural element of the
vessel, such as a bulkhead.

Attaching the drive to the tiller arm (on
left). With a short arm such as this, the
loads in the system are considerable.

The compass sensor must be firmly
mounted somewhere clear of ferrous
metals and other electronics.

Installing the remote control unit at the
helm position, close to the wheel.

Windscreen wiper repair

The majority of marine windscreen wiper systems are relatively simple compared to their automotive counterparts, so diagnosing faults and making repairs is usually a straightforward process.

Unlike a car, where a single motor drives both wipers, most boats have a separate motor to operate each wiper blade. If a wiper stops working, start by following the fault-finding procedure for any other 12V device, and check that power is reaching the unit (see page 152). If one wiper stops functioning, the fault is likely to be with that unit, but if all wipers fail simultaneously it's worth checking fuses and circuit breakers before anything else.

In an old wiper motor, the grease will congeal over time, especially in the gearbox, which will make the unit stiff and difficult to operate. It's worth removing the motor every few years to clean it up. The procedure below will often give an ageing motor a new lease of life. Most wiper motors can be removed simply by unbolting them from behind the windscreen.

Below **Reliable wipers are vital to retain visibility from the helm in rain or rough water.**

After removing it:

- ✪ Unscrew the gearbox from the back of the motor.
- ✪ Clean the old grease off with a solvent and cloth as necessary.
- ✪ Smear a thin film of fresh, waterproof grease over the moving parts.
- ✪ Replace the gearbox cover and refit the motor.

Replacing a wiper mechanism

Ensure the power is turned off and remove the wiring to the motor.

Undo the anti-torque nut that prevents the motor assembly rotating.

Working outside the windscreen cabin, undo the motor securing nut.

Remove the holding nut from the wiper spindle and sealing washer.

The entire unit can now be lifted away from the window.

The anti-torque eye on the side of the motor case is shown here.

Replacing wiper motors

If the wiper motor repeatedly burns out, this is an indication that it is too small for sustained use – some boatbuilders specify motors on the basis that the boat is likely to be only used in good weather. If the vessel is used extensively in inclement weather, it may be worth replacing the motor with the next size up.

> **TIP**
>
> It's worth making a periodic check of the condition of wiper blades. Splits or cracks on the edge of the blade will mar efficiency and indicate complete failure is a possibility.

Marine wiper motors are designed to be fitted to a wide variety of boats, and so generally conform to industry-standard specifications. This includes a ½in (16mm) diameter knurled shaft end with 72 teeth for the wiper arm attachment. Larger boats and commercial vessels, however, may be fitted with a 1½in (approx 38mm) shaft end.

Before fitting, the sweep of the blades must be set to suit your boat, following the manufacturer's instructions. Generally, a choice of 80, 90 and 110 degrees can be selected, although some models have up to eight possible settings.

Replacing wiper arms and blades

The industry-standard fittings help to simplify this process, although an appropriate length of wiper arm will need to be selected to fit your boat's windscreen. As with cars, wiper blades will need to be replaced as they age – they are generally a push-fit that requires no tools.

As with automotive systems, marine screen washers are based on a 12V pump, so problems are generally either associated with the pump or with blocked nozzles. Poking a fine pin or sewing needle into the nozzle will usually solve the latter.

Engine repairs

Engineering skills

Although servicing an engine is usually a relatively straightforward process, when it comes to more major repairs, a greater degree of engineering knowledge may be needed.

There are a number of instances during the repair of an engine or other mechanical item when very precise measurements need to be made. A vernier caliper is a precision measurement instrument, accurate to within one hundredth of a millimetre, so identifying the difference between a metric 25mm propeller shaft and an imperial 1in (25.4mm) one, for example, will prove to be no problem. A micrometer can be used in a similar way, but will only measure external sizes, not the internal diameter of a tube, for example.

Feeler gauges are used to measure the gap between two items that are very close together, such as the electrodes of a spark plug, or the valve clearances of a four-stroke engine. They consist of six to eight thin metal strips, varying in thickness by around a few hundredths of a millimetre. The clearance (size) of the gap is measured by finding out which blade has a slight drag when it is inserted into the gap.

TIP

When undertaking a task for the first time take photographs of each stage of the procedure at the dismantling stage. This record will illustrate how all the components fit back together, and the correct order for reassembly.

Above **Using a vernier gauge to measure the precise size of an item to within 0.01mm.**

Below **Engine access is not always this easy and tools can sometimes fall into the bilge. Keep a magnet handy to retrieve them!**

Torque settings

A common mistake is to overtighten components when refitting them – this often complicates future servicing and repairs. Engine manufacturers specify the tension to which every nut and bolt should be tightened. This is expressed in units of pounds per foot or Newtons per metre, indicating the amount of force that would need to be applied to a wrench of that length to achieve the desired tension.

A torque wrench is used to measure the amount of pressure applied when tightening a nut precisely. This is a vital tool for replacing cylinder heads, for example, after replacing a blown gasket, as each of the nuts must be tightened progressively to specific measurements to prevent the head from warping. See also Mechanical Skills on page 134.

Above **A torque wrench enables nuts and bolts to be tightened to exacting tolerances.**

Left **A compression test will indicate the condition of key engine components, without dismantling the motor.**

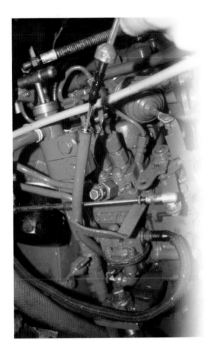

Cleanliness is king

When working on any part of an engine, it's vital to maintain a very clean working environment, as any dust, grit or other impurities that find their way into the motor or fuel system will significantly accelerate wear. One of the reasons modern engines last much longer than those made two or three decades ago is that they are now built in an environment that's cleaner than an operating theatre.

Left **Monitoring oil consumption against engine hours will give a good indication of engine condition and the rate of wear.**

Monitoring wear

As an engine ages, components will, of course, start to wear. However, even an elderly engine, providing it has been properly maintained, may well remain comfortably within acceptable tolerances. It's worth recording any change of oil consumption over time – if this increases rapidly it can be a sign of serious problems. A compression test to show the pressure in each cylinder is also a good indication of an engine's condition – this should be within the tolerances specified by the manufacturer, and on multiple cylinder engines there should not be a difference of more than ten per cent between the highest and lowest readings.

Starter problems

Whether they are mechanical or electrical in nature, most starter motor problems can be resolved reasonably easily, without the need for complex parts or workshop facilities.

As a huge amount of electrical energy, delivered in a short burst, is needed to turn an engine to start it, wiring runs are kept as short as possible, with the starter motor activated by a heavy duty solenoid switch that's mounted directly on top of the starter motor. The starter switch or key on the engine's electrical control panel simply activates this starter solenoid. Problems with dirty or corroded contacts are commonplace – if the starter fails to turn but the battery voltages appear okay, each junction in the wiring should be separated, cleaned and reassembled.

Battery problems

An almost flat battery may have only enough power to drive the solenoid, but not enough to turn the engine. In this case, a distinctive heavy click is heard when the solenoid engages, but then there may be silence. Occasionally, repeated clicks are heard, as the solenoid engages continually, and then disengages as the voltage in the system drops as it tries to start the engine.

Ideally, the idle voltage of the starting battery should be above 12.1V, and it should have enough juice to hold a voltage of more than

Above **This bolt is easy to reach to remove the starter, but some need a socket with extension bar and universal joint.**

10.8V when cranking the engine – any less than this will make it more sluggish to start. A low initial (open circuit) voltage can be remedied by charging the battery; however, if the open circuit voltage appears good, but the value when cranking drops below 10.8V, then the battery is at the end of its life.

Most diesel engines use glow plugs – pre-heaters that warm the intake air – to facilitate starting from cold. There should be one of these per cylinder, and if the engine doesn't start easily when cold, it's worth investigating whether or not these become warm when activated.

Below **Monitoring start battery voltage will minimise the chances of the engine failing to turn briskly on the starter.**

Right **The components of most engines are sprayed the same colour, which can make identification difficult. The solenoid sits on top of the starter motor.**

Brushes

These are the carbon contacts that form the connection between the static wiring and the rotating parts of the starter motor's electrical wiring. Over time, they slowly wear down. If every other part of the system appears to be in order, the likelihood is that the brushes need to be replaced. On most starter motors they can be reached after removing the end cover and will need to be soldered in place.

Below **Key elements of the starter motor and solenoid. The starter drive gear meshes with the flywheel to turn the engine.**

Solenoid

Starter motor

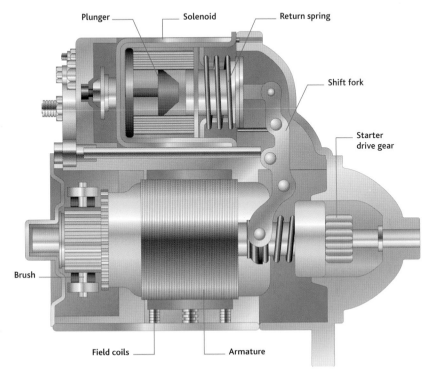

Plunger — Solenoid — Return spring

Shift fork

Starter drive gear

Brush

Field coils — Armature

Mechanical problems

The starter motor spins a pinion that in turn drives the engine's flywheel. This is normally engaged only when the starter motor is spinning – a secondary function of the solenoid is to operate a lever that slides the pinion along the shaft. This pinion can become partially or fully stuck on its shaft, resulting in the starter motor turning but the pinion failing to engage and turn the engine, or a graunching noise that indicates it's hitting the flywheel, but without enough force to engage with its teeth. The solution is to remove the starter motor and solenoid – they can generally be unbolted from the engine as a single entity – and then free and regrease the pinion.

Blocked fuel pipe & water in fuel

Even with the most meticulous care, it's almost inevitable that a little water will find its way into the fuel system. However, if large amounts enter the system then engine failure and mechanical damage are possible consequences.

Water in the fuel can arise from a number of sources, although it's most frequently blamed on refuelling with contaminated fuel. While this does happen on occasion, it's always worth checking the boat's own systems to ensure they are not to blame. The sealing ring for the deck filler pipe is a good place to start, as is the outlet for the tank's vent, as these are sometimes placed in locations where they can be swamped by big waves.

As well as having the potential to cause engine failure, water in the fuel can wreak havoc on fuel injector pumps. These items, that may cost one-quarter of the total price of the engine, are precision devices that depend on the flow of fuel for lubrication. There should, therefore, be a water separator incorporated into the fuel system between the tank and the motor. Any water present will show as an opaque layer at the bottom of the glass bowl, and

TIP

Watch out for the walls of flexible pipes becoming supple and collapsing with age. This can cause a fuel blockage and is not easy to identify, particularly if it occurs on the suction side of the fuel lift pump.

Below **Fuel problems are one of the most common causes of engine failure on boats of all types.**

Right **This plastic drain screw is used to drain water from the glass water separator bowl below the fuel filter.**

can be drained off by loosening the plastic screw underneath by a couple of turns. The separator should be checked at least daily, or after every eight hours of engine running.

If water has risen above the visible part of the separator, check the engine-mounted fine filter casing for evidence of water contamination – if water hasn't reached this point, then it should not have reached the pump either. However, if the contamination is extensive, the prudent course of action is to drain the pipework completely, then refill the fuel system and bleed the air from it (see page 176).

If the problem persists, the tank should be drained and refilled with clean fuel. This is particularly important for diesel tanks, as bacteria can thrive in the interface between the diesel and the water, multiplying to a density at which they can block filters (see page 184).

Fuel pipe problems

Blockage of a fuel pipe is unusual, as the fuel filter should trap any particles first. However, the filter doesn't protect the first length of pipe between it and the tank. If there's a lack of fuel after filters have been changed, this has to be a prime suspect.

That said, an air leak on the suction side of the lift pump is more likely to prevent the fuel system being bled successfully, and should be investigated first. This may be caused by a filter not sealing properly, or a leak at a pipe junction. Either way, it can be the most frustrating type of fuel leak to deal with as there isn't a tell-tale seepage of fuel to show where the leak is.

If the lift pump is not operating, diesel may seep out of the leak slowly. Placing kitchen towel below the primary filter and each joint in the pipework may reveal the source.

Top left **Make sure you know where to find the main bleed screw for your fuel system. You may need to locate it in the dark.**

Top right **Leaks on the suction side of the lift pump can be difficult to diagnose, as air is sucked into the fuel system.**

Below **The walls of flexible hoses become more supple as they age and can collapse under suction. Armoured hoses are better.**

Bleeding an engine

If air has been admitted to the fuel system – because you have serviced the fuel system, run out of fuel or have developed a fuel leak – you will need to 'bleed' or 'purge' the fuel system to remove any air. Bleeding the system is often seen as a daunting job, but it needn't be.

Diesel engine fuel system

A fuel pump on the engine sucks fuel from the fuel tank, via a primary filter/water separator, and delivers it under low pressure to the engine fuel filter and then to the fuel injection pump. The fuel is then pressurised, measured into very small quantities, and sent to each of the fuel injectors at exactly the right time. The amount of fuel delivered is determined by the governor controlling the rpm of the engine according to the load.

Petrol (gasoline) engine fuel system

Fuel is delivered to the engine in the same way as in a diesel engine. It is then mixed with air in the carburettor, where it enters the inlet manifold. On some engines there is no carburettor, so the fuel is injected straight into the manifold, and the air is mixed with the fuel there instead.

The primary fuel filter

This stops fuel tank debris reaching the fuel pump and separates any water from the fuel, prior to delivery to the engine.

The fuel pump

This transports the fuel from the tank to the engine. It is also used manually when bleeding the fuel system.

The engine (fine) fuel filter

The fine filter prevents very small dirt particles from reaching the fuel injection pump (diesel engines) or the carburettor/injection system (petrol engines).

The fuel injection pump

This pressurises, adjusts the quantity and times the fuel to the injectors. Excess fuel is returned to the tank.

The fuel injectors

These inject the fuel to the individual cylinders. Fuel leaking past the injector is returned to the tank or fine filter.

Below **The new filter being inserted prior to bleeding the system.**

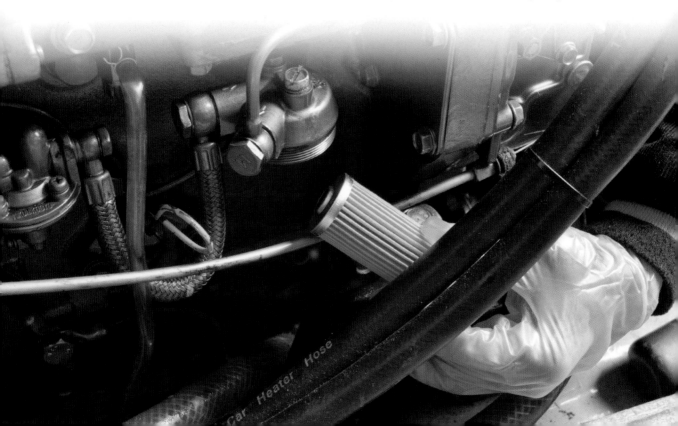

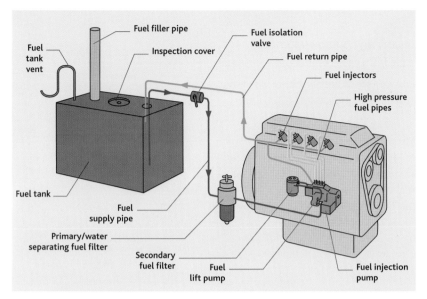

Above Ensure that any sealing rings are properly installed to prevent the filter leaking.

Left A typical diesel fuel system. Older boats may have the fuel supply from the bottom of the tank.

Bleeding the fuel system

⊙ Turn the fuel supply on.

⊙ If the primary filter is lower than the fuel level in the tank, open the filter bleed screw. Pressure due to gravity will force any air out of the pipe. When fuel is running from the bleed screw, close it.

⊙ If the primary filter is above the fuel level in the tank, do not open its bleed screw.

⊙ Open the bleed screw on the engine fine filter.

⊙ Use the manual fuel pump lever/ plunger to pump fuel through the system. If the primary filter could not be bled, this may take some time, as the primary filter bowl will have to be filled as well as the secondary filter.

⊙ When fuel runs continuously from the bleed screw, close it.

⊙ It is unlikely that the injectors will need bleeding.

Bleeding the engine

The engine will not run without fuel, so ensure it's turned on before you bleed the fuel system. Have a container ready to collect any fuel released.

If the primary filter is lower than the level of fuel in the tank, open the bleed screw until the fuel flows out. Close the bleed screw once any air bubbles have gone.

There is a bleed screw on the secondary filter body to allow trapped air to escape. Undo this about two turns and let the fuel flow until all air bubbles have gone.

Pump the priming lever (or plunger) on the fuel pump until the fuel runs from the bleed screw without air bubbles, then close the bleed screw.

Adjusting the belt drive

An engine has one or more rubber belts driving the alternator and sometimes the raw water pump. If the belt fails, there will be no electrical output from the alternator – and if the raw water pump stops working, the engine will overheat in a matter of minutes, rendering it unusable.

Types of drive belt

The most common drive belt is of fabric-reinforced rubber. Generally these are quite adequate. If a heavy-duty alternator is fitted, a heavy-duty drive belt should be used – these often have notches in their contact face.

Measuring belt tension

A slipping belt will cause rapid wear, so it's important that the belt is under sufficient tension. It is often recommended that, to test tension, the belt is pressed as hard as you can halfway between the pulleys. The deflection should be about

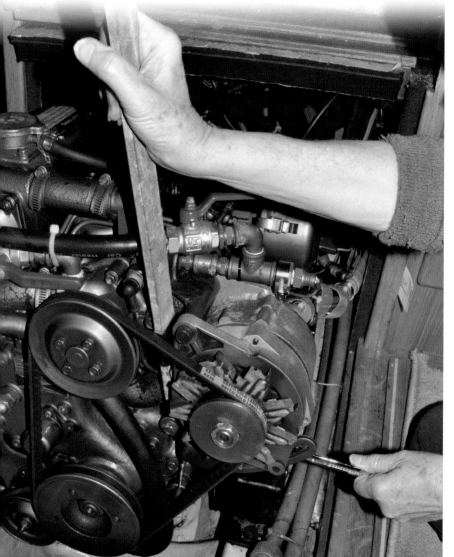

Left Adjusting the alternator belt often requires a lever to tighten the belt while the adjustment clamp bolt is tightened.

Below On some engines, the water pump is driven by a separate belt. This must also be kept tensioned correctly.

Left **A correctly adjusted belt should twist through approximately 90 degrees.**

Rubber cam belts

Some engines are marinised versions of car engines, and these may have rubber cam belts. Failure of these will result in very expensive damage. Cars normally require cam belts and their associated tensioners to be changed at 50,000- to 80,000-mile intervals, which equates to about 1,000 engine hours. Usually beyond the DIY mechanic, this essential maintenance should be undertaken by a professional.

0.5in (12mm). Possibly an easier and more reliable method is to grip the belt, at its mid-position, between your thumb and forefinger and twist. If properly tensioned, it should twist approximately 90 degrees.

Adjusting belt tension

Most engines have a very unsophisticated method of adjusting belt tension:

❂ Loosen the adjustment bolt and the pivot bolt on the alternator or water pump.
❂ Use a long, strong lever to force the alternator or pump away from the engine, first ensuring that the two bearing points of the lever are not resting on any part that could be damaged by the strong force that you are going to apply.
❂ While still applying the strong force with one hand, tighten the clamp bolt with the other.
❂ Tighten the pivot bolt.
❂ Check the belt tension and readjust if necessary.

Drive belts with screw adjusters

❂ Slacken off the clamp and pivot bolts.
❂ Screw the tensioner in the required direction.
❂ Check the tension.
❂ Retighten the bolts.

Below **Once the belt has been tightened, the adjustment bolt is tightened, followed by the alternator/water pump bolt.**

Water pump repair

Most marine engines are water cooled, and use a pump with a rubber impeller to pump the water through the system. Failure of the impeller will render the engine unusable, so you need to be able to change the impeller yourself in case it fails.

How a water pump works

The majority of engines use a pump with a flexible-bladed rubber impeller rotating in a chamber. During part of each revolution, the blades are squashed by a fixed cam, so that the volume between consecutive blades is reduced. This reduction causes water to be forced out of the exit port. As the blades recover their normal shape and the volume increases, water is sucked in through the inlet port.

Priming the pump

These pumps are self-priming, provided there are no air leaks in the 'suction' pipe and that the pump is no more than 15ft (5m) away. If the pump is reluctant to prime, check that the water strainer cap is fully tightened and, if necessary, fill the strainer with water.

Below **This flow of water from the exhaust pipe shows that the sea water pump is operating correctly.**

Changing the impeller

If the pump is inaccessible, it might be easier to unbolt it from the engine first.

Loosen the retaining bolts on the front of the pump and remove the faceplate.

Impeller failure

The impeller is a tight fit in the casing to prevent leakage, resulting in a lot of friction and therefore heat. The impeller and casing are cooled by the water that is pumping. If no cooling water flows, the impeller will rapidly overheat, causing it to disintegrate.

Changing the impeller

⬦ Close the cooling water seacock.
⬦ Remove the screws holding the faceplate in place.
⬦ Remove the faceplate, endeavouring not to damage the sealing gasket.
⬦ Withdraw the impeller from its shaft – this may require partial withdrawal at first, to expose a set screw, which can then be removed.
⬦ Insert the new impeller, having first coated the blades with washing up liquid or grease.
⬦ Clean the mating surfaces of the faceplate, renewing the gasket if necessary.
⬦ Replace the faceplate and screws.

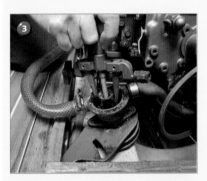

It's best to use a specialist tool to remove the impeller, otherwise use screwdrivers.

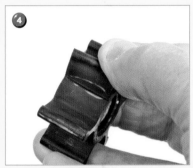

Check the impeller for cracking at the blade roots. This one needs to be replaced.

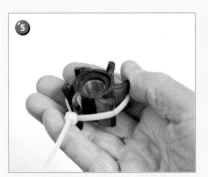

Use a cable tie to pre-shape the blades into the correct position to make insertion of the new impeller easy.

Insert the new impeller in the pump, and slide the cable tie out. Reassemble in reverse order.

Heat exchanger problems

The heat exchangers of indirectly cooled engines can help to extend engine life considerably. However, they are not immune to trouble, with scaling of the waterways being the most common problem encountered on older units.

There are two broad options for cooling a marine engine. The most simple is to pump raw water (taken from the sea, lake, river, etc, in which the boat is floating) around the motor, and pump it out with the exhaust. However, there are a number of drawbacks to this, especially for vessels that operate in sea water, where the salt will corrode internal parts of the engine and narrow the waterways. Such engines are fitted with thermostats that limit their operating temperature to 63°C

(145°F) – around 20 degrees lower than normal. Although this slows the process of corrosion, a side effect is that, as they never warm up to the engine's designed operating temperature, they run at a lower efficiency and wear more quickly.

A better option, therefore, is to use a closed system in which fresh water and antifreeze is pumped around the engine. This water is cooled by pumping through one side of a heat exchanger (eg a pipe) that has 'raw water' (eg sea water, if in the sea)

running through the other side. This allows the engine to run at its designed temperature, which will improve fuel efficiency and maximise the life of the unit, as all the parts will be running at their designed tolerances.

Below **Removing the heat exchanger from a large six-cylinder engine.**

Left **Many engine manufacturers recommend descaling the heat exchanger at least once every five years.**

Below **Cross section through a heat exchanger, showing the fresh water coolant (blue) and raw water (green and white).**

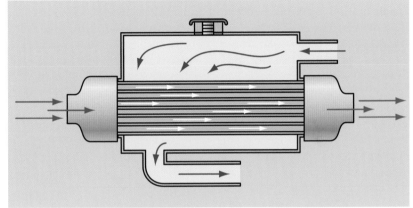

Descaling a heat exchanger

Over time, the waterways on the raw water side of the heat exchanger will become restricted by deposits of scale. If the engine runs warm, but the water pumps, drive belts and exhaust hose are in good condition, this is likely to be the cause.

Before it can be descaled, the heat exchanger should be removed from the engine.

✪ Start by draining both the fresh water and the raw water parts of the cooling system. Some engines have a drain plug specifically for this purpose, while others will require the lowest end of the cooling hose to be removed.

✪ Next, remove any other hoses, followed by the bolts securing the unit to the engine block. The heat exchanger can then be dismantled further on the bench.

Right **Removing a neoprene type end cap from a heat exchanger, revealing the waterways within the core.**

Dismantling a heat exchanger

✪ Start by unbolting and removing the end caps. This will reveal some of the waterways, and can give you a good idea of how badly scaled they are.

✪ At this stage, the components should be soaked in a citric acid solution for at least 24 hours, as this will help to soften and loosen the scale. If a lot of scale persists, a second soaking in acid solution will be worthwhile.

✪ Then, flush the waterways through with water. This should clear the restriction in the waterways, although severely scaled heat exchangers may benefit from mechanically rodding out scale.

Beating the diesel bug

Whenever there is water present in a diesel tank, bacteria are prone to form at the interface between the fuel and the water. This can quickly escalate into a problem of sufficient severity to block the fuel filters.

The first defence against contracting a fuel bug is to ensure that water does not enter the fuel tank. However, there are a number of mechanisms through which this is possible, so it requires constant vigilance. A good practice, that will reduce the chances of taking on contaminated fuel, is only refilling at outlets that have a high turnover of fuel.

Ensuring water cannot enter your own tank is the next line of defence – ensure the filler cap seals well, and that water cannot enter through the vent pipe. Another way which water can form in the tank is through condensation on the tank walls. As the boat is warmed and cooled by the sun each day, air will first be expelled through the vent as it expands on heating, and then more air is drawn back in as it contracts when it cools. As it does so, some of the moisture in the air condenses on the side walls of the tank, and runs to the bottom of the tank (diesel floats on water). A cycle then sets up, in which a little more water is added to the fuel each day.

The best way to combat this is to ensure the tank is kept topped up whenever practical – hence not wanting to buy fuel from an outlet whose tanks may remain less than half full for an extended period of time. Treatment with a propriety diesel bug killer is also a sensible precaution, especially if you notice tell-tale black deposits on the filters when changing them during engine services.

Top right **If water is present in diesel, bacteria can thrive at the interface between the two liquids.**

Below **If possible, always try to refuel at an outlet with a high turnover of fuel. These are less likely to have water in their tanks.**

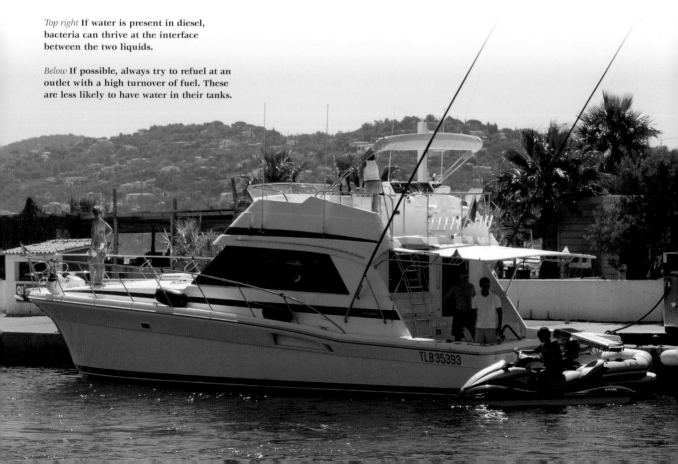

Overcoming the bug

A blocked fuel filter is often the first sign that tanks have become contaminated with bacteria. Although filters can be changed easily, it's still wise to be circumspect and keep a look out for further problems. It's certainly worth treating the tank with a bug killer and check filters much more frequently than normal – the diesel bug killer won't get rid of the bacteria already in the tank, although it should stop it reproducing.

Right **Using a water-separating filter when refuelling will help to ensure as little water as possible reaches your boat's tanks.**

Above **Bacteria rapidly clog filters. If you have the diesel bug, be prepared to change filters more frequently than usual.**

Left **Fuel tanks benefit from periodic draining and cleaning. This is vital following a bacterial infestation.**

If large amounts of bacteria are present, and filters become blocked regularly, the tanks will need to be emptied and thoroughly cleaned. If facilities are available, after decanting the fuel from the boat's tanks, it is possible to remove the impurities from the fuel through a process known as polishing. This uses an electric pump to push the fuel through a fine filter and water separator, independently of the engine. This allows contaminated fuel to be passed through the system several times, if necessary, with a change of filter, until it is perfectly clean.

Water & oil contamination

Finding water in the oil or oil in the water are both indications of serious problems with the engine, generally stemming from a blown cylinder head gasket, or cracked or warped head. Both problems are often associated with overheating.

The first sign of trouble is often a white mayonnaise-like emulsion under the oil filler cap, or on the oil dipstick. This arises from cooling water finding its way into the engine oil, which severely impairs the oil's lubricating properties. Alternatively, oil may be found floating on top of the water in the heat exchanger or coolant reservoir of indirectly cooled engines. A compression test – using a pressure gauge screwed into either a sparkplug or injector socket – will help to confirm the problem.

Removing the cylinder head
Preparation for this varies for different types of engine, but is broadly as follows:
- Drain the cooling system.
- Remove the cooling system hoses.
- Remove the fuel lines.
- Remove the exhaust and inlet manifolds.
- Remove the rocker cover box.

The cylinder head should now be ready for removal. These are usually tightened to a very high torque specification (see page 170), so a good socket set, with a long handle, is essential to unscrew the bolts. This must be done in the order specified by the manufacturer, to ensure the head is not warped further. Start by cracking off each bolt by just a few degrees, then repeat the process, turning each bolt 45 degrees. On the third iteration each can be turned 90 degrees. This step-by-step procedure ensures stresses remain constant across the cylinder head.

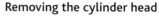

Left **After removing the cylinder head use a blunt tool to remove all traces of the head gasket, together with any carbon deposits.**

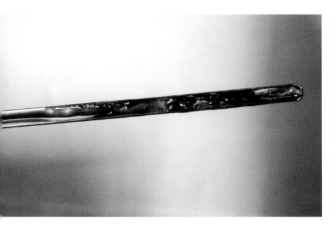

Far left **White emulsion on the dip stick signifies there is water in the oil.**

Left **Likewise the oil filler cap. A compression test will confirm the diagnosis.**

Once all the bolts are hand-tight, they can be removed one at a time, and the head lifted off the engine block. Use a blunt tool to remove all traces of the head gasket from both the cylinder head and the engine, taking the utmost care not to scratch either of these surfaces.

Cylinder head examination

The next stage is to check whether the cylinder head is distorted – this can be done using a straight edge such as an engineer's steel rule and a feeler gauge. Move the edge of the rule over the underside of the head – in all possible orientations using the feeler gauge to measure the largest gap you can find between the head and the rule. This gap must be within the tolerance specified by the engine manufacturer – usually the maximum tolerance will be less than 0.004in (0.1mm).

If your measurement exceeds the manufacturer's specified tolerance, the head will need to be skimmed by an engineering workshop. This process removes a thin layer of metal from the bottom of the cylinder head, leaving it perfectly level.

Refitting the head

This is a reversal of the removal process, but it must be stressed that the process for tightening the cylinder head bolts to the manufacturer's specification must be followed to the letter. After placing the cylinder head on its new gasket, insert all of the bolts and spin them up by hand until a little resistance is felt.

Following the sequence for your engine, use a torque wrench to tighten each bolt in turn, a little at a time, until the required torque value is reached. The inlet and exhaust manifolds can then be refitted, followed by fuel pipes, cooling hoses, and all other items.

Below **The bolts holding down the cylinder head must be tightened in a strict order.**

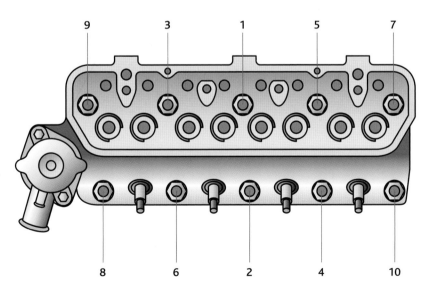

Broken or loose engine mounts

Engine mounts are subject to enormous loads, yet a broken mount can go undetected for a surprisingly long time. This can cause a number of problems, including increased vibration and accelerated wear of shaft seals and gearboxes.

Fuel or oil leaks are the most common reasons for the rubber parts of engine mounts to fail. These liquids attack the rubber and the adhesive that bonds it to the metal parts of the mount. A less common cause results from a rope or other debris fouling the prop. If this stalls the engine, considerable loads are placed on the system, which can bend the prop or shaft, damage the gearbox, or shear an engine mount. As well as damage to stuffing boxes or dripless shaft seals, a broken mount will increase loadings on the gearbox output shaft bearings and the gears themselves, which if left unchecked will result in premature transmission failure.

Diagnosing problems

The first sign of a broken engine mount is often that the engine can be seen to vibrate excessively. This is normal when the engine first starts or is turned off, but otherwise movement should be minimal. With the boat moored, check to see whether the vertical stud is centred over its base – if it's leaning to one side the shaft is out of alignment. Then start the engine and put it in gear – at one-third throttle it should move no more than 0.16in (4mm) between forward and reverse gears.

Before replacing mounts, the engine must be supported by other means, usually by placing chocks or wedges of timber beneath it, allowing the mounts to be replaced one at a time. If necessary, it can also be raised fractionally using a scissor-type car jack. Make sure no hoses or wires will be damaged if the engine moves outside its normal limits during the operation.

Once the engine is supported safely, start by unscrewing the top nut on the mount, then slacken the height-adjusting nut below this. Eventually this mount will no longer be supporting the engine's weight, which will allow the bolts securing the mount to the engine beds to be removed safely. The old mount can then be removed and its replacement slipped into position.

Left **Carefully chocking the engine to support it will enable damaged mounts to be changed one at a time.**

Above **The rubber parts of engine mounts will decay rapidly if oil or fuel is allowed to drip onto them.**

Left **Engine mounts are relatively simple to change, but the engine must be realigned afterwards.**

Realigning the shaft

After installing new engine mounts, the alignment of the engine/gearbox with the prop shaft will need to be checked and adjusted. Unbolt the shaft boss from the plate on the back of the gearbox, and slide the shaft aft a fraction. Then, check the gap between them with a feeler gauge – this should be constant right round the circumference. If not, the engine mounts should be adjusted until it is.

Before starting this procedure it's worth checking the condition of the cutlass bearing – if it's excessively worn, the shaft cannot be aligned accurately. See page 192 for replacing the cutlass bearing.

Bottom left **A refurbished engine bay with the new engine mounts in position, ready for the engine to be installed.**

Bottom right **The new engine in position. Before the gearbox and propeller shaft are connected, the engine alignment must be checked.**

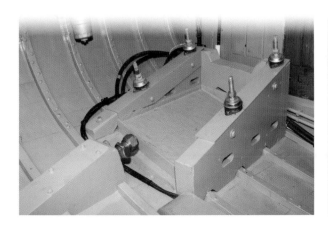

Damaged engine controls

Loss of engine control has the potential to disable a vessel without warning; however, in most cases, symptoms start to become apparent long before the controls fail.

Most marine engines use a single lever control that operates both the gearbox (forward, neutral and reverse gears) and the engine's throttle, via mechanical cable linkages. Irrespective of the brand, these all work on the same principle, and parts are frequently interchangeable, although cable lengths always vary between installations on different boats.

Right **A single-lever control for a sailboat. Make sure you know how to access the back of the control in the event of problems.**

Below **The system is more complicated for motor boats with multiple helm positions, although the latest engines have electronic controls.**

Diagnosing problems

If the levers start to become harder to move, the problem can only lie in one of three areas: the cable, the connection to the throttle or transmission, or the control unit. Start by disconnecting the cable at the engine/transmission and operate the throttle or gear selector by hand. The lever should move smoothly with light to moderate force.

While the cable is still disconnected from the engine, operate the control lever. If this is now easy, it will confirm the diagnosis of problems at the engine or gearbox. However, if the lever remains stiff to operate, the problem must be either with the lever or with the cable. Removing the cable from the lever will identify which of these is at fault.

TIP

If the button in the centre of the Morse lever doesn't spring out, it will be impossible to engage gear. After starting the engine, never cast off before returning the lever to the upright position and checking all is okay.

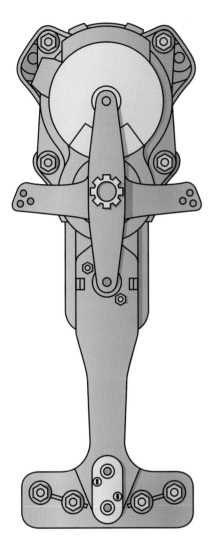

Fitting and adjusting cables

Cables are sold in increments of 1ft (30cm). Always round-up measurements to the next longest size, as a cable that's too short will not adopt a perfect alignment, and will therefore fail prematurely. Try to minimise any sharp bends, and make sure no bend has a radius of less than 8in (20cm).

Problems can also arise with the little button in the centre of the control that is used to disable the link to the gearbox so that the engine can be revved in neutral when starting. The spring that pushes this out automatically will weaken with age, while at the same time corrosion, or a build-up of salt, can create significantly more friction. If the button becomes jammed in the inner position, the plate attaching the cables can be unscrewed from the back of the unit – this reveals access to the blind side of the button,

Above **Trace each control cable to the engine or gearbox – it may be possible to operate the throttle or gearbox manually to get you home.**

and it can be pushed out manually. Even if this problem has only happened once, you can be sure it will recur. The control should therefore be cleaned thoroughly, dried, and the button lubricated with light oil. If it's possible to source a new spring at the same time, this will also improve the operation.

Above **View of the back of a single-lever control – these operate both gear and throttle cables.**

Right **Many problems stem from long runs of control cables that turn several corners to reach remote helm positions.**

Replacing cutlass bearings

Cutlass bearings are one of only two supports for the propeller shaft – the forward end of the shaft being supported at the gearbox. They play a vital role, and are frequently a pointer to engine alignment problems.

The bearing is formed of two components, usually a nitrile (ie oil-resistant) rubber set in a bronze or marine-grade brass boss. They should be replaced when the shaft has around 0.08in (2mm) of play – this figure can be increased slightly for shafts larger than 1.25in (35mm) diameter, but reduced for smaller ones.

Normal lifespan is several years; however, if wear is rapid or uneven, this points to shaft and gearbox alignment problems (see page 188). In addition, fishing line can be drawn into the bearing very easily, which will accelerate wear

significantly. Similarly, if the boat often operates in water with a large amount of muddy or sandy sediment, this will also speed up wear, as will marine growth on vessels that are not used for extended periods of time. The bearing is lubricated by sea water, so when the engine is running, the shaft should not touch the bearing directly, provided it is correctly aligned. Most wear, therefore, takes place when engaging gear, and when returning to neutral, and engines that run a large number of hours may not experience significantly more wear than a lightly used craft.

Procedure for removal

The prop shaft must be removed before the cutlass bearing can be replaced (see page 200). The bearing will be held in place with a pair of grub screws, so these must be removed first. However, there's every chance it will also be corroded in place – don't be tempted to try knocking the case of the bearing out with a drift, as this risks damage to the P-bracket and its attachment to the vessel. Instead, use a puller that clamps around one side of the P-bracket, while allowing pressure to be put on the other side with a screw thread.

Below **Like all underwater gear, cutlass bearings are easy to forget – but excessive wear can indicate bigger problems.**

Fitting a new bearing

After removing the old cutlass bearing, the aperture in the P-bracket or shaft log should be cleaned up, with any signs of corrosion removed. The new bearing can then be slid into place – this should be an easier operation than removing the old one. Once the bearing is in situ, tighten the grub screws to secure it, then refit the shaft and propeller.

Left **Check for wear at the bearing by moving the propshaft both vertically and from side to side.**

Below left **Measure the shaft with a vernier gauge to ensure exactly the right size of replacement cutlass bearing is fitted.**

Below **Cutlass bearings are usually made of nitrile rubber, which is both hard-wearing and oil-resistant.**

Alternatively, a handsaw can be used to make three longitudinal cuts through the bearing's shell, taking care not to damage the P-bracket or shaft log. The individual elements of the bearing can then be collapsed inwards and removed.

The cutlass bearing must be a perfect match to both the shaft and the internal diameter of the P-bracket or shaft log. Accurate measurement of these with a vernier caliper is essential (see page 170).

Dripless shaft seals

Although dripless shaft seals need less regular attention than traditional stuffing boxes, it would be a serious mistake to ignore them entirely.

A wide variety of dripless shaft seals are fitted to many boats in preference to a traditional stuffing box. Different models vary enormously in complexity, and therefore in maintenance and repair procedures, but in all cases it's important to understand the model fitted to your vessel. As with all rubber materials below the waterline, such seals should be inspected regularly for wear and chemical deterioration, noting that most manufacturers recommend replacement as a precautionary measure every five or six years.

Principles of operation

The majority of these seals are water lubricated, although some earlier models rely on oil for this purpose – with these models the oil reservoir must never be allowed to run dry. When launching a boat with a water-lubricated model, any air that's trapped in the seal must be purged. This is done by squeezing the seal with one hand until water squirts out – a process generally known as 'burping'.

Failure to carry out this procedure is the largest single reason for premature failure. The other common reasons for early failure stem from broken engine mounts and/or a misaligned engine and prop shaft (see page 188). Water leaks are the most obvious indication of an aging seal. These may start as an occasional small drip, but will slowly turn into a more regular flow with the engine running. Seals designed for large shafts, and therefore big engines, need a considerable flow of water to provide cooling to the bearing surfaces, as well as for lubrication. Water is therefore piped directly to the seal from a skin fitting. Limescale will reduce the diameter of this pipe progressively over time, leading to potential overheating of the seal; however, replacing the pipe is an easy matter.

(see page 188)

> **TIP**
>
> While it's possible for a skilled marine engineer who's familiar with the procedure to change dripless shaft seals while the boat is afloat, it's more prudent for an amateur mechanic to do so with the boat hauled out ashore.

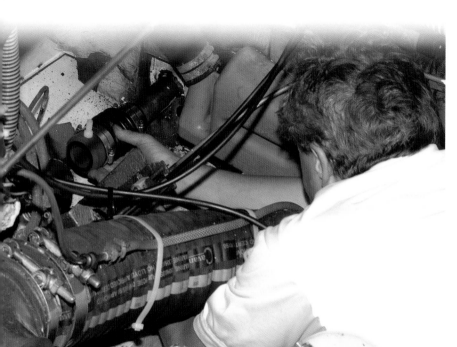

Below **Sliding the new seal onto the end of the propeller shaft. Make sure no dirt or grit is allowed to contaminate the seal.**

Above **'Burping' the seal to expel air after launching. Typically these seals rely on water for lubrication.**

Removal and replacement

The shaft doesn't need to be removed entirely to replace a shaft seal; however, it must be removed from the back of the gearbox, to allow it to be slid back enough to remove the old seal and get the new one onto the shaft (see page 200). The hose clips securing the unit in place can then be loosened, and the old unit slid forwards off the shaft.

Replacement is a straightforward reversal of this procedure, but note that O-rings and lips of the seals are prone to damage when the unit is being removed or installed – if there's a burr on the end of the prop shaft, for example, it should be filed smooth before fitting the shaft seal.

Make sure you grease the unit before launching – generally a small plastic tool is supplied to facilitate inserting grease under the lips of the seal. Otherwise, a wide plastic drinking straw, containing around 5ml of grease, can be inserted under the lip of the seal and squeezed into the unit. Once the boat is afloat, burp the seal and check it for leaks at a variety of engine speeds.

Right **Two popular small dripless seals for small shafts. Larger models may have a feed for oil or water, which provides cooling as well as lubrication.**

PSS shaft seal

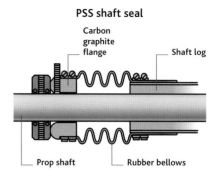

Carbon graphite flange · Shaft log · Prop shaft · Rubber bellows

Volvo shaft seal

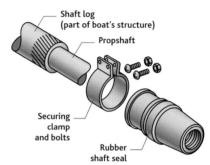

Shaft log (part of boat's structure) · Propshaft · Securing clamp and bolts · Rubber shaft seal

Replacing a shaft seal

The PSS Shaft Seal service kit as delivered from the manufacturers.

Back out the grub screws in the rotating ring to prevent them damaging the shaft.

Use plenty of soapy water to allow the ring to slide easily while being adjusted.

Mount the fixed part of the seal and tighten both hose clips evenly.

Compress the hose assembly and tighten the rotor grub screws.

Connect the water feed to the spigot on the hose assembly.

Propeller evaluation

To get the designed performance from a boat's engine, the propeller needs to be matched precisely to the engine's power, the motor's speed when developing its maximum output, the boat's displacement, and the type of vessel.

There are two key measurements that define a propeller: diameter and pitch. The latter indicates the angle of the blades to the axis of the propeller shaft. It's defined as the distance the propeller would move forward through the water in one revolution, given a perfect grip on the water, in the same way that one revolution of a particular corkscrew will always move it the same distance through a cork.

> **TIP**
>
> Most marine engine manufacturers have online propeller size calculators that will calculate the size of the propeller needed, given the type of boat, its displacement, and the engine installed.

A prop with a fine (eg small) pitch will therefore move a relatively short distance for each rotation, whereas the distance covered by one with a coarse pitch will be much greater, hence the same engine being able to move a heavy boat slowly and a light vessel quickly. In effect, the prop is a vital element in ensuring the engine is geared to suit the vessel.

For example, a small 15-knot RIB and a 26ft (7.9m) yacht weighing 3 tonnes, with speed under power of 5 knots, might both be powered by the same 15hp outboard engine. However, each rotation of the RIB's propeller will need to move it forward three times as far as a single rotation of the prop driving the yacht.

If the RIB's coarse-pitched prop is fitted to the yacht's engine, the motor would not be able to move the boat fast enough to allow the prop to spin at the engine's cruising speed – this is the classic sign of an engine that's over-propped – it will never be able to reach maximum revs. Conversely, if fitted with the yacht's propeller, the motor on the RIB would rev freely, without moving the boat through the water adequately – it won't achieve more than 5 knots.

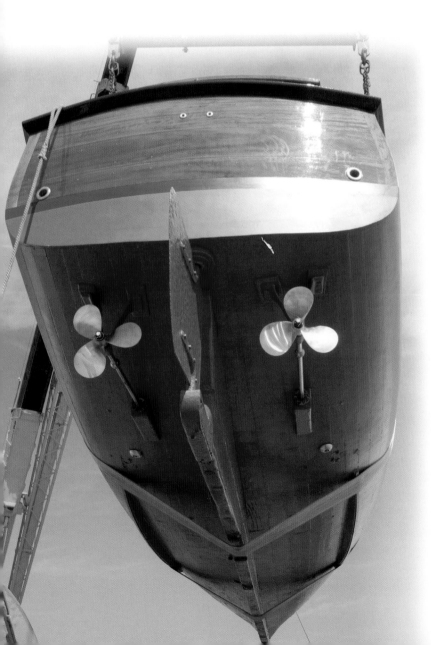

Left **Propellers must be matched to the boat and its engine/gearbox configuration to give optimum performance and economy.**

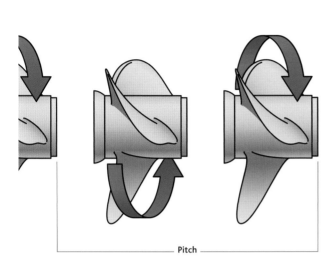

Pitch

Sailboat vs motorboat props

There are further differences between motor and sailboat props, because the latter must avoid excess drag when sailing. Therefore, a smaller diameter three-bladed prop is usually selected as a compromise; however, some out and out motorsailers are fitted with the four-bladed models that might only otherwise be found on motorboats.

Performance sailing boats are often happy to accept a further compromise to reduce drag, and opt for a fixed two-bladed prop, or a folding or feathering model. The latter are more complex and expensive than folding props, but suffer fewer disadvantages – in particular, performance in reverse

Above **A four-blade prop on a motor sailer derived from a heavy fishing boat design. Here the priority is to maximise thrust.**

Above left **The pitch of a propeller is the distance it will move through a body of water in one revolution.**

is improved, and there's more grip on the water overall with a feathering model.

Above **A folding two-blade prop is the ultimate in low drag for sailboats, but produces less thrust when under power.**

Left **Sailboat propellers tend to have fewer blades and are of smaller diameter, which reduces drag when under sail.**

Prop & bracket damage

Apparently innocuous damage to the edge of a propeller blade can result in a significant loss of efficiency. In addition, propellers and P-brackets are at risk of dezincification if not properly protected by anodes.

The tips of propellers must be in perfect condition if water is to leave the surface without forming energy-sapping vortexes. Don't underestimate the importance of this – there are many boats in operation with props that lose a considerable amount of efficiency. Although outboard engine propellers are particularly at risk of damage from grounding, those on inboard engines can also easily collect damage over time, particularly if fouled by rope, chain or other debris (see page 202).

Fortunately, even quite extensive damage can be repaired by specialist workshops, so this rarely spells the end of the prop, although the repair, and subsequent balancing, is beyond the scope of the facilities of the average boatowner to undertake themselves. In addition, it's often possible to change the pitch of a propeller (see page 196) so that it becomes a better match to the boat and engine.

Metal underwater components are always at risk of galvanic corrosion, so the prop, shaft and P-bracket should always be protected by zinc anodes. If the metal shows evidence of dezincification – a pink colouring when the surface is scratched indicates a loss of the alloy's zinc content and an excess of copper – the bracket or prop should be replaced at the earliest opportunity.

Below **A considerable amount of force may be needed to shift the shaft nut on a large propeller.**

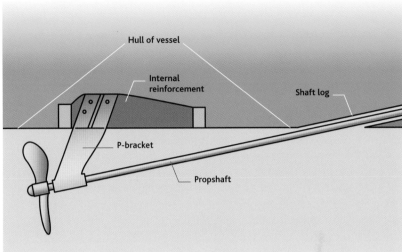

A- and P-brackets

These support the aft end of the prop shaft, just ahead of the propeller. Having two legs, an A-bracket provides greater support; however, drag is increased, so these are rarely used outside displacement motorboats. The fibreglass around the root of the bracket should be checked carefully each time the boat is hauled ashore, and after any incident in which the prop is fouled. Small gel coat cracks can be ground out and refilled, but more extensive damage must be cut back to sound material and reglassed.

Above left **P-brackets can be subjected to a huge twisting force if the prop is fouled. The cracked fibreglass here is indicative of a structural problem that needs attention.**

Above **P-brackets are secured to substantial internal stiffening members.**

The exact procedure for replacing a bracket depends on how it's fitted to the boat. Some have a palm at the top of the external part of the bracket that is bolted through the hull, while others pass through a slot cut in the hull, and are then bolted through stiffening bonded to the inside of the hull. In both cases, the whole lot is often laminated over with fibreglass mat and resin, so it may not be possible to ascertain exactly how the bracket is fitted until this has been removed. Before bonding in a new bracket, it's important to fit the shaft and check its alignment (see page 188). When this is accurate, the bracket can be secured in its final position.

Left and far left **Photos of a prop before and after reconditioning. In many cases, bent or damaged blades can be repaired for a fraction of the cost of a new propeller.**

Replacing the prop & shaft

The prop shaft needs to be removed when replacing the cutlass bearing or fitting a new shaft seal. In addition, it may need to be replaced when a new engine is installed, as many new engines are physically smaller than their predecessors.

In a few cases it's possible to remove the shaft with the propeller still attached; however, on many boats this will foul the rudder. It's therefore best to start the process by removing the prop. The end of the prop shaft is normally tapered, with a nut on the end of the shaft used to press the propeller tightly onto the taper. There is also a rectangular keyway that needs to be a really good fit – this is vital for transferring thrust from the shaft to the propeller. After removing the nut, the best way to slide the prop off the shaft is with a puller, although a sharp tap may still be needed to help break the inevitable bond between prop and shaft.

Removing the shaft

Removing the coupling that connects to the back of the gearbox from the prop shaft is often a challenge. To ensure there is no play that could cause vibration, and hence accelerated wear, these components are machined to exacting tolerances. This creates problems when they need to be separated, as any corrosion that forms on the inside of the coupling will tend to lock the shaft in place. To remove the shaft:

⚙ Start by unscrewing the grub screws that pass through the coupling, and then unbolt the shaft coupling from the gearbox coupling.

⚙ Then, slide both the shaft and coupling aft, treat with penetrating oil and, if possible, leave for 24 hours.

⚙ A spacer can be placed between the shaft and the gearbox coupling, and the two elements reconnected, using longer bolts if necessary. Progressively tightening these bolts will then force the shaft out of its coupling. However, great care must be taken – try to keep the tension even across each of the bolts by only

Below **Use a long, well-fitting spanner to loosen the shaft nut. If necessary, apply easing oil 24 hours before starting work and use heat to loosen the grip of the nut.**

Right **Inserting a replacement shaft. In many cases the rudder will need to be removed to allow the shaft to pass.**

tightening each one a little at a time, and by tensioning them in opposite pairs. If too much force is required it's prudent to stop, otherwise there's risk of breaking the flanges on the gearbox side of the coupling.

Assessing prop shaft condition

Once removed, the shaft should be examined carefully for excess pitting and wear at the shaft seal. It's also important that it is absolutely straight and balanced so that it doesn't vibrate when rotating quickly. The only viable way to get these aspects checked is to take the shaft to a specialist engineering workshop.

Before refitting the shaft, clean the inside of the coupling and examine the rectangular key – everything must fit together with no play. The shaft will almost certainly need to be tapped back into place – ideally this is a two-person job, with one person gently tapping the end of the shaft at the propeller with a mallet, while the other guides it into the coupling.

Above **In the event of the shaft becoming detached, a hose clip will prevent it sliding backwards out of the boat.**

Left **Loosening the bolts that attach the propeller shaft to the gearbox flange.**

Clearing a fouled propeller

A fouled prop is a major headache for any boatowner, and can create problems that extend well beyond the immediately obvious loss of power.

A fouled prop can disable a boat, yet in many cases it is not safe to enter the water to remove the obstruction. However, you can often do something to resolve the situation from on board, especially as it's more common to pick up debris such as plastic sheeting than for a rope or net around the prop to stop the engine completely.

Debris such as sheeting can often be unwound from the prop at least partially by running the engine in reverse. In many cases, it will be wound tightly around the prop, so more reverse action is needed than

might be anticipated. It's also worth alternating between forward and reverse gears. Although it's rare for this action to completely clear the prop, it will often remove sufficient debris for the boat to be able to reach a place of safety in which the problem can be properly rectified.

A rope that stops the engine can be much more difficult to unwind, although it's worth seeing what happens when the rope is pulled by hand with the gearbox in neutral, and whether it's possible to engage reverse gear with the engine running, even briefly. In the latter

case, to avoid potential for injury, crew must be well clear of the line before the engine is started.

An endoscope can allow a prop to be inspected, and the scale of the problem identified, without entering the water, making this a worthwhile item to carry on boats that operate in areas that have a considerable amount of debris in the water.

Below **Marine growth has a more pronounced effect on a prop's performance than the same growth on the hull.**

Left **Engaging a diver might be a cheaper option than lifting the boat out of the water to clear a fouled prop.**

Below **Plastic bags and sheeting are the most common items to foul a prop but fishermen's nets can also get caught.**

Bottom **Never underestimate the damage a plastic bag can cause. This propeller had to be removed to clear the mess from the shaft.**

Marine growth

Propellers rotate very quickly, so even a small growth of marine fouling will have a dramatic effect on the prop's efficiency. However, many boatowners are unaware of the scale of the loss of drive this causes. Unfortunately, the prop's speed of rotation means antifouling rarely stays attached. The best option is often to polish the propeller, which may help prevent growth getting a grip. Work through increasingly fine grades of abrasive paper, starting from around 240 or 400 grit, depending on the condition of the metal, and working up to 800-1,200 grade.

Consequential damage

If the engine has been stopped by a fouled prop, it's rare that there is no further damage, especially if the motor was running at speed. At the very least, the edges of the prop are likely to be dinged, but more severe problems are also possible. The engine mounts are subjected to the entire power of the engine, so a failed mount is a possibility, as is damage to the gearbox, or to the mounting of the P-bracket.

If a prop has been fouled by small-diameter items such as fishing line or nets, although it may not stop the engine, it will certainly reduce the efficiency of the propeller severely. In addition, the line can work its way into cutlass bearings (see page 192) and the gearbox oil seals of outboard engines (see page 286), causing considerable long-term damage.

Fitting a new engine 1

Marine engines have to work in a very hostile environment, and it's usually saltwater corrosion that puts them beyond economic repair. Very rarely will a leisure boat engine wear out – they simply don't do enough hours.

A replacement engine may be needed due to shortage of spares, severe corrosion or a terminal breakdown. Alternatively, you may simply want a quieter, more efficient and more reliable unit to enhance your cruising pleasure.

Some owners opt to refurbish their engines, but often find that labour costs escalate as mechanics encounter seized fittings and sheared-off bolts.

If you go for a newer, second-hand unit, it is often a gamble unless it is from a reputable source. If you go for a brand new engine, the boat will rarely repay the investment in resale value. It will, however, certainly repay with better reliability, more economy and less noise over the long term.

Below **Motorboat engines tend to corrode before they wear out. This 1970s Bertram is probably due for an engine change.**

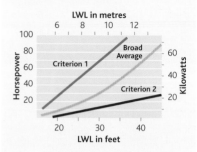

HOW MANY HORSES?

If you change the size of your engine, you need to ensure that you have the right horsepower. To save money, you may want to retain your existing gearbox, prop shaft and propeller, and when swapping like-for-like this won't be a problem.

Increasing the horsepower or altering the gear ratio will usually require a completely new propeller.

The graph shows the typical horsepower required by a displacement yacht, according to its length. Blue water yachts require Criterion 1 to punch into very bad weather, and to power voyaging ancillaries. Lightweight racing yachts can get away with Criterion 2, and a happy medium is the Broad Average.

The same formula applies to displacement motorboats, but planing craft have their own requirements. The manufacturer of the boat, or specialist marine engine suppliers will be able to advise on the best combination.

Source: *Boat Data Book*, Ian Nicolson. Adlard Coles Nautical

TIP

Even a badly corroded or elderly engine may have some residual value, especially for parts. It can pay to advertise it for spares to help defray the costs.

Disconnecting the engine

First, disconnect the gearbox couplings to the propeller shaft – usually just a case of undoing a few bolts. Keep these bolts safe.

Drain the fuel tank, and then disconnect the fuel lines. Many owners who repower their boats tend to refurbish the fuel lines, filters and fuel tanks at the same time.

Disconnect the wiring loom. Label each wire for reconnection. Faulty wiring is a major cause of breakdowns at sea, so many owners opt to completely rewire the engine bay to increase reliability.

Remove the rubber exhaust hose from the manifold. This is usually held by just a pair of jubilee clips. Check the state of the hose. It may benefit from renewal.

Unbolt the engine from the engine beds. If the nuts are corroded into place, the solution is to drill right through the nuts with a hardened

Above **Removing the old engine is usually fairly straightforward. Here the drive shaft and exhaust have been disconnected.**

steel drill-bit (cobalt-tipped drill bits work well). The nuts can then be split open with a cold chisel.

Lifting the engine

Check the engine will fit through the hatch. Engines are often installed in new boats before the deck is attached, and will only come out again once exhaust manifolds and alternators are removed. Measure the clearance, and if necessary 'undress' the engine block so it will fit through.

Employ the boatyard crane and some handy strops for the lift. Even quite small marine diesels are deceptively heavy, so watch your back. Let the crane take the strain.

Above **If the nuts holding the engine feet are rusted solid, the easiest solution is to drill through them and split them open with a cold chisel.**

Above **To lift out the old engine, attach strops and employ the boatyard crane. You may need to partially 'undress' the engine so it fits through the hatch.**

Fitting a new engine 2

With the old engine out of the boat, now is the time to refurbish the engine bay. Inaccessible wiring or seacocks can be rerouted, and the entire engine bay cleaned up and repainted. The biggest challenge, however, is realigning the new engine.

When a yacht is re-engined, most owners take advantage of this opportunity to access the engine bay and completely refurbish all the systems. Fuel tanks are often removed to be steam cleaned and checked for potential problems. The most critical part of a re-engine, however, is to ensure that the angle of the new engine is correct, and this may mean altering the engine beds.

Like-for-like engine swaps are normally relatively straightforward, but if you are fitting a different make of engine – or changing to a shaft drive arrangement – this could involve some surgery. Several manufacturers offer a service whereby they will modify the position of the feet so the new engine straddles the old engine beds properly.

Realigning the engine

The first task is to check the structure of the engine beds, ensuring they are still solid. It may then be possible to use a manufacturer's jig – a lightweight cage that shows how the engine will fit – or one that you have made yourself using wood offcuts, so you can see how the gearbox needs to be aligned with the prop shaft.

There will be tolerances recommended by the manufacturer as to how steeply the engine can sit; down-angle gearboxes can help level it out. The engine feet will have a degree of adjustment, so the gearbox and prop shaft flanges should align perfectly (check them using a feeler gauge as the feet are adjusted). Sometimes, the location of the engine is completely changed. In the boat shown, it could have been moved under the cockpit to free up space in the saloon, although this

Left **A new Lister Alpha diesel in place in a 40 year old sailing boat. The use of a down-angle gearbox has allowed the engine to be installed almost horizontal.**

Above **Engine bay after refurbishment. The yellow string is aligned with the prop shaft to help position the new unit.**

Above **A repower also gives the opportunity to upgrade the ancillaries such as this new water lock, fuel filter and stern gland.**

re-engineering can be expensive.

The exhaust runs of the new unit may be different and of a wider diameter, especially if you are increasing horsepower. All these factors need to be considered, and allowed for, before the new engine is finally dropped in. You also need to check the clearance of the new engine with regard to the main hatch – some engine parts may need to be undressed for it to fit through.

Once lowered into position, the feet are bolted to the engine bed, and the engine is adjusted until the gearbox flange aligns perfectly with the shaft coupling. To allow for any discrepancies, a flexible shaft coupling is advisable; this will also eliminate some noise and vibration, especially where perfect alignment is difficult.

It is then just a case of reconnecting all the systems, and checking carefully for leaks as the new engine is run for the first time.

Engine beds

When fitting a different make of engine, or a more powerful unit, you may need to make some considerable adjustments to the engine beds and/ or to the position of the engine feet. This is particularly true if adding a smaller or more compact modern engine where a larger or wider unit used to be, or if you are adding a considerably different type of engine, such as a saildrive. A whole new frame may need to be made to support the new installation, which can add considerably to the cost of the project.

Upgrading your systems

If you have access to the engine bay, it is a good opportunity to upgrade all the systems that will serve the new engine, and a good investment for future reliability. A new water lock will prevent a backrush of water into the engine, causing it to seize. Exhaust runs, pipe feeds, filters and other systems should be relocated if, in the past, they have been inaccessible or undersized.

Left **Sometimes a lot of work is needed to make a new engine compatible. Here a new frame is being made so this Lister can straddle the original engine beds.**

Troubleshooting engines

Irrespective of whether they are fuelled by petrol or diesel, most marine inboard engines have similar systems for starting and for cooling the motor.

Overheating

Most overheating problems are caused by a failure of the raw water system that uses water from the sea, river or lake in which the boat is floating, to cool the engine. Cooling may be done directly, by pumping the water through the engine itself, or indirectly via a heat exchanger.

The most common problems are failure of the water pump impeller (see page 180), a blockage of the inlet strainer, or the drive belt that powers the pump breaking (see page 178). While these will result in a total failure of the cooling system, many instances of overheating are the result of problems that reduce the system's efficiency and therefore only become apparent when the engine is run at high speed for a prolonged period. These include:

- ✪ Slipping drive belt (see page 178).
- ✪ Damaged water pump impeller (see page 180).
- ✪ Constrained waterways in raw-water cooled engines or heat exchangers (see page 182).
- ✪ Insufficient coolant in the fresh water side of indirectly cooled engines.

Another possibility is a partially delaminated exhaust hose that prevents cooling water flowing

TIP

If a diesel engine is fitted with decompression levers, these can be used to reduce the energy needed to start the motor – with the levers lifted the electrical power needed to turn the engine is reduced significantly. After turning the engine for three to four seconds on the starter motor, the lever(s) can be lowered, and the engine should start, assuming there are no other problems.

towards the exhaust outlet. This is a problem most commonly experienced after a previous incidence of overheating, in which the heat generated has caused internal damage to the hose.

Above **Holding the decompression levers open significantly reduces the electrical energy needed to start a diesel engine.**

Left **The raw water inlet strainer is the first place to look if there's not a strong flow of cooling water from the exhaust.**

Electric start problems

If the engine fails to start because it doesn't turn quickly on the starter, the electrics should be checked before anything else. First, check the voltage of the starter battery – this should be at least 12.1V. Next, repeat this process, with the starter turning the engine for five seconds. The reading will drop, but should remain above 10.8V. If it's below this figure, the battery should be recharged; if it still won't maintain adequate cranking voltage it should be replaced.

If the battery is capable of supplying enough energy, but the engine still doesn't turn quickly, the connections in the wiring between the battery and the starter motor are the next point of focus. These are a frequent source of problems, and any terminal that becomes hot is a sure sign of energy being lost. These should be dismantled, cleaned, dried and reassembled. Continue with all the connections, until the cranking voltage measured between the positive wire to the starter motor and the engine block is within 0.2V of the cranking voltage at the battery.

Never operate the starter motor for more than around 10 seconds – they are not designed for sustained running. In addition to depleting the battery, this will reduce the motor's lifespan. Another problem with sustained starter operation is the possibility of siphoning water from the exhaust into the cylinders, which can cause significant damage.

Above **Loose drive belts are a common cause of under-performing battery charging systems and ineffective cooling.**

Below **The flow of water from the exhaust should be checked every time the engine is started, and regularly while it is running.**

Troubleshooting diesel engines

If a diesel engine won't start – despite turning over quickly on the starter motor – or if it suddenly loses power, the problem almost certainly lies with the fuel system.

Diesel engines operate by compressing a carefully calibrated mix of atomized fuel and air to a very high pressure – one at which the diesel will spontaneously ignite. They are therefore much less complex than petrol motors, which require a precisely timed spark to ignite the fuel. To operate reliably, the simplest diesel engines require only clean fuel that is free of air and water. However, some models also require an electrical input, either to a solenoid valve that shuts off the fuel when the engine is stopped, or, in the case of larger and more recent models, for complex engine management systems.

Below **Wear disposable gloves when working on the fuel system as exposure to diesel can cause dermatological problems.**

Above **Many leaks in fuel pipe connections are a result of old copper washers being reused when the joint is reassembled.**

If the engine stops, or won't develop full power, bleeding air out of the fuel system (see page 290) may give a temporary reprieve that will buy time to solve the problem. However, in many cases this will only treat the symptom, rather than the initial problem. This is most likely to be connected with a low fuel level in the tank, or clogged / partially clogged fuel filters (see page 174).

This type of problem often manifests in rough water, when the sediment that inevitably forms over time in the bottom of the fuel tank becomes shaken and stirred up. Although changing the fuel filters will help get you to port, the tank should be drained and cleaned at the first practical opportunity (see page 174 and page 184). The problem can be exacerbated if the fuel tanks are relatively low on fuel, as the pick-up pipe may be in air at times if the boat is rolling heavily. Modern sailing yachts are especially prone to this as they often have very shallow fuel tanks.

One situation in which air can get into the system is through a leak in the pipework on the suction side of the low-pressure fuel lift pump. A leak here will suck in air, instead of squirting out diesel, which means it can be difficult to trace. However, it's a prime suspect if the filters are clean, and a loss of power can be solved temporarily by bleeding the system.

If a slow decline of performance is noticed over time, and this can't be explained by growth of marine fouling on the hull, the injectors should be cleaned by a specialist diesel engineer and, if necessary, overhauled. On non-turbocharged engines, black smoke – indicating unburnt fuel – emitted when the engine is run at full throttle, is a classic sign of injector problems.

TIP

Always check the obvious when troubleshooting. Is there plenty of fuel in the tank? Are there shut-off valves at the tank, or elsewhere in the system? Are these switched on? Are there any signs of fuel leaks, loose wires or other problems? Has any work recently been undertaken on the fuel system?

Above **Never assume there's sufficient fuel in the tank. You can check the level effectively with a dipstick.**

Right **Operating the small handle on the fuel lift pump to bleed the fuel system.**

Troubleshooting petrol engines 1

The electrical systems needed to create the spark on which petrol engines rely create an additional level of complexity compared to diesel motors. It's here that problems are most likely to be encountered.

Electrical system

Energising each of the spark plugs in turn with a pulse of very high voltage electricity creates the spark that ignites the fuel of petrol engines. In older engines, voltages of 10–12,000V are reached, although the latest units can see more than twice this figure. Traditionally, the spark is created by opening and closing a pair of contacts (the points) in a 12V system, connected to an induction coil, which produces the high-voltage pulse in the HT (high tension) side of the coil. This pulse is then sent to each cylinder in turn via the distributor.

Systems of this type have a number of potential failure mechanisms, with many instances of engine failure being the combination of several relatively small faults. The most common are pitting, and dirt on the contact points – these should be cleaned (or replaced if deeply pitted) and the maximum gap between them set to the engine manufacturer's specifications, and checked with a feeler gauge.

Multi-cylinder engines have a distributor to direct the high-voltage pulse at each cylinder in turn. This consists of a rotating arm under the distributor cap that delivers the high-voltage current to each of the spark plugs in turn. Each of these contacts degrades over time –

ideally, the distributor cap and rotor arm should be replaced annually, but, if necessary, the contacts can be cleaned with emery paper. Keeping these items dry on a boat can be a major challenge, but it's essential for the engine to remain reliable.

In modern systems, the high voltage is created electronically, which is more reliable and makes a higher voltage feasible, therefore creating a stronger spark. However, the same problems with the distributor cap, rotor arm contacts and high voltage leads are still possible.

Below **Cleaning the contacts on a distributor rotor arm with fine wet and dry paper will improve running.**

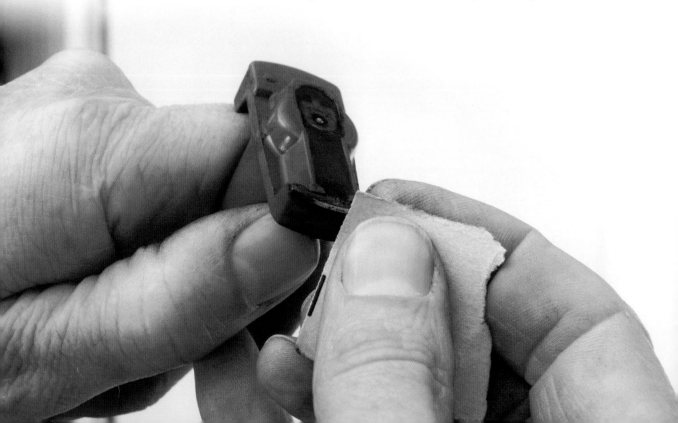

Right **Distributor cap of a four-cylinder engine. Contacts should be clean, and the inside should be dry.**

Testing for a spark

The strength of a spark can be tested by removing each spark plug, holding it close to the engine block, and turning the engine over. Traditional contact breaker ignition systems will produce a spark that can jump a gap of around 0.2in (5mm), while electronic ignition will double that distance. Ensure you're well insulated by wearing thick (ideally rubber) gloves, and hold the spark plug using insulated pliers.

Above **HT leads must be pressed firmly home on the spark plugs to ensure a good connection.**

Left **These petrol engines fitted on a power boat depend on complex electrical systems to keep them running smoothly.**

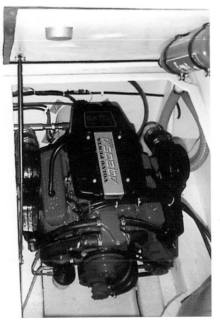

If a petrol engine won't start, yet turns easily on the starter motor, and has an ignition system that appears to be in good order, the fuel system should be investigated for possible problems.

Fuel system

Petrol engines may use either a carburettor or fuel injection system to measure the exact quantity of fuel that needs to be introduced to the cylinder on each combustion cycle, and ensure it is atomized into a spray that will ignite cleanly when the spark plug is energised. Carburettors tend to be fitted to older and smaller engines for this purpose – they are much simpler than injection systems, but also more prone to problems, particularly with two-stroke engines. However, many of these are easily remedied. The most common is a restriction of the jets in the carburettor – a warm

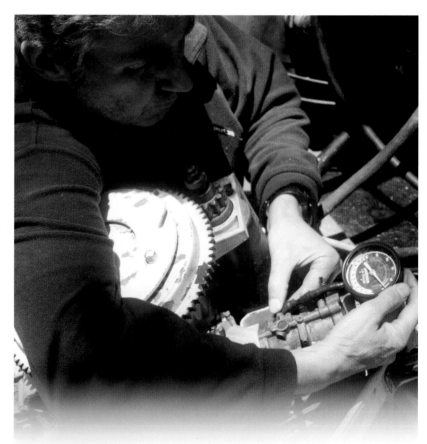

engine that runs better when given some choke is the most obvious symptom of this (see page 284).

If the engine starts easily when warm, but is reluctant to start from cold, the operation of the choke should be checked. When operating correctly, this should cover the air intake into the carburettor (see page 284).

Left **Spark plugs should be a light grey/ brown colour. The jet black colour of this one indicates oil fouling, or unburnt fuel.**

Above **Using a pressure gauge to check the operation of the (low pressure) fuel pump.**

Fuel filters

As with diesel engines (see page 210), there should be fuel filters and a water separator in the system. If these filters become blocked or clogged, the supply of fuel to the engine will be reduced – it may, therefore, run at low speeds, but won't deliver full power. If filters that have been replaced at the recommended service intervals are found to be dirty, this points to a build-up of dirt in the fuel tank, which should be drained and cleaned.

However, if changing the filters does not solve the problem, the low-pressure fuel pump (as distinct from the injector pump on fuel-injection engines) may be at fault. The diaphragms of these are prone to becoming perished, particularly if older engines are run with fuel that contains a high proportion of ethanol (biofuel) – modern engines use a different grade of rubber that is resistant to degradation by ethanol. The effectiveness of the electric pump can be tested by measuring the pressure on the output side of the pump with a gauge. Alternatively, some pumps can be separated easily into two components, which expose the diaphragm, allowing it to be examined visually.

Right **Typical components of the fuel system of a marine petrol engine.**

Below left **For non-fuel injection engines the choke should be fully open in the normal running position.**

Below right **The choke should completely cover the inlet to the carburettor in the cold start position.**

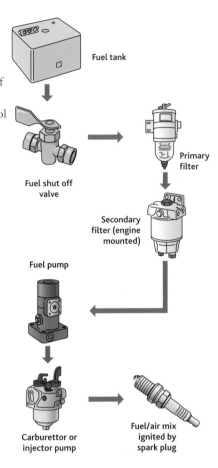

Fuel tank

Fuel shut off valve

Primary filter

Secondary filter (engine mounted)

Fuel pump

Carburettor or injector pump

Fuel/air mix ignited by spark plug

FRIZZANTI III

Motorboat
repairs

Fitting trim tabs

Trim tabs, which are fitted to a boat's transom, can improve ride comfort, safety and fuel economy significantly. They are relatively straightforward to replace, or fit from scratch.

Trim tabs help keep motorboats at an optimum fore and aft pitch to maximise speed and fuel economy. A different setting is needed when operating the boat at different speeds, and for different loads being carried – for example, when the number of people on board varies. One of the most popular upgrades therefore is to replace trim tabs that can't be adjusted by the driver with models that have electric or hydraulic actuators.

Aside from changing worn-out units, other reasons for replacing trim tabs include fitting a more powerful model, or upgrading to

hydraulic systems. These tend to have fewer problems relating to water ingress in the electrical components and are therefore inherently more reliable.

Size and position

Most trim tabs are 9in (23cm) long, and, as a rule of thumb, the width should be roughly one inch per foot of boat length. However, 12in (31cm)-long trim tabs may be appropriate for semi-displacement boats and other relatively slow vessels with a cruising speed of under 14 knots. Boats with limited transom space, such as those with multiple

outboard motors or outdrives, can also be fitted with a 12in (31cm) model. They should be located around 0.24in to 0.32in (6–8mm) above the bottom of the transom, and 1in to 4in (25–100mm) inboard of the edge of the chine.

Many trim tabs are held in place with self-tapping screws, rather than being bolted through the transom. To ensure the screws have maximum grip, it's vital to ensure the correct size of pilot drill is used for making

Below **Trim tabs can increase speed and reduce fuel consumption. Upgrading is a popular and worthwhile modification.**

Fitting new trim tabs

Position the tabs 4in (10cm) in from the chine and mark the position of the screw holes.

Bed the tabs on sealant and screw the fastenings into pre-drilled pilot holes.

Attach the actuator strut base to the tab, then drill holes for the transom mount.

Connect up the hydraulic hose or wiring, as appropriate, before...

...finally fitting the top of the strut, bedding it on marine sealant.

With this system the actuating motor can be placed in a dry place below deck.

the screw hole. A marine adhesive sealant should be inserted into the screw holes, as well as around the edge of the fitting. Avoid the temptation to overtighten the screws, though, or you will squeeze all the sealant out.

Electric and hydraulic trim tabs

Electric trim tabs have powerful motors that draw a large electrical current, albeit for only short lengths of time, so they should be wired with large diameter cables to minimise power losses between the battery, switchgear and motor.

Electric models have the actuator within the piston, so to prevent

Right **A newly installed trim tab. The base of the tab should be 0.24in to 0.32in (6–8mm) above the bottom of the hull.**

damage from water ingress, it's important to ensure a good seal between this and the transom. Hydraulic models, however, have their electrics remote from the piston, so they can be fitted somewhere where they won't get wet. The key to installing the hydraulic element is to make certain everything remains meticulously clean – the smallest amount of dust or grit will rapidly accelerate wear on pistons and seals.

RIB & centre-console boats

One of the thrills of fast powerboats is their acceleration and handling in waves, but this can place enormous loads on the deck fittings. How securely seats, consoles and grab rails are attached must, therefore, be beyond doubt.

It is extremely important that the console and seats of powerboats are fixed securely to the deck – there have been numerous instances of crew sustaining injuries when falling overboard after one of these items detaches itself from the deck. However, there is normally no access to the blind side of through-deck fittings on RIBs and centre-console boats, so it's often not obvious how fittings should be attached.

Never succumb to the temptation of relying on self-tapping screws to secure the console or seats. Such an arrangement is almost bound to fail at some time during the boat's normal lifespan, even if the screws are backed up with an adhesive sealant.

Most vessels of this type are built with longitudinal metal strips (usually aluminium) bonded into the deck below the floor. These are designed as the secure attachment points for consoles and seats, enabling you to drill a hole for a bolt and tap a thread in the aluminium, so that effectively it becomes both the nut and the backing pad.

Right **A console through-bolted to two plywood frames laminated to the deck of an older rib.**

Below **Seats and centre consoles must be securely attached to the boat – either bonded in or bolted through the floor.**

With an older boat, don't rely on
the previous fittings having been
located correctly – many RIBs and
centre-console boats were fitted out
at small dealer workshops, rather
than the boat builder's factory,
so the standard of work can vary
enormously. It is not unknown, for
example, for consoles to be attached
with self-tapping screws through the
fibreglass floor. Over time fittings
may also have been changed or
moved by well-meaning but badly
informed owners.

Below **Fitting a new console. After drilling
the holes, threads can be tapped in the
under-floor rails for the securing bolts.**

Fitting new items

If replacing consoles or seats, the
position of the under-deck rails must
be positively identified first, and their
location marked with tape or a marker
pen. They can normally be found
using the electronic device sold
for locating wiring and water pipes
in walls. Once this is known, new
fittings with fixings at the appropriate
spacing can be sourced.

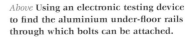

Above **Using an electronic testing device
to find the aluminium under-floor rails
through which bolts can be attached.**

If the aluminium rails are missing
or cannot be found, it may be possible
to laminate a frame onto the deck
with fibreglass, to which the console
can be fitted. If doing this, it's vital
that the frame is attached to the
deck securely – any deck paint and
gel coat must be ground off before
laminating starts.

The attachment of fittings that
may encounter large loads, such as
grab handles, also demands careful
consideration. If not an integral part
of the seats or console structure,
they should be attached with through
bolts, penny washers and marine
plywood backing pads.

Repairing an outdrive

Outdrives are complex pieces of machinery and, as they operate at very high speeds and are always immersed in sea water, are prone to damage. Regular inspection is the best way to prevent expensive problems.

The outdrive leg is a drive unit that allows a powerboat's engine to be located right aft, freeing up the maximum amount of internal living space. Owing to its constant immersion in sea water, a number of critical seals are required to stop water ingress, and the usual cause of failure is when one of these is compromised.

Servicing an outdrive

Servicing an outdrive leg is within the remit of an experienced DIY engineer, particularly the routine tasks, such as changing anodes, bellows and gear oil. Inspect the leg, too, for signs of problems, before they become expensive to fix.

The easiest way to service an outdrive is to remove it from the boat and take it to a workshop. The drives are relatively easy to dismantle, providing there isn't too much corrosion.

Some of the common repairs that may need to be made are:

Bellows failure: A set of rubber bellows protects the drive shaft as it emerges through the transom plate and connects with the leg's drive train. Another set lower down carries the control cables. Both create a flexible, watertight link between the outdrive and the boat, but because they are exposed to

Above **The rubber bellows should be closely inspected for splits, and replaced every two years as a matter of course.**

sunlight, they can become brittle with age. A cracked bellows will allow water into the boat and the gearbox, rusting the universal joint and emulsifying the gearbox oil. The bellows should be secured with marine-grade stainless steel clips, and inspected regularly. Replace the bellows every two years, even if they appear in good condition.

Locking mechanism: The outdrive will have a trim and tilt mechanism, with the earlier units mechanically operated. Later units use hydraulic rams. If the springs fail, or the cables become stiff, then the outdrive will kick up when reverse is engaged. It may also lock in the down position, making tilt impossible. To repair it, take the mechanism apart, and clean or replace the springs and cables.

Left **This pair of duo prop outdrives is suffering from oxidisation of the aluminium casing. A lick of paint should fix this problem.**

Above **The lock down clamp can become stiff and should be regularly cleaned or reverse gear will become inoperable.**

Worn clutch: Older outdrives have a cone clutch, a relatively simple sliding mechanism for engaging reverse and forward gears. If the gears engage with a 'clunk' then all is well. Perversely, if they engage smoothly this means the clutch is worn beyond its tolerances and you will lose power through slippage. A tell-tale sign that this has happened is very dark gear oil, rather than the usual honey colour. The outdrive will have to be stripped down to access the clutch mechanism, which will need complete replacement.

Above **Check the edge of the cooling water intake pipe to ensure the edge is sound, as any breaks here will reduce suction.**

Right **The main elements of a duo prop outdrive.**

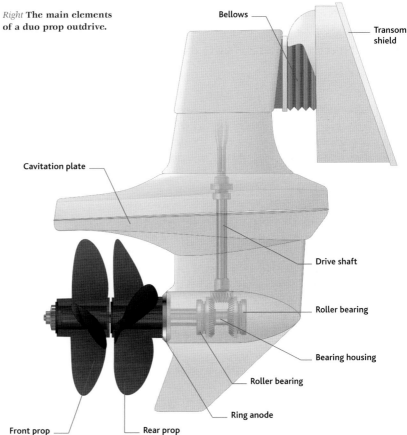

Bellows

Transom shield

Cavitation plate

Drive shaft

Roller bearing

Bearing housing

Roller bearing

Ring anode

Front prop

Rear prop

Water intake: The cooling water for the engine is drawn in through the intake pipe, which is a vulnerable part of the outdrive. The clip must be of the highest grade of stainless steel to prevent any corrosion, and during a service you should remove the rubber hose and ensure that the metal of the pipe is still in good condition. Any failure here will compromise the engine's ability to cool itself.

H-bracket: A key part of the supporting framework for an outdrive is the H-bracket, and this is supported by bushes on each side. Check the top of this bracket closely for any cracks, which are caused by the bushes becoming worn. Worn bushes allow the drive to flop around, stressing the top of the H-bracket.

Anodes: Check the anodes regularly and replace when showing signs of 50 per cent wastage. An outdrive leg has several areas that have dissimilar metals separated by rubber seals, and if the anodes dissolve away, then crevice corrosion will quickly attack these areas instead, creating a number of problems.

Repairing duo props

Duo props – counter-rotating twin propellers – are, as with all propellers, easily damaged by semi-submerged debris, and can be expensive to replace. Knowing how to remove and inspect them for damage is, therefore, very important.

TIP

If you are removing your duo props for the first time, have an exploded diagram handy, or take a series of digital photos to remind yourself how the components fit back together.

Duo props are designed to sit on a pair of counter-rotating shafts, each with its own internal seal, and are made from either aluminium or stainless steel. In between the inner and outer props is a powerful rubber bush, designed to take several tons of load for long periods. Replacing this bush isn't a DIY job, although you can inspect them for wear and tear.

Inspect the blades regularly, because even a slight dent can throw out the prop's balance. Pay close attention to the tip of the blades, where they are most likely to get damaged.

Below **Duo props provide more power through the water, and better handling at low speed. Here a stainless steel inner propeller is being fitted. Note the new ring anode.**

Replacing duo props

Removing and changing duo props is not difficult, but care must be taken to ensure that all the components go back in the right order, otherwise the props could become damaged.

- If removing the props while afloat, raise the outdrive right up, take the keys out of the ignition and ensure the battery switch isolator is off, so the engine won't start accidentally.
- Jam the props with a piece of wood under the cavitation plate so they are locked together, or shift the gear lever to the forward position to lock the drive. Undo the bolt in the hub, and then carefully remove it.
- The outer prop should now pull off the shaft, exposing the nut that

holds the inner prop in position. Shift the gear lever to reverse, or reinsert the wooden block to jam the prop again.
- Using a special castelated tubular tool, undo the locking bolt for the rear propeller, and then draw the prop off the shaft. Wipe the propeller shaft clean and inspect it for fishing line. Check and, if necessary, replace the ring anode.
- Reassemble the duo props, carefully smearing the shafts with a specialised grease to make them easier to remove in future. You will also need a torque wrench for tightening the propeller bolts.

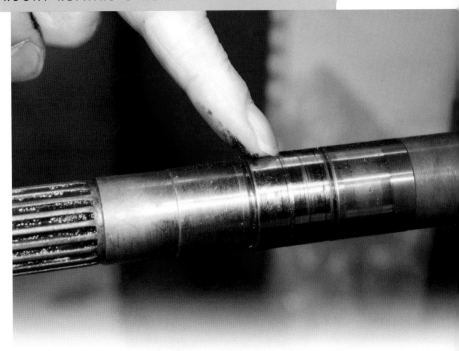

Right **This shaft has been scored by a fishing line or a damaged seal, which will allow water to seep into the gearbox.**

Seal inspection

If the unit is on dry land, it is a good idea to check the seals when you have removed the propellers. There are three in total, one on each shaft, and a large one at the base of the leg. Checking the gearbox oil will indicate if there is a problem with the seals – if it is milky, then water has been getting in. Fishing line often fouls shafts and can cut into the seals, allowing water to leak in.

Occasionally, wear in the prop shaft in the area around the seals leaves grooves which can cause water ingress, so oversized seals may be needed. If the wear is excessive, the shaft itself may have to be replaced, and it can be drawn out of the base of the leg by freeing up the two main retaining bolts.

Damaged blades

An experienced propeller specialist can usually repair damaged aluminium duo props. The damaged area is either beaten out or cut back, and then built back up again with fresh aluminium. The propeller is then checked for pitch, balance and alignment. Stainless steel propellers generally give better performance than aluminium ones, and are far less prone to damage. However, they are considerably more expensive.

Replacing worn props

Lock the props with a wedge of wood and undo the central nut.

Withdraw the outer prop, taking care to catch the thrust washer.

Repeat for the inner prop. You can now remove the ring anode.

Before fitting the new props, coat the shaft with recommended grease.

Sailboat repairs

10

Rigging & sailmaking skills

Regular inspections are the key to keeping a boat's rig and sails in good order. However, there is always the possibility of more significant damage that requires repair.

As sails age, areas of stitching will chafe through well before the cloth becomes damaged, and a small area of broken stitching can quickly run along the entire length of a seam. Ideally, any badly chafed seams should be run through a sewing machine as a precaution, before the thread finally breaks. Most domestic sewing machines are capable of sewing through up to three or four layers of sailcloth, provided an appropriately heavy-duty needle is used.

Alternatively, seams can be hand-stitched – using the original needle holes makes this an easier process. This is, however, still a time-consuming task, so hand stitching is generally reserved for short-term repairs, such as oversewing both sides of a length of damaged stitching to prevent it unravelling further. Use double-sided tape to hold the two panels together in exactly the right place while it's being stitched.

However, long-distance cruisers which don't carry a sewing machine on board may have to undertake a considerable amount of hand-stitched repairs. That's a very strong incentive to carry out repairs the moment damage is first noticed!

Small holes in sails can be repaired using self-adhesive sailcloth, providing the sail is cleaned of salt water, and thoroughly dried before the patch is applied. Larger holes, or those in very high stress areas, particular the leech, clew and near mainsail battens, will also need to be stitched to survive extended use in strong winds. See pages 244 for more on sail repairs.

Below **A traditional rig built with modern materials. Rigging skills are useful whatever type of rig you have.**

Rig problems

If remedial work is needed on rigging at deck level – for example, to replace a damaged clevis pin, chainplate or bottlescrew – the mast can be supported by taking halyards down to secure deck fittings near the chainplate, and applying moderate tension to the lines. However, it may not be safe to climb the rig in this state, so if any standing rigging above deck level needs to be replaced, the mast should be lowered first. Before doing so, count the number of turns on each bottlescrew, so that the rig can be returned to its original tension and tuning.

Ropework

If a braided rope has significant chafe, there's little that can be done to remedy it, short of creating two much shorter lines from it. Historically, such remnants of three-strand ropes were spliced together to form another line that was only marginally shorter than the original. Splices are also used to create eyes in the ends of ropes. This is easiest with three-strand lines (as illustrated), but is also possible with braided ropes such as those used for halyards.

Right **The correct way to adjust rigging screws, using the right size spanners. Don't be tempted to use a screwdriver as a lever.**

Eye Splice Sequence

1 Separate the three strands, then tape the rope to prevent it unravelling further.

2 Open the lay of the rope, thread a strand through it, and pull until the tape is reached.

3 Thread the second strand through the next lay of the rope, and turn the rope over...

4 ...to reveal the last lay of the rope, through which the third strand is threaded.

5 Keep going following the same pattern, working away from the loop.

6 At least three tucks of each strand are needed. Five will give a more secure splice.

Aluminium mast repairs

A metal mast has to absorb plenty of strain, particularly from compression loads. The early detection and remedy of potential problems will help avoid expense, inconvenience and possibly danger, too.

For such a vital piece of equipment, a yacht's mast rarely receives the regular checks and maintenance that it deserves. Apart from rigging failure, the most common reason for dismasting is weakness in the metal caused by dents or corrosion, which can lead to a loss of structural integrity.

Full inspections are best carried out when the mast is off the boat; however, regular checks should also be made throughout the season from a bosun's chair, or even using a pair of binoculars from the deck.

Dents

Masts are usually dented when they are off the boat, although careless handling of spinnaker poles and other equipment can lead to them being dented afloat. The mast is basically a compression post, so a dent will amplify the inward forces in that area, creating a weakness. If you have found a dent or crease in your mast, it pays to check it out.

Depending on where the dent is, how deep it is, and how close to vital load-bearing areas it is, there are several possible cures. The most favoured repair is to plate it over, preferably from both inside and out, with a piece of similar grade metal. Sometimes, if the dent is in the middle of a spar, the spar is cut in half near the dent and the dent knocked out. A collar is then placed inside the mast and pop riveted for some distance either side of the join. This method is common practice in mast production, and is well proven.

Left **Preparing a mast for removal. A rigger is attaching a crane strop under the spreaders. Note the mast steps that make regular inspection much easier.**

Left **The most effective way to repair a mast is to cut off the damaged area, add an inner collar, and rivet on a new section.**

Above **Corrosion eats away at the aluminium, and is usually caused by reactions between dissimilar metals.**

Smaller dents may be treated with just an external plate, with the corners rounded to prevent any hard spots. This avoids having to gain access to the inside of the mast.

Some repairs aboard can be made with a hard-setting epoxy, but aluminium can react badly to some chemicals, so the repair may have a limited life and actually make the situation worse. Wrapping the mast in carbon fibre may cause even more damage due to galvanic action.

Corrosion

Corrosion is a far more common problem, and occurs when dissimilar metals are used – for example, stainless steel screws on an aluminium spar. Any dissimilar metal fixing used on a mast should originally have been coated in an anti-corrosion compound, but these can break down with time, and their use is sometimes overlooked.

Look for a white powder around fittings such as the spreader caps, winch bases, light fittings and end caps, as this is an oxide caused by the metal breaking down. Any frayed electrical cables can also leak current into the mast, rapidly accelerating the process. Check for loose fittings, too, as this may indicate that the surrounding metal is crumbling.

A preventative cure for corrosion is to remove the item and clean it and the affected area with hot water to dissolve the salts. Any loose rivets should be drilled out and replaced, and if the holes are larger than standard rivets, use machine screws instead. The fixings should also be smeared with an anti-corrosion compound, such as zinc chromate or barium chromate.

Most aluminium masts are anodised using an electrochemical technique that produces a protective anti-corrosion layer of just a few microns thick. Others are painted after treatment with an etching primer. Extend your mast's life by gently washing it with warm water and mild detergent, and use an aluminium polish for spars to help revitalise the anodising.

Below **Corrosion can also take place inside the mast, such as on this mast base, where water from halyards has run down the spar.**

Glue failure in a wooden mast

The 1950s and 60s saw a huge increase in the use of glues in boatbuilding, particularly for creating lightweight, hollow wooden spars. Fifty years later, many of these spars are suffering from glue failure. So what's the best way to give these old sticks new life?

TIP

If you spot a crack in the mast while under way, it may be prudent to reduce sail, brace the spar, and proceed to the nearest harbour on a reach, rather than subject the mast to sudden jolts by motoring into a heavy sea.

The first sign of problems is likely to be a black line along the join, where water has crept in. Or the join may already have started to part. It's tempting to simply clean out the crack with a knife, slide in a bit of glue, clamp it all up, and be done with it. And in some cases this might well do the trick – at least for a while.

The likelihood is, however, that you won't be able to clean the surfaces properly to create a good bond, in which case all you've done is reglue one bit of failed glue to another. In a few months' time, you'll have to start all over again. More significantly, if the glue has failed in one place, then the chances are it will fail elsewhere, and no-one wants to go to sea knowing that the mast might fall apart at any moment.

The most sensible course of action is to completely dismantle the spar, thoroughly clean all the surfaces, and then stick it all back together. This might sound daunting, but in most cases should only be two to three days' work.

Below **The boom and mast of this 1930s classic yacht were split open and reglued with epoxy, hopefully giving them another 70 years of life.**

Dealing with glue failure

Remove any fastenings and open up the offending join by running a spatula or thin knife down its length. The objective is to break the glue join. If the join doesn't part easily, then try prising it open with wooden wedges. Be careful not to damage the faces of the join. If it doesn't spring open readily, then think again. Perhaps the glue is still good!

Once the join is open, smooth the two faces using a plane or a belt-sander, or a combination of the two. If using a belt-sander, be careful not to take off too much wood. Once the old glue is removed, stop sanding! If using a plane, the bigger the plane the better. Once the faces are clean, check they meet without a gap, and sand/plane off any high spots.

Prime both sides with neat epoxy. This prevents the liquid epoxy being 'sucked' out of the joint when you apply the thickened glue. Once the primer is dry, mix up another batch of epoxy and thicken it with microfibres until it is the consistency of double cream. Apply it evenly to one side of the join.

Clamp the two faces together using clamps, giant hose clips, Spanish windlasses, or anything else that comes to hand. Insert short lengths of scrap timber under the clamp jaws to protect the mast. Remove clamps and clean off with an electric sander, or with whole sheets of sandpaper folded in three.

Repairing rot in a wooden mast

If you discover rot in your wooden mast, the viability of repairing it will be determined by the extent of the rot and where it's located.

As a rule of thumb, it's worth repairing a wooden mast if the section of rot extends for less than one third of the spar's entire length. However, if the middle section contains any signs of rot, the entire mast should be replaced because of the high level of stress that it's subjected to around the hounds and the crosstrees. If the spar is made from more than one piece of wood, it's important to ensure that the glue joint is still sound, and that it does not move when it comes under pressure.

Scarphing new wood onto an existing spar

Feather scarph joints should be used to join the new wood to the spar. The scarph's ratio should be 12:1, so that the length of the scarph is 12 times that of its width. Some wooden spars may consist of both hollow and solid sections, and with these it is worth cutting the scarph joint on the mast before buying your new length of timber, in case the rot extends further than first thought.

A possible reason for the rot is failure of the glue joint separating

TIP

When doing a dry fit, make marks along the spar and the new piece(s) of wood, so that when you come to glue them together, it's easier to line everything up.
Peter Graham, International Boatbuilding College.

the hollow and solid sections of the mast, resulting in water ingress. If this is the case, simply move the position of the scarph joint along the spar, remove the affected wood, and buy a longer piece of timber.

Gluing the new wood to the spar

Once the scarph joints have been cut to shape, make sure you do a dry fit, clamping the new wood in position to make sure the scarphs have been cut correctly. If everything fits together as planned, key the mating surfaces with 80-grit sandpaper, remove any dust or debris, and then mix up the glue. Resorcinol resin glue is more suited to this purpose than epoxy, because it is ultraviolet resistant. However, it is not a gap-filling glue, and so the joints must fit as tightly as possible.

Left **The new wood has been glued in position and is being planed to match the spar's profile.**

If you do this, when cured, little of the dark-coloured glue will be visible. If using resorcinol, be aware of the ambient temperature when the glue is curing. If the temperature drops below 16°C (61°F) it could undermine the integrity of the glue joint. In winter months, it's a good idea to place the spar in a plastic tent (sheets of bubble wrap laid over a suspended ridge pole are effective) and warm the tent gently using oil-filled electric radiators. Once the scarph joints have been glued, leave the spar overnight to allow the glue to cure properly.

Above **To achieve a constant level of pressure while the glue cures, use as many clamps as possible.**

Above right **The chalk marks indicate the amount of wood that will be removed to form the staggered scarph joints.**

Shaping new wood

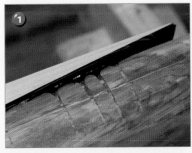

The glue has cured and the new wood is ready to be shaped.

The majority of the shaping work can be carried out with a plane.

Run your fingers along the new wood to detect any changes in profile.

The new wood smoothed and shaped to match the spar's original profile.

Repairing seized blocks

Blocks have to work under harsh conditions with heavy loads, and often need some attention. If the sheaves become stiff or seized, it could be a case of overdue maintenance, or, worse, distortion, which will involve a complete rethink of the type and size of block being used.

There is a wide choice of blocks available on the market, and depending on their location within the rig, these range from very simple affairs, made from a tough, ultraviolet and salt-resistant plastic with stainless steel pins, to more sophisticated race-pedigree lightweight models, fitted with hi-tech bearings for minimal friction.

If the pulley, known as the sheave, is stiff or seized, remove the block from the rigging and inspect it closely. A common failure is buckling or distortion, either because the block is too small for the loads it is carrying, or because it is badly misaligned. This causes the block's cheeks to become compressed against the sheave, stopping it from turning properly.

A clue to overloading will be elongation in the holes on the attachment point. Spinnaker halyard blocks fail regularly as a result of distortion, as they are often pulled hard in many directions in a short space of time, and so need to be fully articulated on the mast.

Evidence that the lead is wrong is a groove worn into the inside cheeks of the block. Overloading a block will cause the head of the housing to lift upwards into a bridge, or begin to

Above **The old hot water trick. Boiling water does wonders to free up salt-encrusted blocks.**

pull the shank through. Overloading may also distort the pin that runs through the sheave, causing it to stop turning properly. If the block has been distorted badly, there may be

Below **Modern yachts are fitted with a variety of blocks and turning blocks, all of which have the potential to seize up.**

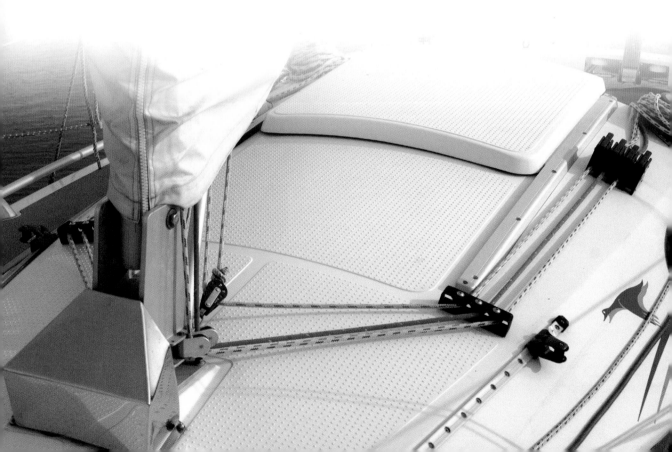

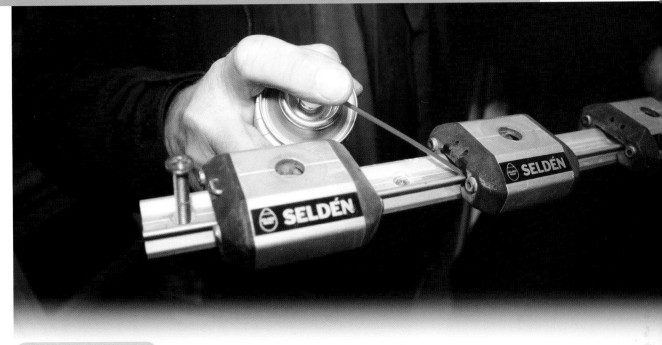

Above **Silicone lubricant should be injected from above to free a seized bearing.**

Right **Some blocks are designed so that the sheave is easily removed, making future repairs much easier.**

TIP

If you are getting consistent problems with a block, it may be the wrong type for the job. Blocks that have to handle static loads, such as those at the base of a mast, should not be of the ball bearing type, as these will suffer from 'flats' in the bearings. A more robust plain bearing block should be used.

no choice but to replace it with a larger, more robust model with better articulation.

If the block appears to be in good shape, and not distorted, then it should be rinsed thoroughly with fresh water. To dissolve salt deposits effectively, use hot or warm water. Leave the block to soak for a while, then dry it thoroughly and spray some Teflon lubricant into the interface between the sheave and its pin. This combination of desalting and lubrication should free up the block. If not – and if it is the type that can be taken apart – then the bearings may need to be replaced.

This also applies if the block has a flat spot, or appears to 'graunch' as it goes round.

When checking genoa and mainsheet blocks, ensure that the sheaves are smooth, as ultraviolet damage can cause the outer edges to break up, and this can quickly chafe the sheets. Crash-gybes can also cause fractures within the housing around a genoa car, and distortion of the swivel pin. Each manufacturer will have a set of instructions for maintaining these blocks, and a list of spares. Most, but sadly not all, blocks can be stripped down for repair.

Repairing seized winches

If your winch starts to seize up, or the gears don't work, then the solution is to strip it down and investigate. The cure is usually just some routine maintenance.

The winches used for controlling a yacht's running rigging all work on much the same principle: the drums freewheel until a winch handle is used, and this causes metal pawls to deploy in the mechanism. These then engage precision-engineered single- or two-speed gears, allowing the most unruly of sails to be brought under control.

Winches are robust items, but they still have some small internal parts that need to be checked, cleaned and lightly greased every so often. Manufacturers' recommendations are that winches should be stripped down at the beginning of the season, and lubricated every couple of months. They should also be stripped down and serviced prior to laying-up for the winter.

Most manufacturers have comprehensive maintenance manuals that you can download from their websites, and it's a good idea to keep copies of these on board. Winch maintenance can be a therapeutic pastime for a quiet day at anchor, and most come apart easily. The trick, however, is to keep all the components safely in a tray during the process, and to ensure that you have the spares needed so that the winch can be put straight back into action. Again, most manufacturers sell service kits, and these are often supplied with recommended lubricants, and two of everything, as winches are usually serviced in pairs.

Below **Complex rigs require a number of winches to properly control. These usually include two-speed and self-tailing models.**

Reasons for winch failure

The main cause of winch failure is the pawls refusing to engage. Oddly, this can be caused by over-greasing, but it's more usually down to corrosion of the stainless steel springs that are supposed to force the pawls out of their housings. Salt build-up in this precision part of the winch can also cause problems. Occasionally, an undersized winch can become distorted due to excessive loads – an average 40ft (12m) yacht, for example, can have up to 1,000lb (453kg) pulling on a drum in heavy weather.

Stripping down a winch

The exploded diagram of a typical Lewmar winch gives a good indication of how everything fits together around the central shaft.

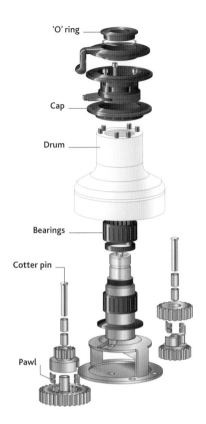

Above **An exploded diagram of a Lewmar sheet winch. These winches are easy to strip down and spares are readily available.**

'O' ring

Cap

Drum

Bearings

Cotter pin

Pawl

Stripping down a winch

Access may vary. This Lewmar has a plastic cap, which exposes two locking pawls...

...but this Anderson requires the removal of several Allen screws instead.

Carefully lift off the drum, as components may be caught up inside.

Slide off the bearings, and then tease out the cotter pins to free the gears.

The usual culprit – replace the spring inside the pawl.

When reassembling, ensure the cotter pins are fully bedded down.

To strip a winch down, you will need: a tray or bowl to store the components in, cloth, spare parts, reference material, a brush, a screwdriver (for teasing out circlips) and pliers. The following steps should then be taken:

✪ Winches are usually accessed from the top, so start by removing the screws or circlip so that you can lift off the main drum housing. The area under the main drum needs close inspection. The small doors, which work as spring-loaded flaps, are depressed when the winch is free running, and engage when the winch is driven. If they fail to spring out because of excessive or salt-hardened grease, or because of salt corrosion, the winch won't work.

✪ Lubricate the bearings lightly, and, using a brush, remove any salt build-up from inside the gears. The cotter pins can sometimes be slightly raised if the winch hasn't been installed or reassembled properly, which can cause the drum to lock solid. Make sure they are fully recessed during reassembly.

✪ Look for signs of distortion or uneven wear in the shaft. This is a sign that your winches are undersized, and may need to be changed.

Repairing seized roller furlings

A roller furling system enables a headsail to be permanently hoisted while allowing it to be furled by simply pulling on a line. However, as with all metal parts on a boat that are exposed to the elements, regular checks should be made to ensure their integrity.

If you are finding your headsail increasingly more difficult to furl, there could be a number of potential causes. Firstly, check that the backstay is tensioned correctly. If it has not been set up properly, the mast may lean forward, causing the roller furler's spar or stay to sag, which in turn will mean that more force is required to haul in the sail. Equally, it is worth checking that the headsail halyard has not slackened off during the course of the season, and that the furling line runs freely through its blocks.

Above **Roller furling gear comes in all shapes and sizes. Decorative teddy bears are an optional extra.**

Forestay corrosion

If possible, check any visible parts of the forestay for signs of corrosion or metal fatigue. Many boatowners overlook the replacement of the forestay within the roller reefing system when they replace the standing rigging, because it can be a tricky job to extract the old forestay and fit a new one. The consequences of ignoring this essential element of standing rigging can, however, be devastating, as it could lead to your rig coming down.

Left **The furling line is lead aft through blocks attached to the stanchions. More tension on the line is required to prevent it jamming inside the drum.**

Clogged up furling drums

If there appear to be no problems with the rig tension, the most likely explanation is that dirt or salt has built up inside the furling drum and clogged up the ball bearings, preventing it from running smoothly. In these circumstances, clean the furling drum with soapy water to wash away any salt, and then inject silicone grease into it to get things moving again. If this fails to work, it is possible that the ball bearings have started to break down and that new ones are required.

On some systems, it may not be possible to replace the bearings without help from a professional rigger, or the original manufacturer, because the furling drums are sealed. However, on those systems where you can access the bearings easily, problems with the furling drum may be resolved with a new set of bearings. Before buying any replacement parts, though, it's worth checking the whole system thoroughly, to make sure there are no other problems. For example, if one or more sections of the main furler spar require replacement, it may be more cost effective to consider buying a new furling system.

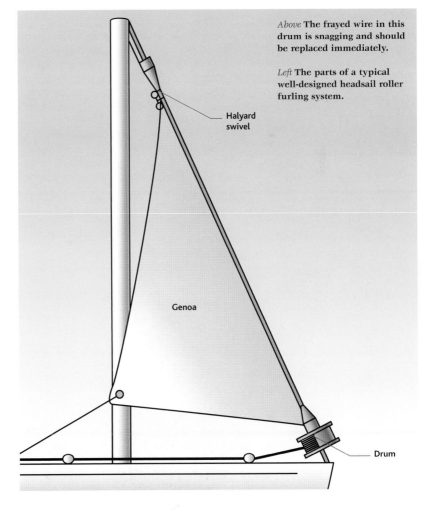

Above **The frayed wire in this drum is snagging and should be replaced immediately.**

Left **The parts of a typical well-designed headsail roller furling system.**

Halyard swivel

Genoa

Drum

Installing or relocating winches

Upgrading to larger and/or self-tailing winches helps to make a boat easier to handle. Extra winches may also be needed if a cruising chute or spinnaker is added to the boat's inventory.

Winches are subject to considerable loads, with primary winches in particular being one of the most highly stressed items on board. It's therefore vital that they are fitted as securely as possible – large backing plates that spread the load out over a wide area are the key to this.

A potential problem with fibreglass boats arises from the way in which the decks are constructed. Most incorporate a layer of foam or balsa wood sandwiched between two layers of fibreglass laminate. This creates a stiff, lightweight structure; however, the core material is easily compressed, and it is not suitable for a winch to be bolted directly onto.

The solution is to remove the core material under the new winch. Start by cutting away the lower fibreglass skin, below the new fitting's location, to expose the core material. Once this has been removed, the core material can be replaced with a piece of hardwood set in a mix of resin and filler. Then, laminate new fibreglass onto this, overlapping the surrounding area so as to spread the load as far as possible, and make good the section of the lower fibreglass skin that was removed.

Old bolt holes can be filled by masking the underside of the holes, then mixing fibreglass resin with silica or glass bubbles to a onsistency that will just flow off the end of a mixing stick. Leave space at the top for the final layer of gel coat, which will need to be colour matched to the shade of the deck moulding.

Locating winches

When selecting the position of a new winch, there are three key factors that must be taken into consideration:

- ❂ Firstly, crewmembers must be able to throw their full upper body weight at winching – simply using arm muscles is inefficient and can become tiring very quickly.
- ❂ Secondly, the line led to the winch must have a fair lead, as friction will be significantly increased if it has to run around too many tight corners.
- ❂ Finally, to minimise the possibility of riding turns, the line must meet the winch drum at an angle of around five to ten degrees below the horizontal axis of the drum.

Left **Winches should be placed so that it's possible to use your body weight, not just your arm muscles, to turn the handle.**

Left **One person may be able to reach both sides of the fastenings for coachroof winches, but otherwise it's a two-person job.**

Adding deck gear to newer yachts

Many yachts designed since the mid to late 1990s already have provision for additional deck gear to be added without major modifications to the boat. Instead of the foam or balsa core, these boats have aluminium plates bonded into the deck in the locations that optional fittings may be positioned at a later date. This means that boltholes can be drilled through these plates, and a thread tapped so that the metal plate becomes, in effect, the nut.

This arrangement speeds up the process of installing deck gear enormously, but it's important to know where these plates are located. The boat's owners' manual will detail this – if you don't have a copy, obtain one from the builders or, if the builder is defunct, from an owners' association.

Above **Penny washers or larger backing plates are needed to spread the loads that a winch transfers to the deck.**

Left **Use epoxy resin filled with silica or glass bubbles to fill old bolt holes, having first masked the underside of the holes.**

Sail repairs 1 – seams and patches

Long-term repairs to damaged seams and torn sails are best carried out by a professional sailmaker. However, if a problem occurs during a long passage, it may be necessary to carry out a short-term repair that will last until you reach dry land.

If the stitching starts to give way while the sail is in use, it should be lowered as quickly as possible to prevent further damage to the seam, or distortion of the sailcloth. If the seam has to be re-stitched to complete the voyage home, it is vital that a needle of the appropriate size for the weight of the sailcloth is used, otherwise you could cause yet more damage to the sail. If possible, use sailmaker's double-sided adhesive tape, and apply it to both sides of the sail. The tape will take a great deal of strain and hold the seam together until a permanent repair can be carried out ashore.

To avoid problems with your sails, check them thoroughly before you stow them for the winter months. In particular, check where the sail rubs against the shrouds, and make sure that all the stitching is intact. If there are any signs of abrasion, or areas where the stitching has started to come loose, then the sail should be repaired.

Above **If the stitching along the seams is starting to come loose, it should be repaired without delay or it will quickly spread.**

Below **If a sail is torn or the seams begin to give way it should be swiftly lowered to minimise the damage.**

Repairing a torn sail

A torn sail should be lowered as quickly as possible to prevent the rip spreading any further. It is worth carrying a sail repair kit on board, which should consist of needles, thread, palm, sailmaker's double-sided adhesive tape, and some pieces of sailcloth to use as patches. The spare pieces of sailcloth should be of the same material that your sails are made from, so that if used in a repair, they stretch in sympathy with the sail. Unlike the seams, there is a little more leeway when fitting a patch, because it is easier for a sailmaker to cover an untidy temporary patch.

When fitting a patch it is vital that you line up the two torn sections correctly. A sailmaker will use two spikes to do this when the sail is on the loft floor, but a pair of spring-loaded cramps attached to the saloon table can be used when effecting an emergency repair.

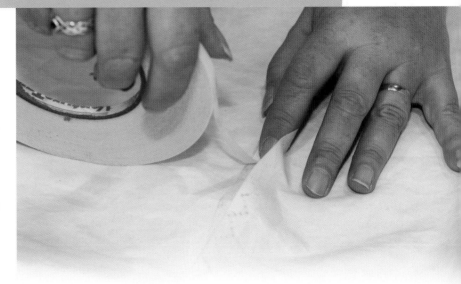

To repair a torn sail

- Apply double-sided adhesive tape over the tear.
- Cut a piece of sailcloth to the appropriate size to form the patch.
- Apply double-sided adhesive tape along the edges of the patch, and glue in position.
- Turn the sail over, and apply double-sided tape to the other side of the tear, before adding a patch.
- Both patches can then be stitched in place to complete the repair.

This repair is a good temporary solution; however, a more permanent repair should be carried out as soon as possible. Sailmakers will usually apply patches over the original sailcloth if the tear is small, but, if the tear is quite big, they will generally remove some of the damaged cloth to save weight.

Above **Double-sided sailmaker's adhesive tape can be used to hold a seam together while a repair is carried out.**

Repairing a torn sail

A pair of sailmaker's spikes is used to line up the two torn sections.

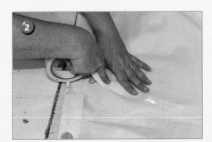

Double-sided adhesive tape is applied to both sides of the tear.

The edges of the patch are heat-sealed with an electric rope cutter.

Double-sided adhesive tape is applied to the edges of the patch.

The patch is stitched in place – either by machine or by hand.

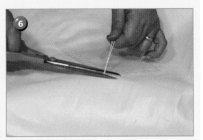

The surplus thread is removed to leave a perfect finish.

Sail repairs 2 – attachments

Over the course of a sail's working life, it might be necessary to replace a reef point or bolt rope, or repair a damaged batten pocket. If the sail is in otherwise good condition, this is a cost-effective solution to prolonging its useful life.

Bolt ropes

Before the advent of modern pre-stretched ropes, shrinking bolt ropes – the rope sewn around the edges of the sail to strengthen it – used to be a major problem. Huge advances in rope-making technology have made a difference, but, occasionally, bolt ropes do shrink and need repairing. These days, the shrinkage is unlikely to be more than 4–6in (100–150mm), so the best solution is to ease the bolt rope off at either the tack or the head of the sail, and sew in a small length of new rope to allow for the amount of shrinkage. This method does not weaken the sail in any way, because the two parts of the bolt rope are hand-stitched in position.

If the entire bolt rope has to be replaced, attach a thin line – a mousing or messenger line – to the old bolt rope. This will be pulled through the bolt rope pocket as the old rope is removed. The new bolt rope is then attached securely to the mousing line and pulled into position, before it is stitched firmly in place.

Below **A mousing line is used to pull the bolt rope up the luff pocket, before the rope is firmly stitched into place.**

Batten pocket repair

Stitching the batten pocket back in place with a sewing machine.

The surplus thread is removed for a smart finish. Hand-stitching is also possible.

Testing the repaired pocket with a batten to make sure there are no obstructions.

Batten pockets

One of the common problems with batten pockets is that the elastic on the inboard end of the pocket deteriorates with age and becomes overstretched. When this happens, the sail batten becomes loose in the pocket and no longer supports the sail. Fortunately, this is a straightforward problem to rectify. Simply unpick the stitching around the inboard end of the pocket until the elastic is exposed. Replace the damaged elastic and then stitch the pocket back in place.

Batten pockets will occasionally rip on the inboard end if the sail has been stowed badly. This kind of damage can be fixed by unpicking the pocket's stitching around the ripped sailcloth, and fitting a small patch underneath. In these circumstances, a sailmaker will usually take the opportunity to replace the elastic, too, before sewing the pocket back in position.

Top **Unpicking the thread of a damaged batten pocket to begin the repair.**

Above **Holding the inboard end of the sailcloth that forms the batten pocket.**

Right **Unpicking the thread around the edge of the damaged reef point. The reinforced reef point is subsequently replaced to leave a virtually invisible repair.**

Reefing points

Sometimes, reefing points get pulled out when the mainsail is hoisted without the reef having been shaken out fully. When this occurs, a quick and usually undetectable method of repair is to remove the remaining reinforcing piece around the reefing point, and replace it with a small patch, through which a new eyelet is punched.

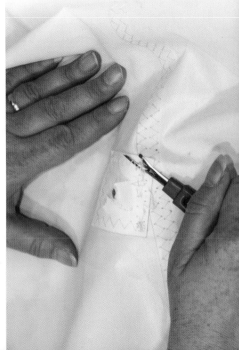

Halyard repairs

Unless a halyard is long enough to allow for a repair, the only real option available in the event of it failing or suffering serious abrasion is to replace it immediately.

A halyard will typically endure the highest rate of wear of all the ropes and warps on board a boat, particularly where it passes through sheaves, rope clutches and winches. Therefore, it is worth checking these parts of the halyard regularly, and if you spot any signs of abrasion, replace it before it jams or snaps.

Traditionally, if part of an existing halyard was damaged, boatowners would simply splice ropes together to form a new halyard. On a modern yacht, however, splicing ropes together is rarely worthwhile, not least because the spliced section may be too thick to pass through the halyard's associated blocks and rope clutches. It may also introduce a potential point of weakness in the halyard.

When buying a replacement halyard, one option is to buy a longer length of rope to allow for the replacement of an eye splice, should one become damaged in the future, therefore saving money in the long term. Equally, a halyard's working life can be extended by turning it end for end to equalise the wear along its length.

Replacing a halyard

If a halyard has broken, and you need to replace it, you will need to drop a weighted messenger line down the mast via the upper halyard sheave. To 'fish' it out of the bottom of the mast, you may need to remove the lower sheave to gain access. The new halyard can then be attached to the messenger line and pulled through the mast. Alternatively, if the old halyard is to be replaced, and is still in one piece, attach the messenger line to the old halyard and pull it through the mast. The new halyard can then be attached to one end of the messenger line and pulled through.

Left **Once an eye splice is finished, the surplus strands of rope are removed with an electric cutter to leave a neat finish.**

Above **A messenger line, or 'mouse' can be used to feed a replacement line down a hollow boom or mast.**

Eye splices

Before using a halyard, it's worth checking the condition of the eye splice, including the stainless steel thimble. If a thimble starts to show any signs of damage or metal fatigue, it should be replaced. Equally, a new splice will be needed if the halyard is turned end for end. The splicing method you use will be determined by the type of rope you want to splice. Dinghies and small yachts are often rigged with three-strand ropes, which is the easiest type to splice. The majority of modern yachts, however, use braided rope, and this requires a special fid and pusher to produce a successful eye splice. See page 228 for more on eye splices.

Braid on braid splice

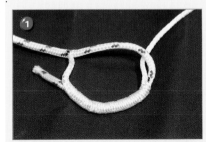

The (red & white) sheath has been pushed through the (white) core.

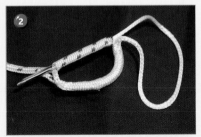

The fid (needle) provides a channel for the core to pass through part of the sheath.

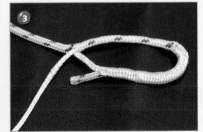

The core is pulled through the sheath until the slack is taken up.

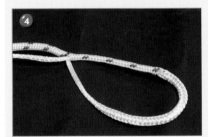

The slack parts of the rope are now smoothed out.

The stainless steel thimble is fitted as the splice nears completion.

The surplus core is removed with an electric rope cutter.

Rigging terminal repairs

If a rigging terminal is subjected to an uneven pull that involves considerable force, or shows any signs of damage, the only course of action is to replace it as soon as possible.

Above **If any loose strands of stainless steel wire are spotted above a rigging terminal, it should be replaced without delay.**

Rolled swage terminals

Rolled swage terminals are the most commonly used direct link between stainless steel rigging wire and the rigging screws. Essentially, they consist of a sleeve that fits closely over the end of the wire, which is then placed in a hydraulic press and, under extremely high pressure, squeezed to create a join that is as strong as the wire itself. When the swage terminal emerges from the hydraulic press, the joint should be straight, smooth sided, and have a constant diameter. Failure to achieve this result may lead to the development of a hairline crack along the sides or at the end of the terminal, which will allow corrosion to occur.

Loose strands

If the rigging terminal is subjected to an uneven pull, it should be inspected immediately to see if there are any shiny or loose strands of wire just above the swage terminal. If either is spotted, the shroud should be replaced without delay, because they are both early warning signs of an imminent failure of the joint between the wire and the terminal. Once the first strand

Above **A hydraulic press is used to compress a rigging terminal over rigging wire to create a piece of rigging.**

Left **The pressure applied by the press actually elongates the rigging terminal.**

Below right **As rigging screws age, they become susceptible to seizing up if they are not regularly lubricated.**

Seized rigging screws

Rigging screws have consisted of stainless steel forks and bodies for many years. However, as this type of rigging screw ages, it becomes more susceptible to seizing up, especially if the screw has not been adjusted for some time, or the boatowner has not applied grease to the threads regularly. The risk of this happening can be reduced, if you opt for rigging screws with stainless steel forks and bronze bodies.

emerges from the terminal, it is only a matter of time before the rest of the wire pulls clear, and this could result in the loss of your mast.

Other problems to look out for include corrosion at the top of the terminal. This is usually caused by water collecting at the bottom of the plastic tubing that is fitted to the shrouds of some boats, to protect the sails and/or sheets against abrasion. One method of preventing this problem is to fit a small plastic ball between the terminal and the plastic tube. This will maintain a gap between the tube and the swage terminal to allow any water to run off.

The shroud should also be replaced if the stainless steel wire is kinked or, if the terminal is bent, because it is not possible to straighten stainless steel without weakening it.

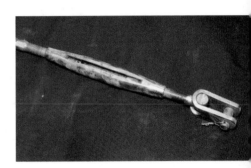

Damaged hardware

Unlike most things on a boat, mast sheaves, shackles and halyard pins are relatively cheap to replace should they break, or become distorted.

Sheered halyard pin

The sheaves at the head and the base of the mast are usually secured in place by stainless steel clevis pins. If the pin shows any signs of distortion during the course of a voyage, you should stop using the halyard that runs around the sheave, and replace the pin at the first available opportunity to avoid the risk of its failure when the halyard is in use.

Below **The bigger the boat, the more complex the rig, and the more gear there is to go wrong.**

Sheaves

If the mast sheaves show any signs of damage or cracking, you should stop using the relevant halyard until the sheave can be replaced. If it starts to break up while it is in use, the resulting sharp edges can quickly damage a rope. Equally, if a new halyard is showing unexpected signs of abrasion, it is worth checking that the sheaves are the correct size for the rope. If they are too narrow or small in diameter, they can damage the running rigging. Ideally, the rope should fit snugly in the pulley groove, and

should not be compressed or flattened by it while under load.

A seized sheave can ruin a rope very quickly, too, because more friction is generated as the rope passes over the immobile sheave. It is therefore important to ensure that you inspect the sheaves and lubricate them with a thin oil regularly. The sheave should also be withdrawn as part of your long-term maintenance programme, so that the pivot hole can be inspected. If it starts to become oval shaped, it will rotate less freely and, ultimately, seize up.

Above left **If any of the sheaves show any signs of damage, stop using that halyard until the sheave can be replaced.**

Left **If a shackle moves sideways it can be subjected to an uneven load and ultimately fail. The problem can be avoided by sewing washers either side of the headboard hole.**

Main halyard

Unevenly
strained
shackle

Headboard

Latching pin
with cam
and key

Washers
sewn to
headboard

Bent shackles

Shackles are the most commonly used direct link between a halyard and a sail. It is important that the shackle fits the sail's headboard as snugly as possible, because if the shackle is able to slide sideways there is a high risk that the headboard will slip to one side. This will result in an uneven load being placed on the shackle pin, which could cause it to bend and, eventually, fail. To avoid this problem use a shackle of the right width. However, if this is not possible, then it is worth sewing washers either side of the headboard hole to ensure the shackle remains centred. If the shackle pin shows any sign of distortion, it should be replaced immediately.

Above **A shackle pin that's this distorted is not only impossible to undo but liable to fail at any moment.**

Pop riveting

Pop rivets, or 'blind' rivets, to use their technical name, are a means of securing two pieces of metal where it is difficult to access the reverse (blind side) of a structure. This makes them ideal for applications on masts. Pop rivets are easy to use, strong and very versatile.

The Leicester-based United Shoe Machinery Corporation invented the blind rivet as a way of joining two thin layers of material together, but its use is now widespread for a number of fixing applications.

Types of pop rivet

A pop rivet comes in many sizes and types, but essentially it is a short tube of malleable metal with a shaft called a mandrel through the middle. At the top of the tube, the mandrel flares out slightly, rather like the head of a nail. The pop rivet is inserted into a pre-drilled hole of a specific diameter, and then a special tool is used to grasp the protruding mandrel. As the trigger on the tool is worked, metal teeth grab the mandrel and pull it out, forcing the innermost end to compress and mushroom inside the mast. At a predetermined pressure, known as the 'blind setting', the mandrel snaps off, leaving the rivet locked firmly in place.

This method of securing items to an aluminium mast is widespread, especially as pop rivets are available in small increments in size, making them very versatile. They are also available in a number of materials, including aluminium, Monel, copper and stainless steel, although pop riveting in stainless steel is very hard.

> **TIP**
>
> When making a number of holes for pop riveting, use a cobalt-tipped drill bit. Although more expensive than standard drill bits, they remain sharp for much longer when drilling metal.

The shape and profile of the rivets vary widely, with some pop rivets having a secondary shell designed to peel back like a banana skin when joining lightweight or fragile materials. Mast applications tend to use the conventional rivet design.

There are several different tools available for pop riveting. For heavy

Below **A riveting tool is placed over the protruding mandrel, before it is pulled back and the rivet 'popped' into place.**

How to 'pop' a rivet

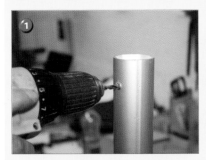

Drill out the old rivet with a sharp drill slightly larger than the original rivet.

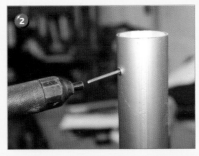

Clear away the debris, and insert the new rivet into the hole.

Attach the riveting tool, and start to pull the mandrel back until it snaps off.

The body has mushroomed on the 'blind' side, locking the fixing into place.

duty or large amounts of rivets, a pneumatic pop rivet gun is recommended. For smaller jobs, most riggers use a 'lazy tongs' hand riveter, as it is much easier on the hands.

Pop riveting kits are inexpensive, and for mast applications it is recommended to use Monel rivets, due to the metal's greater strength and resistance to salt water. It is very important to drill a hole of exactly the right diameter as your rivet for a good fit.

Replacing rivets

The old rivet can be drilled out using a sharp drill bit of the same diameter as the original hole. This will break open the tube and cause it to fall apart. To replace the rivet:

❂ Make a new hole, by marking the mast, punching a centre, and then using a drill of the right diameter.
❂ Insert the new rivet into the hole. The outer collar stops it dropping through.
❂ Insert the rivet gun over the mandrel, and then work it with a series of arm movements. The mandrel is held tight and pulled outwards, causing the flange at the top of the rivet to start crushing the tube as it moves along it. You can see the distortion on the blind side quite clearly. The mandrel snaps off flush with the outer collar, and the rivet should now last for many years.

Left **Two sizes of pop rivet. Those made from Monel last longer as they are more resistant to saltwater.**

Replacing standing rigging

Stainless steel 'standing' rigging should last around ten years, or 40,000 miles of sailing. However, regular inspection is recommended to prevent common problems such as failure of individual strands in the end fittings, cracks in T-hooks, and corrosion in the mast terminals becoming more serious.

Standing rigging, aptly named as it keeps your mast standing, can be made from a number of materials, including traditional rope on classic sailing yachts and exotic carbon fibre materials for hi-tech racing machines and superyachts. However, the most common type is stainless steel wire.

This type of rigging consists of a very high grade of polished stainless steel, and is available in a variety of thicknesses, with racing yachtsmen trying to get away with the thinnest diameter possible to save weight aloft, and long-distance cruisers usually oversizing to maximise safety. This oversizing means that cruising yachts are generally only exerting about 15–20 per cent of the breaking strain on their wire when sailing fully pressed.

Any metal item that is subjected to repeated strain, or cyclic peak loading, will eventually suffer from metal fatigue, but if a yacht's rig is set up properly, there is no reason why it should not last for up to 60,000 miles. However, a hot climate, a lot of atmospheric pollution and regular hard sailing in strong winds will reduce the rigging's lifespan to around five years.

There is very little routine maintenance to be done to standing rigging, except to clean and lubricate the bottlescrews; however, regular inspection for cracks, misalignment of rigging terminals and broken strands is essential.

Left **Standing rigging keeps your mast in place, and most cruising yachts use oversized wire, meaning the rig is never pressed beyond 20 per cent of its capacity.**

Left **A rigging terminal machine allows riggers to compress high quality wire into end fittings for a reliable connection between the shroud and the mast.**

Problem areas

The usual trouble spots are at the neck of the terminals, where the wire is literally compressed into a metal sleeve. If the terminals are misaligned, this can cause a single strand to snap, and so weaken the entire rig.

Another common type of end fitting is the T-hook, which slots into a plate on the mast. Fractures can occur under the T-piece, and across the plate itself, and may be very small, so close inspection is needed – something that is not always possible when the mast is stepped.

T-hooks should always be regarded with suspicion.

Sometimes, the rigging will appear rusty, but this isn't always a sign of failure. The polishing process during the manufacture of the wire can be at fault, as it can cause iron oxide (rust) to travel down the wire and collect around the neck of the terminal.

Replacing your rigging

Rigging is best replaced with the mast unstepped, although individual shrouds can sometimes be replaced with the mast still standing. Give the rig a full inspection at the same time, as this is also your chance to upgrade the wire size if you are planning any long-distance sailing, and to check the correct alignment of the various blocks and turnbuckles. Remember to label each shroud to aid reassembly.

The best defence against future problems is to ensure the rig is set up properly to avoid 'snatch' when the yacht is sailing, and to sight up the mast to check its alignment when under full sail with 18–20 degrees of heel. Selden Masts recommend that when new rigging has been fitted, small adjustments are made on each tack until the lee cap shroud is just going slack, and the mast is straight athwartships, and has a slight forward bend at the spreaders. The forestay should have a similar tension to the cap shrouds, and the backstay slightly less.

Common problem areas

This loose strand means that the shroud should be replaced immediately.

A hairline crack in this mast T-hook plate means failure is imminent.

A common problem with T-hooks is a fracture on the inside, which is hard to spot.

Rust at the bottom of a shroud may be harmless run-off from poor polishing.

Making a new mast boot

Many yachts have keel-stepped masts, which means that the mast penetrates the deck and anchors itself to a fitting in the bilge. This arrangement means the spar is secure, but it leaves a hole in the deck that needs to be sealed. The answer is a mast boot.

A mast boot is a simple conical seal to stop water entering a yacht's accommodation through the hole in the deck. They are made from a flexible, waterproof material such as leather, rubber or plastic, and are secured to the mast and its deck support by large stainless steel clips.

As with all perishable materials, the effects of ultraviolet, salt water and movement can weaken a mast boot, eventually causing it to fail.

Replacement is easy, but does involve a bit of manipulation to achieve a good fit, especially when working with rubber.

Signs that your mast boot needs replacing include small cracks in the rubber, or, if made of leather, the stitching breaking up, as well as water running down the mast and pooling in the cabin. Temporary repairs can be made with duct tape, but the best repair is to make a new boot.

The most flexible and waterproof material to use is neoprene, which has a good resistance to salt and ultraviolet. A typical mast boot on a 25ft (7.6m) keel-stepped boat would be made from 0.08in–0.12in (2–3mm) neoprene, with a seam overlap of 1–1½in (30–40mm) and a height of about 8½–10in (22–25cm).

Below **Mast boots are often found at the base of unstayed masts, such as on this famous junk-rigged Folkboat, *Jester*.**

Making a mast boot

The easiest way to make a mast boot is to create a cardboard model. For this, you will need an old cardboard tube, such as a kitchen towel insert, some cardboard, brown paper, a piece of neoprene rubber, some sandpaper, a glue gun, a knife and a pencil.

✪ First, measure the diameters of the mast and the deck sleeve, and use a compass to draw two circles of these dimensions on the cardboard.

✪ Cut the cardboard tube to the height you want the boot to be, then stick the two circles on each end of the tube to make a tapered bobbin.

✪ Now, roll the model over the paper, and trace its track. This will result in two curved lines.

✪ Cut out the shape, and use it as a template on the neoprene. Remember to allow enough material for an overlap.

✪ Roughen the edges of the rubber with sandpaper, and wipe with a solvent such as acetone to degrease it.

✪ Mask off with tape, and then coat each surface to be bonded with a rubber glue, the strongest variety usually being a two-pack.

✪ With the second coat of glue tacky, position the two overlapping halves and then force them together with a roller. Remove the tape, and allow to cure for 24 hours.

✪ To fit to the mast, slide the boot on upside down, so that the widest part of the cone is at the top. Fit the stainless steel clip, and then roll the boot down over the clip to hide it. When the mast is re-stepped, the lower part of the boot can be secured with another clip. Don't overtighten, as you could pinch and tear the neoprene.

✪ Finally, smear petroleum jelly around the mast at the top of the boot to make it watertight.

✪ If the mast is already up, the new boot can be fitted by wrapping the neoprene around the spar, and then gluing it together. This method is harder, though, as it is difficult to apply pressure to the join, and therefore get the glue to seal well.

Right **Note how the boot tapers out to cover the circular metal deck plate, and how the top is folded over to hide the metal clip.**

Getting well booted

Using measurements from the mast, make a bobbin to create a template.

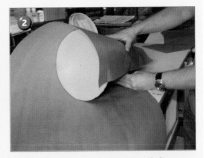

Wrap the template paper around the bobbin, allowing for some overlap.

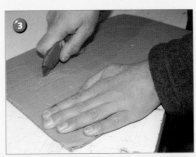

Cut out the template, lay over the neoprene, and then cut out the boot itself.

Roughen the overlap, apply glue, and then press the two edges firmly together.

Making a solid wooden spar

Aluminium and carbon fibre spars may offer practical advantages over wooden ones, yet wood is still the material of choice for many owners of classic boats.

Wooden spars are usually made from either Sitka spruce, or the denser yet cheaper Douglas fir, because both species are flexible, relatively lightweight, and can be obtained in clear, knot-free lengths. If possible, choose your timber in person, and try to make sure the timber is within 1in (25mm) of the spar's final diameter, so as to avoid any risk of distortion, which can occur when the timber is reduced to a smaller size and the wood's natural inner tension released.

Solid spars are, in fact, much more stable when they are constructed from two pieces of wood glued together, rather than a single piece.

If the spar length is greater than that of the available timber, you may need to scarph an additional piece on to one end. If you decide to do this, scarph joints must have a minimum ratio of 12:1.

Preparation work

It's crucial that when you make or repair a wooden spar that you support it evenly along its entire length, so that it can't sag or distort. The best way to do this is to use trestles, and although there are no set guidelines as to the maximum distance between them, they should be placed close enough that the spar can't sag. They should also be set at

a comfortable working height. To make sure the trestles are level, run a string line between the two furthest trestles – if they are level, the top of each one should touch the line when it is pulled tight.

Checking for twist

If you are making a spar using two pieces of wood, glue them together using an adhesive such as resorcinol. Once the glue has cured, select one side of the spar and check for any twist. This can be done by placing three 'winding sticks' upright on the timber, one at either end and a third in the middle. You can then 'sight' across the top of the sticks. If they don't line up, it means there is twist in the wood which can be eliminated by planing the wood flat.

The next step is to mark out the centreline, as well as the final

Below **A No7 hand plane, with a nice long sole, is ideal for shaping a wooden spar.**

diameters, and any tapers and steps in the mast. This can be done using a chalkline, followed by a pencil.

Rounding off

Transforming the square-section spar into a round-section spar is a laborious process that involves turning the four sides of the spar into eight, and then 16, and finally 32, using an electric plane or No7 hand plane.

Spar gauges can be used to mark the required lines on the four sides of the spar, with the pins arranged to reflect a ratio of 7:10:7 for the first stage. A ratio of 5:9:5 should be used for the second phase, while the final stage, when the spar is converted into a 32-sided spar, should be done by eye.

By this stage, the spar should be virtually round, so use a smoothing plane to finish it off. Final fairing should be done using a 3ft (1m) long piece of sandpaper, which is wrapped around the spar. Parcel tape applied to the back of the sandpaper will help prevent it from ripping. The sandpaper should then be 'worked' along the spar to remove any remaining humps and bumps. A round scraper, followed by 120-grit sandpaper, should be used to eradicate any cross-grain sanding marks. When you have finished sanding, seal the spar with a 50:50 mix of varnish and thinners.

Above **An old saw blade with a radius cut out of it can be used as a round scraper for the final part of the mast-shaping process.**

Shaping the spar

A spar gauge is used to mark out the first set of cuts.

A circular saw set at 45 degrees transforms the four-sided timber into an octagonal.

A set of dividers is used to mark the cuts required to turn it into 16 sides.

The indents made by the dividers are marked out in pencil.

The cut lines are clearly marked down the whole length of the timber.

An electric plane is used to turn the eight sides into 16, and then remove any corners.

Making a hollow wooden spar

A hollow wooden spar is ideal if you want to reduce the weight of the spars, without losing the aesthetic appeal of a wooden one. It also has the added benefit that the instrument wires can be run discreetly up the middle of the mast, rather than on the outside.

The process of making a hollow wooden mast, using two identical lengths of timber, initially follows the same procedure as that used to make a solid spar (see page 260). The differences begin once the two halves of the spar have been formed. On reaching this stage, mark out the centreline, finished diameters, tapers and steps of the mast on both halves, as these must be shaped to the required profile before the hollowing-out process can begin.

Below **The two hollowed-out halves are glued and clamped together to create a light and yet strong hollow spar.**

Hollowing-out the two halves

- Mark out the hollow section on each half. Although one of the main reasons for having a hollow spar is to save weight, it must not be at the expense of strength, so the wall section should be at least $\frac{1}{5}$ of the spar's maximum diameter. The ends of the hollow section must culminate in a spherical radius to avoid point loading of stresses.

- The initial profile of the hollow section will consist of steps that have been cut by a router.
- Remove these steps using a moulding plane, followed by sandpaper wrapped around a curved sanding block.
- To form the ends, use a gouge and finish with sandpaper to eliminate any sharp edges.
- On completion of the hollow sections, seal them with a coat of epoxy. Use a hot air gun to warm the epoxy and allow it to penetrate the wood, without forming a thick pool at the bottom of the hollow.
- Once the epoxy has cured, use a wide, flat sanding block to remove any excess epoxy.

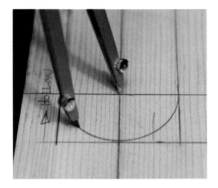

Above **Marking out the extent of the hollow section which must culminate in a radius to avoid point loading of stresses.**

Right **Using a template to check that the hollowed section is the required shape.**

Joining the two halves together

Resorcinol is the most common glue used to join sections of a spar together. As a non-gap-filling glue, it requires good flat surfaces to achieve a tight join, and a constant level of pressure to achieve the strongest bond. As soon as the glue has been applied, use as many G-cramps as possible to keep the two halves of the spar together. Wooden pads should be used between the cramps and the spar to spread the load across its width, and prevent it from crushing the hollow section.

When tightening up the G-cramps, do so lightly to start with, and fix a couple of cramps sideways to stop the two halves of the spar moving apart as the other cramps are tightened up. When everything has been tightened up, keep an eye on the spar to ensure there is no

movement. Make sure the sideways-positioned cramps are not too tight, so that they don't force the two halves of the spar apart, and undermine the integrity of the glue joint.

When the glue has cured, shape the spar by following the same steps used when making a solid spar (see page 260).

Alternative methods of construction

Hollow masts can also be made by gluing together strips of wood known as staves. There are two methods for doing this, one that uses four staves, and another that uses eight. When four staves are used, they are glued together to form a box-section mast, whereas, if a rounded spar is required, eight staves are used.

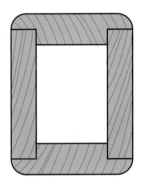

Box

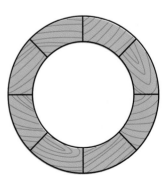

8 Staves

Right **Hollow masts can also be made by gluing either four or eight staves together.**

Dinghy
repairs

11

GRP dinghy repairs

Dinghies are normally lightly constructed, yet they are often subjected to harsher treatment than larger vessels. This is particularly true for yacht tenders that are dragged up stony beaches, or for those that sustain damage when tied alongside a quay.

Rubbing strakes, whether timber or rubber, are often one of the first components to show wear. The most common problem with the rubber types that wrap around both sides of the gunwale is that they pull through their fastenings. Refitting these with larger washers will often give the rubbing strake a new lease of life.

Rubber types that slot into an aluminium backing can be more difficult to deal with if the rubber pops out of place. Patience will often pay dividends here – in winter, heat the rubber carefully with a hairdryer to make it softer and more malleable. A few blobs of adhesive will help keep it in situ.

Wooden rubbing strakes rarely sustain damage along their entire length, so a graving piece or short length can be scarphed in to replace a damaged section (see page 84).

Bilge runners

These can be vulnerable to significant wear, especially on tenders that are frequently beached, or dragged into the water from a concrete slipway. Plastic or brass rubbing strips can protect the bilge runners to a certain extent, although the screw holes may allow water ingress into the hull.

With moulded fibreglass bilge runners, start the repair by cutting away any damaged material. Thoroughly dry the hull, before filling any voids and screw holes with a mix of resin and colloidal silica or microfibres. Additional layers of fibreglass can then be laminated on top of the runners to restore them to the original strength specification.

On a larger vessel, impact damage can be repaired in a similar manner

Above **Yacht tenders can have a very hard life, yet the safety of the crew depends on them being kept in good repair.**

Below **Dinghies tend to be lightly built, so damage that might be cosmetic on larger vessels may turn out to be structural.**

to fibreglass repairs (see page 26). A knockabout tender can be repaired easily, possibly without too much attention to achieving a perfect cosmetic finish. However, it's a different matter for a specialist racing dinghy, where a good fairing job will be needed to make a perfect finish (see page 40 for more on finishing work after GRP repairs).

Above **Dinghies with a double hull can be unsafe if a layer is damaged, as the void between the two skins can fill with water.**

Small fibreglass repairs

At first sight this looks as though this is relatively light damage...

...but once the loose material is removed the problem extends further.

The hole, with all unsound material removed and ready for laminating.

With three layers of fibreglass mat in place, it's ready for final finishing.

Double-skin dinghies

Many dinghies and other small boats are built by joining two fibreglass mouldings together, with the void in-between filled with foam. When these boats are new, they have the advantage of ample built-in buoyancy. However, if either of the two skins is punctured – or the join between them is damaged – water can flood between the two compartments. A major problem with this is that there's no way of measuring how much water has got in.

Most frequently, the problem is that the joint between the two mouldings has been damaged. The best solution is to separate them, remove the foam, repair any other damage, and then rejoin the two sections, ensuring the joint is completely waterproof. This can be achieved by bedding them together on an adhesive filler, made by mixing epoxy resin and microfibres. Laminating two layers of fibreglass over the join will then ensure it remains watertight.

GRP hull repairs

A large hole in a fibreglass dinghy can be awkward to repair, especially if it's on a corner, a chine, or through a part of the hull made inaccessible by a watertight chamber. The method shown can be used to repair a much larger boat, if for any reason the inside of the hull cannot be reached.

When a dinghy is damaged in the lower part of the transom, there is likely to be a watertight buoyancy chamber on the inside which will make access difficult or impossible. The trick is to make a former, which can be inserted through the hole and bonded to the inside of the hull. This makes a 'wall' to support the lay up.

The first task is to clean up the edges, and then grind them back with a coarse (P60) grit disc on an angle grinder to make a shallow 2in (5cm) feathered depression all round.

The opposite corner of the boat is used as a mould. Clean the hull, allow to dry, and then apply three layers of release wax. Lay some 6oz woven GRP cloth over the corner and thoroughly wet out (ie saturate) with epoxy, forcing it down with a roller until it has taken the shape of the underlying hull. Cover with peel ply and allow to cure.

Lift off the mould, and transfer it to the opposite side, orientating it to fit. You will be able to see the hole through the material, so now draw the outline of the extremity of the feathering. Cut around this outer line with a bandsaw or scissors. The resulting cutout will form a backing plate, which will be flexible enough to insert through the hole. Key the insides of the hull around the hole as well as you can with coarse sandpaper prior to fitting.

Drill a small hole in the middle of the cutout, and fit a screw to act as a handle. Liberally coat the edges of the cutout with a quick-drying epoxy where it will meet the hull, and then push it through the hole. Using the screw, pull the cutout firmly back so the glue can make contact, and hold it until the glue sets.

Below **Fibreglass dinghies are prone to damage, especially those regularly used for landing on rocky shores or against hard quayside steps.**

Right **The buoyancy tanks inside this dinghy make this a tricky repair. Here, the edges of the hole have been trimmed and feathered to create a depression.**

Place a clear polythene sheet over the reinforced hole, and draw a series of rings to represent the ½ in (1.25cm) contours of the feathered depression. These contours will be used to shape a series of reinforcement patches. Cut out the patches according to the contours,

Patching a hole

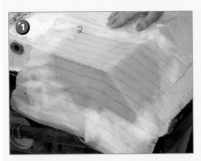

To create a backing pad, apply three coats of release wax to the undamaged corner. Wet out some woven roving, cover with peel ply, and allow to cure.

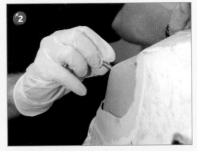

Remove and trim the backing pad. Apply quick-drying epoxy to the edges, insert it into the hole, and use a screw to pull it up tight.

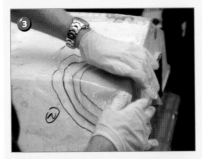

Use a clear sheet of polythene as a guide for the repair patches. Wet them out together, with the largest diameter pad at the bottom.

Remove the polythene, apply the patches, and smooth with a brush. Once cured, apply epoxy filler to fair the hull prior to sanding and painting.

and then lay them on the polythene, starting with the smallest one and progressively getting bigger so the largest is at the top.

Pour activated epoxy onto this patch sandwich, and gently work over it with a spatula until all the patches are thoroughly wetted out. Pick up the polythene from underneath, and then lay it over the hole so the patches come into contact with the feathered depression. Use the contours as a guide. You want the widest patch to meet the hull first, with the increasingly smaller ones making the layup thicker towards the centre and forming a plug.

Peel away the polythene. The resulting layup may be a little distorted, so work it over with a brush or roller until it is as smooth as possible. Once cured, you can apply epoxy filler, which can be sanded flat. A final decorative touch is to sand the entire hull and give it a coat of two-pack paint. If faired and painted properly, the repair will be invisible.

Buoyancy tank leaks

Dinghies are prone to capsizing and swamping, and so must have sufficient buoyancy to support their own weight, plus that of an outboard motor, anchor, and any other gear carried. However, this safety feature can easily become compromised.

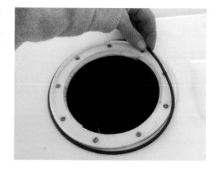

Testing buoyancy tanks at least once a season is the only way to be sure of their continued integrity. There are two approaches to doing this: submerging the boat for 30 minutes, or lightly pressurising the tanks with air and checking the pressure is maintained for at least ten minutes. The former has the advantage that any leaks will be immediately obvious thanks to the stream of bubbles that will stem from the smallest of deficiencies.

However, it may not always be easy to achieve this, especially if working on the boat at home, as dinghies are not designed to support the weight of a full load of water inside when onshore. This is particularly true of lightweight racing dinghies and small speedboats.

The alternative is to lightly pressurise the tanks with air from a foot pump – many inflatable dinghy pumps will fit the bung (drain) holes at the bottom of the tank. Leaks can be found by putting a detergent solution around the edges of the tanks and any fittings, including inspection hatch covers.

In most cases, it is these fittings that will need attention – they should be removed, cleaned and re-bedded on a marine-grade adhesive sealant, before being screwed or bolted back in position. If the screw holes have become enlarged, follow the procedure on page 272. The rubber or plastic seals on inspection hatches have only a finite life, so these may need to be replaced.

If the problem is with the tanks, leaks are most likely to be where they join the hull or deck. These seams can be sealed by the following method:

✪ Sand both sides of the join with a medium-grit abrasive paper.
✪ Thoroughly clean and dry the entire area.

Above **Some inspection covers have a rubber seal that becomes perished over time. This is often sold as a spare.**

Below **Effective buoyancy is vital for all dinghies, to prevent the boat sinking in the event of a capsize or becoming swamped.**

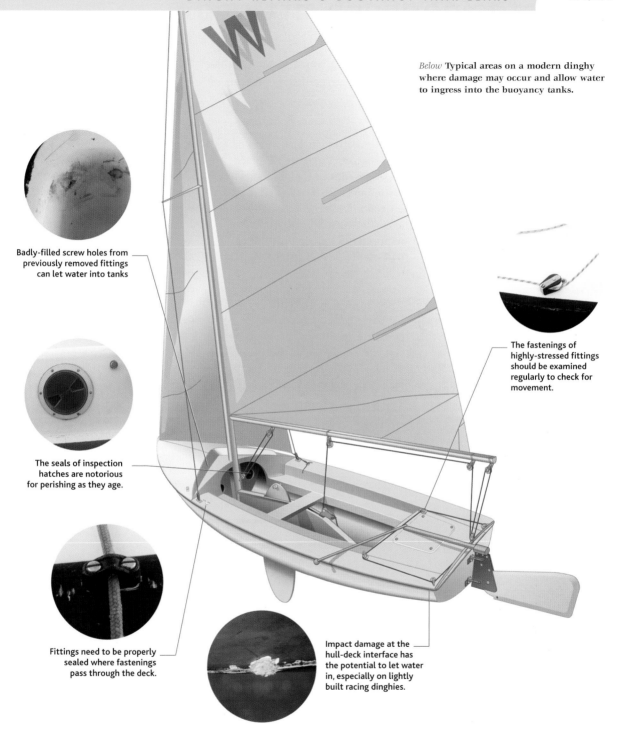

Below **Typical areas on a modern dinghy where damage may occur and allow water to ingress into the buoyancy tanks.**

Badly-filled screw holes from previously removed fittings can let water into tanks

The seals of inspection hatches are notorious for perishing as they age.

Fittings need to be properly sealed where fastenings pass through the deck.

The fastenings of highly-stressed fittings should be examined regularly to check for movement.

Impact damage at the hull-deck interface has the potential to let water in, especially on lightly built racing dinghies.

⊕ Laminate fibreglass tape over the top of the seam. Two layers – the first of 1in (25mm) wide tape, and the second of 2in (51mm) – is ample for this, and will create a strong join. A neater job can be made if the fibreglass on each side is sanded away further, so that the repair lies below the height of the original gel coat.

⊕ A new gel coat – colour matched to the original – can then be applied and faired in to blend in with the original material.

Refastening loose fittings

Many dinghy deck fittings are subject to relatively small loads, and are therefore attached with self-tapping screws. However, if they pull out of the deck, some lateral thinking may be needed to refit them securely.

As a dinghy ages, the fastenings on the deck fittings inevitably experience movement when under load. This eventually leads to the screw holes becoming enlarged, and failing to grip. Simply replacing the screws with longer ones is often not feasible, as most fittings are designed for a certain size of fastening, so a larger one will not fit. In any case, this doesn't address the root cause of the problem.

If there's easy access behind the fitting, replacing screws with bolts and large washers is likely to be all that's needed. If there's no way of reaching the blind side of the fitting,

an alternative that can work well for a wooden or heavily constructed fibreglass dinghy is to fill the old screw hole with a mix of resin and microfibres. As the resin starts to set, insert the screw to create a thread, then remove it before the epoxy hardens to prevent it becoming stuck in place.

This process may not, however, work with the thin laminates of modern lightweight racing dinghies. In some cases, the location will lend itself to cutting a hole for an inspection hatch, which will allow a hand to reach the blind side of the fitting. If this is not

possible, though – either from a structural or aesthetic perspective – a marine plywood backing pad can be positioned behind the fitting, providing there's an inspection hatch within a couple of metres.

Start by running a mousing line from one of the screw holes to the hatch, as this can be used to pull the backing pad into place. Epoxy adhesive can then be squirted through the screw holes using a syringe, to fix the backing pad in place. The fitting can then be screwed to this, ensuring it's bedded down on a marine-grade sealant.

Below **Loose fittings should be attended to immediately. If left, screw holes will grow larger and a bigger repair will be needed.**

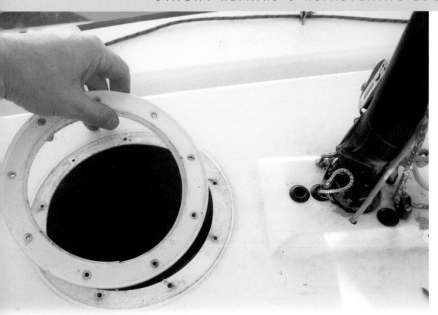

Aluminium spars

Screws or rivets that pull out of aluminium spars can also pose a problem, especially where corrosion of the metal is evident. It may be possible to bolt the fitting through the spar, but this risks further weakening, especially in highly stressed areas, such as the gooseneck and the mid-section of a boom. A better solution is an aluminium backing plate, shaped to match the inside profile of the spar. This can be pre-drilled with holes for pop rivets, or bolts, and a thread tapped so there's no need for nuts on the blind side.

To fit the plate, take the end-cap off the spar, run a mousing line from the damaged screw holes, and pass the line through the fixing holes drilled in the backing plate. Then, use the mousing line to manoeuvre the plate into position, and fit the new bolts or rivets.

Above left **Leaking hatches are a common problem and can be solved by re-bedding with a marine-grade sealant.**

Above **These stainless steel self-taping screws for a vang attachment have corroded the aluminium mast. As they are at the end of the spar, access is easy and they can be replaced with bolts.**

Resealing fittings

Mask around the edge of the fitting – this helps with cleaning up excess sealant.

Use a marine-grade adhesive sealant. This will last much longer than silicone types.

Apply a single bead of sealant that encircles the screw holes and links them together.

Wooden dinghy repairs

As wooden clinker dinghies age, they may incur some form of localised damage, or start to develop minor leaks that can be rectified without you having to replace entire planks.

If a wooden dinghy has been stored ashore for several years, and allowed to dry out completely, it may leak considerably when relaunched. However, before you resort to extensive repairs, it may be possible to make the dinghy more watertight by carrying out some basic remedial work. Firstly, check the fastenings, as the leak may be caused by one or more of these failing. Another simple solution is to relaunch the boat and allow the wooden planks to take up (swell). When wood dries out it shrinks, and, conversely, when it is saturated it swells, so you may find that after several days afloat, the hull planks have swelled sufficiently to either reduce the leaking significantly, or cure it completely.

Removing hard, old paint

Another common problem on old wooden clinker dinghies, is the build-up of several layers of paint between the lands (overlapping edges) of the planking. Eventually, this paint will go rock hard, and no longer flex with the natural expansion and contraction of the planking. This can cause a leak by preventing the wood swelling. Curing this problem is a straightforward process, albeit time consuming:

✪ Start by turning the boat over and stripping off the paint. When the bulk of the paint has been removed, the areas where paint has accumulated between the lands should be evident. Remove any lumps of paint using a hacksaw blade.

✪ Next, hand sand the seams.

✪ Apply an oil-based mastic along the seams, and work it in-between the lands with a putty knife. Remove any excess with an old rag dipped in white spirit. When the dinghy is relaunched and the hull begins to take up, the mastic will flex enough to maintain an effective watertight seal between the planks.

✪ If all of the planking has been stripped back to bare wood, it is worth applying a coat of a linseed oil-based wood preservative. This should be left to soak into the wood for a couple of days, so that it is totally dry before you start repainting it.

Below **The stresses and strains on wooden sail boats mean they are prone to leaking – but they can also be easily repaired.**

Left **The damaged section of a sheer plank on a clinker dinghy is removed with a router. Note use of ear and eye protection.**

Refastening tired hood ends

The hood ends (the forward and aft ends of the planking) are one of the most vulnerable parts of a wooden clinker dinghy. On older wooden dinghies, these may start to crack and split, allowing the fastenings to pull out. If the planking immediately forward of the transom is completely sound, you may be able to fit a fashion piece to the inside face of the transom, and resecure the planking to this.

Alternatively, if most of the hood ends are damaged, and the transom is also quite tired, it might be worth replacing the transom with a slightly enlarged one that is fitted a little further forward, to a point where the planks are all sound. A new transom knee may also be required if the position of the transom has changed. The original integrity of the boat will be restored by securing the new transom to the undamaged part of each plank, although the dinghy will inevitably be shortened by a few centimetres.

Resealing leaking planks

Strip off the old paint with a hot air gun and scraper, taking care not to scorch the wood.

Sand down the seams by hand – an electric sander won't reach in corners.

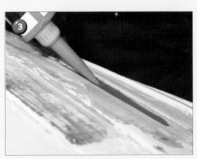

Apply an oil-based mastic along the seams – avoid silicone sealants at all cost.

Remove excess mastic with an old rag moistened with white spirit.

Inflatable dinghy repairs

Inflatable dinghies operate in a harsh environment, yet their very nature means they are made of lightweight and flexible materials. Despite this, good-quality dinghies have the potential to be long lasting, provided they are treated well.

Inflatable materials

Two materials are used for the overwhelming majority of inflatable dinghies: Hypalon (a rugged synthetic rubber) and PVC impregnated into a fabric cloth. Hypalon is widely regarded as the superior choice, and has potential for excellent longevity, with many 30 year old boats still in service.

Vinyl is cheaper and more popular, but degrades faster in ultraviolet light, and repairs are awkward to make because it's difficult to get glue to stick to the shiny surface. The cheapest PVC dinghies have glued seams, but better quality models have seams bonded through a heat welding process. These can almost rival Hypalon for longevity.

Care of inflatables

Abrasion is the biggest enemy of all inflatables. Avoid dragging the boat across the ground when launching, landing and handling on shore, as this will rapidly wear the surface of the material. Similarly, when stowing the dinghy on board take care to avoid contact with anything that could cause the material to

Above **A spoon is an ideal implement to smooth out air bubbles when applying a patch to an inflatable dinghy.**

Below **Wear and tear is often found in the join between tubes and solid transoms. This dinghy has a commendably high level of reinforcement in this area.**

Right **Examine both tubes and floor at regular intervals for signs of damage.**

chafe. In a rough sea, even a small amount of movement can create problems.

Over time ultraviolet degradation will weaken the material, especially with PVC dinghies, so if possible avoid leaving the boat outside where it will be exposed to sunlight for extended periods.

The boat should be washed with fresh water and dried thoroughly before being stowed. The practicalities of stowage on most boats mean dinghies are often packed into the smallest possible volume, but this inevitably creases and weakens the fabric. A better option is to store the boat ashore, ideally somewhere it can be left unrolled and partially inflated.

Repairing leaks

To repair small holes in the fabric, inflate the dinghy and pour a weak solution of detergent over the tubes. Bubbles will form around any leaks. The area should then be dried and the surface roughened with 100-grit sandpaper to provide a key for the adhesive, then thoroughly cleaned and de-greased. Ideally two applications of methyl ethyl ketone (MEK) should be used for cleaning, although acetone can be used for non-critical patches.

It's important to use the correct repair kit for the fabric type, and to follow instructions to the letter. Low humidity and moderate temperature (15–23 °C) are also important if a long-lasting repair is to be achieved. Note that the adhesive has a short shelf life – as little as one year – and once opened readily absorbs water, so a part-used container should not be kept for use at a later date.

In the absence of a repair kit, cleaning the area and applying a blob of marine adhesive sealant such as Sikaflex 291 can provide an effective temporary repair.

Far left **Transoms are vulnerable to chafe if the dinghy is dragged along the ground when launching or recovering.**

Left **Check the painter for chafe and to ensure the attachment is firmly bonded to the boat.**

Trailer mechanical repairs

Boat trailers operate in a harsh environment, but are often left languishing without care for long periods. After a period of standing, they should be inspected thoroughly, and any problems fixed.

A few top-of-the range trailers have sealed-unit wheel bearings, which are almost impervious to water ingress. However, most will succumb to frequent dunkings in both fresh and salt water, and will require attention if they were not serviced before they were laid-up. A rumbling noise from a bearing indicates excessive play and metal-on-metal contact, and this is a precursor to imminent failure. Wheel bearings are easy to remove, clean and regrease:

❋ Support the trailer securely on stands.
❋ Remove the wheels.
❋ Remove the dust cap from the hub.
❋ Slide out the split pin that holds the castellated nut in place.

❋ Unscrew the nut and remove the wheel hub.
❋ The bearings will now be visible and can be removed.
❋ Clean them in a solvent, such as paraffin (kerosene).
❋ Work grease into the rollers.
❋ Replacing the bearings is a reversal of this process, and the hub should be well packed with grease, allowing for expansion.
❋ Use a torque wrench to tighten the castellated nut to the settings recommended by the manufacturer, and fit a new split pin.
❋ After refitting the wheel, rotate it to check that it spins freely. You should also wobble it by taking hold of it with two hands on opposite sides – no play should be felt.

Below **Most trailers use non-marinised bearings and brake systems. Those that aren't pampered after use are likely to fail.**

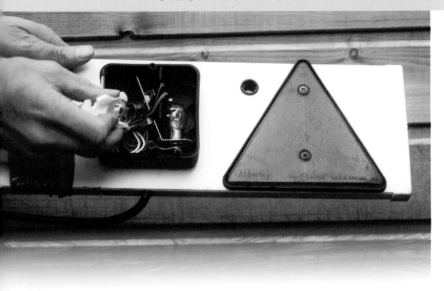

Left **Lighting boards are subject to considerable vibration, especially on empty trailers, so bulb failure is common.**

Storing trailers

If a trailer is to be stored for any length of time, start by giving it a full service – this will minimise the amount of deterioration, especially key parts such as brakes and wheel bearings. Lift the trailer on a jack, and place chocks beneath it to take the strain off the tyres and suspension units. The brake should also be released.

When recommissioning a trailer that has not been used for some time, it's vital to ensure it's in a fully roadworthy condition. If it was decommissioned as above, then a check of the wheel bearings, braking system and condition of the chassis and suspension units (see page 280) is likely to be all that's required. However, if the trailer's history is unknown, it should be assumed that, as a minimum, a full service is needed, with any problems found in the service rectified.

Braking systems

Brakes are fitted to all but the smallest of boat trailers – any boat weighing over around 881lb (400kg) may need a braked trailer, depending on the size of the towing vehicle. Many boat trailers rely on braking systems designed for trailers that are never submersed in water. This means cables are prone to corrosion, and can jam in their outer sleeves. Components may also seize within the brake drum. Once this has happened, the only remedy is to replace the cable, or strip the brake system apart. Following the sequence for servicing wheel bearings will also reveal the brake components.

Below left **With this type of hub, the outer wheel bearing must be removed before the brake drum can be taken off.**

Below right **When removing brake shoes, pull one towards you to ease pressure on the springs and make them easier to release.**

Trailer body & other fittings

The structural components of all types of boat trailer are prone to corrosion, so rust must be kept at bay. If severe, but localised, rusting is present, a new section of the trailer may need to be welded in place.

Boat trailers are almost universally made from mild steel that's prevented from rusting by good paintwork or by galvanising. The latter has a longer lifespan, but in both cases rust will eventually eat into the trailer, eventually affecting its structural integrity. If the boat is launched into salt water, the first defence against corrosion is to rinse the trailer with fresh water every time it's used. Touching-up any chips or other damage to the trailer's paintwork, at the earliest opportunity, will also help considerably, as it is the paintwork that protects the steel from corrosion (see page 102 for more on painting steel).

Damage assessment

Tapping the trailer's framework with a small hammer will give you an indication of the metal's condition – if the metal is sound, it will ring like a bell, with a clear note. However, if only a dull thud is heard, a considerable amount of corrosion may be present, and the steelwork must be looked at more closely.

If the damage is localised, the steel can be cut away with an angle grinder, and a new section welded in. Once the old material has been cut away, check the thickness and condition of the remaining metal – most trailers are made from 0.12in (3mm) thick box section, so this gives a good guide to the thickness you should be expecting. Checking the condition of the remaining metal will also reveal whether the trailer is too rusty to be worth repairing. See page 100 for more on preparing steel for welding.

Above top **Checking for corrosion on a galvanised trailer. This should be ground back and regalvanised or painted.**

Above **Tyres of boat trailers rarely wear out, but they should be replaced frequently to avoid age-related failure.**

Below **Many boat trailers operate in a harsh environment of salt and/or grit. Safety demands that they are kept in good repair.**

TIP

A towing coupling or hitch, which hooks onto your vehicle's towbar, should be easy to use, and freshly greased. If it has seized, either partially or fully, it's worth soaking the moving parts in penetrating oil to see whether they can be coaxed into movement. However, if the hitch has signs of significant rusting, it is safer to replace it.

Left **Examining the condition of the security coupling of a small non-braked trailer. This stops it breaking free if the tow hitch fails.**

Breakaway cables and security couplings

Breakaway cables and security couplings are simple safety devices that are crucial in the event of a trailer becoming separated from its towing vehicle. Surprisingly, however, considering their importance, they are often missing or defective on many trailers. A security coupling is used on an unbraked trailer, and is a length of wire with a loop at each end. One end is attached to the trailer, while the other is hooked over the towing vehicle's towbar. If the trailer's coupling unhitches itself during the journey, the trailer will still be attached to the towing vehicle via the security wire.

The greater weight of braked trailers means that security couplings are not strong enough, so these trailers should be fitted with a breakaway cable that will apply the trailer's brakes should the trailer

Above **Never assume a trailer, however new, is roadworthy. The suspension units of this two year old trailer have significant corrosion.**

become unhitched. As the name suggests, when the load on the cable becomes too large it will fail, but by this stage the trailer should be slowing anyway.

Suspension units

These are normally sealed units that require no routine servicing. However, they are also made from painted or galvanised mild steel, and on older trailers, rust is commonly seen here. It's vital, therefore, when inspecting the underside of the trailer, to check that these are in good condition, and any problems with the paint system should be remedied.

If corrosion is significant, the only solution is to replace the entire suspension unit because a lack of suspension may cause damage to the boat and reduces the grip of the tyre on the road. On smaller trailers these may simply be bolted to the frame – if so they're easy to replace. However others, particularly those on larger trailers, can only be removed with specialist tools.

Outboard repairs

12

Diagnosing starting problems

If an outboard engine proves difficult to start it can usually be traced to a relatively small number of issues, especially on two-stroke models where fuel problems are more common. A good starting technique is also an important factor.

Modern large outboards have fuel injection and sophisticated engine management systems that make starting them, in theory at least, as easy and reliable as starting a contemporary car. However, older and smaller models, especially those with carburettors instead of fuel injection, can prove more temperamental.

If starting a cold two-stroke engine, it will need around one-quarter throttle and full choke. This effectively closes off the air supply to the carburettor, creating a rich fuel/air mixture for starting. However, if the choke is not flipped off almost immediately it starts, the engine will die due to lack of air. If the engine is warm then the choke should not be needed, but if the engine hasn't been used for an hour or two, although it is still partially warm, it can be harder to judge how much choke is needed – it may be full choke or just half.

Dealing with a flooded carburettor

The easiest time to flood the carburettor with fuel is when the engine is partially warm, and on some units this may happen after just half a dozen pulls of the starting cord. If you can smell petrol, then chances are you've flooded the carburettor. If you're lucky, however, a flooded engine will start if the choke is turned off and the engine given full throttle to let the maximum amount of air in, therefore weakening the fuel/air mixture. If attempting this, reduce the throttle setting as soon as the engine fires – over-revving of an engine on starting rapidly accelerates wear.

If this doesn't work, a little patience is usually all that's needed, so don't be tempted to try to start the engine repeatedly as this will simply exacerbate the problem. After around five minutes (maybe a little less in hot weather, but more in a cool climate), the problem will often literally evaporate and the engine should start easily without using the choke.

Left **Many problems with outboard engines are relatively quick to solve given a few basic tools and knowledge.**

Left **Two-stroke outboards can be sensitive to the choke control – often it must be flicked to the running position as soon as the engine starts.**

TIP

If starting a pull-start engine you might be surprised at just how long the starter cord is. Make sure you give it a good long pull, if possible using your body weight in addition to your arm muscles.

Blocked jets

When petrol mixed with two-stroke oil evaporates, it leaves behind a gummy black varnish, which can build up into a progressively thicker layer over time. If a two-stroke engine runs rough when warm but improves given a little choke, that's a sign of a partially gummed up main jet in the carburettor.

Dismantling the carburettor and cleaning the jet will solve the problem, but it can be avoided in the first place by ensuring the carb is drained of fuel whenever you expect not to use the engine for a week or more.

Right **Examining carburettor jets – in this case they look perfectly clean, but if black gunge is found it must be cleaned out.**

Below **Removing a carburettor from the engine is easier than it might sound and only takes a few minutes.**

Replacing gearbox oil seals

The oil seals between the gearbox and prop shaft are easily damaged if the prop becomes fouled with fishing line or nets. The seals are cheap to buy, although in some cases replacing them can be a tricky operation.

If the outboard engine's gearbox oil has a white, milky consistency this is a clear sign that water has entered the gearbox. This has the potential to cause serious damage, even if the engine is not used. Most maintenance schedules recommend changing gearbox oil only once a year, but the consequences of water contamination are severe enough to warrant checking the condition of the oil at least on a monthly basis. If water is present in the oil, and the seals cannot be replaced immediately, the oil should be drained and the gearbox refilled with fresh oil to protect the unit. To avoid further damage, the outboard should not be used before the oil is changed.

Sources of water ingress

There are three common routes by which water can find its way into the gearbox. By far the easiest to solve is water ingress via the seals on the two plugs used for refilling the unit with oil. New seals cost next to nothing and should be replaced every time the plugs are removed.

Alternatively, the seals around the top of the gearbox, where the drive shaft enters, could be damaged. A more likely scenario, however, is the oil seals around the prop shaft, as these are particularly vulnerable to damage from fishing line. A sensible precaution to avoid damaged seals is therefore to inspect the prop for evidence of nylon line every time you use the boat.

Below **Gearbox oil seals can be damaged by fishing line or other debris, so they can be a problem irrespective of the age of the engine.**

Replacing a seal

After removing the prop, unscrew the two bolts securing the back cover of the gearbox.

Remove the bolts, taking care to ensure the threads tapped into the soft aluminium casing are not damaged.

The cover plate may need to be levered off – many have notches in the casting to facilitate this.

Lift the cover plate away with the propshaft. Note the position of the elements in order to replace them.

Pressing one of the new seals into position – these are a tight fit, so it may help to heat the casting first.

Refit the propshaft before replacing the cover plate casting, checking that the seal makes a snug fit around the shaft.

Replacing seals

The exact procedure for replacing seals varies according to the engine model, but in all cases it starts with removal of the propeller.

⊙ Once the propeller has been removed you'll be able to see the screws of the plate that holds the prop shaft in position. Remove these screws and then slide the plate off the shaft.

⊙ The seals should now be visible and can be prised out, noting their correct orientation. They are normally fitted in pairs – one to keep the oil in, the other to keep water out – and must be replaced with any lips facing in the same direction as the original seals.

⊙ Finally, refill the gearbox with the grade of oil recommended by the engine manufacturer. To do this, remove the two plugs in the gearbox casing; then, with the engine upright, squirt oil into the lower hole until it comes out of the top hole. This ensures no air locks can form as the gearbox is filled. Once the top plug has been fitted, the filler pipe can be removed and the lower plug inserted. If water was present in the gearbox, then the new oil should be changed after the engine has been run for an hour.

Faulty outboard controls

It is easy to take engine controls for granted, but they are prone to damp and corrosion, especially in salt water environments. In addition, cables and the plastic inserts of linkages will wear over time.

The controls on most outboards are relatively easy to trace from the user control to the point of adjustment on the engine itself. If there are any problems it should, therefore, be straightforward to identify the exact source of the trouble, whether it's a broken or seized cable or a linkage that has simply sprung apart.

To prolong their life, cables should be lubricated annually with a light oil to help prevent them sticking within their cases. However, a cable whose movement is already severely restricted needs to be replaced, as do cables where the wire is starting to fray. This is generally a straightforward operation – one end of the cable will end in a captive ferrule, while the other end will be adjustable. The adjustable end should be removed first and replaced last. If detailed instructions for your engine are not

available, it's worth taking a series of photographs when removing the old cable to use as an aide-mémoire when reassembling it.

Remote controls

These essentially operate in the same fashion as the engine-mounted controls on a smaller outboard, and problems can be traced in a similar manner. However, there is an extra level of complexity and a helper will almost certainly be needed if you can't easily see the engine when operating the controls. Although most remote controls are operated by a single lever, this actually moves two cables – one for gear changes, the other for the throttle. It's therefore important to trace the

Above **Without fuel injection the correct operation of the choke can be checked after removing the air intake housing.**

correct cable when fault finding. Correct adjustment of the cables is crucial to smooth operation – again, this is easier with two people as the second person can confirm the cables work correctly while operating the engine controls.

Left **With a high-speed boat it's vital that the controls are utterly reliable and function correctly.**

Right **Tightening the screw securing the carburettor end of the throttle cable – a hole in the air intake housing allows access.**

Above The bolt in the leg that holds the gear control rods together must be loosened before the lower unit can be removed.

Steering problems

Steering racks on the transom of RIBs and other outboard-powered craft need regular greasing. They are fitted with a grease nipple for this purpose and so should be given a few pumps from a grease gun every couple of months. However, don't be tempted to over-grease the system – this will just cause it to gum up.

If the steering appears to be seized, or the wheel won't turn easily, a seized steering rack is the most likely cause of the problem. Before dismantling and cleaning the system, it's worth seeing whether it's possible to get it moving again by squirting easing oil into the mechanism while trying to move the wheel gently from side to side. Once it's operating smoothly, give the steering rack a couple of squirts of fresh grease to further lubricate it.

Freeing seized steering

Disconnect outboard link arm from end of steering cable. Grease before reassembling. Remove the rubber cover from the flange through which the steering cable passes.

Undo the nut securing the outer steering cable to the motor.

Pull the steering cable out of the tube in the motor. This may be seized in position and require copious amounts of penetrating oil to free it off.

Moving to the helm position, remove the steering head from the console. If the bolts are seized, more penetrating oil will be needed to free them off. It may also be possible to cut them off. The steering head can now be dismantled.

Once the cover is removed the gears can be freed off using penetrating oil. Once free they will need a generous greasing with water-resistant grease to ensure they remain free.

The steering cable can be removed from the main gear and if it is stiff have oil poured through it to try to free it. It is usually necessary to change the cable once internal corrosion has set in.

Fuel blockage & contamination

Fuel tanks on small boats are prone to getting water in the fuel, especially when used in rough conditions. Other contaminants may also be present in the fuel and build up in the tank over time, leading to blockages in the system.

Petrol is able to absorb a small amount of water in solution – up to around 0.5 per cent – but an excess of water in the fuel will lead to a number of problems. Older and smaller engines with carburettors will run rough or stall if exposed to too much water, but larger and newer engines with more sophisticated fuel injection systems can be seriously damaged if an uninterrupted flow of water reaches the injector pump.

Other impurities are more likely to cause a blockage in the fuel filters. The first indication of a clogged filter is usually a slight loss of power, with the problem escalating over time and eventually leading to engine failure.

Problems with blocked fuel lines are relatively rare, but if you suspect a problem after changing fuel filters, a pressure test will identify whether or not there is a blockage. It's also worth noting that the walls of older flexible fuel pipes on the suction side of the fuel pump can collapse, restricting the flow of fuel.

Below **A blockage or other form of contamination is most likely to become apparent at high speed.**

Above **Using a low-pressure gauge to check the fuel pump output.**

Cleaning the fuel system

To clean a fuel tank, start by draining its contents. Ideally, built-in tanks will have an inspection hatch that will enable the final few cups of fuel at the bottom of the tank to be sponged out, along with any other debris that has collected. Alternatively, once drained, a tank can be cleaned using a high-pressure hose (a steam cleaner is even better) – although it's vital to ensure any water is drained after this process.

Installing a water separator

Most engine-mounted fuel filters are of limited capacity and don't provide protection against water in the fuel. The best long-term measure to maximise reliability and avoid potentially expensive damage to

Below **The small in-line fuel filter fitted to many engines clogs easily if contaminated.**

the engine is therefore to install a high capacity pre-filter and water separator. These are normally fitted on the transom of open boats, where the water separator's glass bowl can be easily monitored.

If a portable remote fuel tank is

Above **A tank that has had contaminated fuel should be drained, thoroughly cleaned and dried before reuse.**

used, the flexible pipe from the tank can be taken to the supply side of the filter, with a second flexible pipe installed between the filter and the engine to allow the engine to tilt and swivel for steering. However, if the boat has an integral tank then the filter will need to be incorporated in the pipework before the flexible pipe leading to the engine. In both cases, standard-sized connections are available for filters and pipework, so it is a straightforward task.

Descaling waterways

The waterways along which the water used for cooling an outboard must pass are frequently very narrow. This means they are prone to a build-up of calcium deposits, particularly if the engine is used in salt water, and these can restrict water flow.

An excess of scale is one of the key reasons for premature failure of outboard engines, so it's worth trying to prevent it from building up. Regularly flushing with fresh water is the first line of defence but, once scale has started to build up, soaking the waterways in an acid solution will help to remove some of it. A number of descaling products are available from chandlers, although central heating system descalers will also do the job, the most effective of which are sulphamic acid-based. Vinegar or citric acid can be used too, but these are generally less effective. A small outboard engine can also be run in a tank of acid solution because the heat created when running it will help to soften the scale further.

Right **The gear shift rod must be disconnected before removing the lower leg.**

Below **Small outboards are particularly prone to becoming restricted by limescale.**

Right **With the lower leg dismantled, scale can be scraped from the waterways and water pump body.**

Descaling big engines

Larger outboard engines can have a tank containing an acid solution connected to the 'ear muffs' used to join the cooling intake to a fresh water hose for flushing the cooling system.

✪ Warm up the engine to normal operating temperatures using fresh water from the hose as a coolant.

✪ Now stop the engine, swap over to the acid solution for the tank, restart the engine and run it just long enough for the solution to start pumping out of the exhaust.

✪ Leave it to cool for an hour or so, before reconnecting the fresh water and running the engine for another 10 minutes to flush the acid through.

Below **Once the scale is removed, the pump body can be cleaned with fine emery paper to discourage the build up of further scale.**

Mechanically removing scale

A severely scaled-up engine may benefit from being stripped down to enable the scale to be removed mechanically. A Dremel-type rotary tool is ideal for this, although it's always worth carrying out the flushing process outlined above first, as softening the scale will help speed up its mechanical removal.

✪ Start by removing the cylinder head, following the instructions in the engine's workshop manual. Take care not to shear any of the bolts when loosening them (see page 136 and 170 for more on removing stubborn bolts).

✪ After removing as much scale as possible, fit a new head gasket and tighten the cylinder head bolts to the specification detailed in the manual (see page 186 for more on refitting cylinder heads).

Outboard dealers are often reluctant to touch older outboards because descaling them can absorb an uneconomic amount of workshop time. However, owners who have the patience to do this work can often keep an outboard that's already decades old running for many more years to come.

Glossary

A

alternator A device mounted on the engine that generates alternating current (AC) electricity, which it then converts to low voltage direct current (DC) to charge the battery, and supply the boat's low voltage electrical demands. It is usually belt driven from the engine crankshaft.

anchor rode The chain, rope or a combination of both that connects an anchor to the boat.

angle grinder A very useful power tool that cuts by grinding at high speed (usually around 11,000 rpm). A number of attachments can be used to cut through fibreglass or stainless steel quickly, creating feathered edges in laminate, or removing rust from keels.

anode A sacrificial piece of metal, usually zinc, that protects other metal items in contact with sea water from galvanic corrosion, by eroding instead.

antifouling Paint applied to the bottom of a boat that is kept afloat, to prevent marine growth developing on the submerged areas of the vessel.

athwartships The orientation of anything that runs from one side of a hull to the other, such as a thwart on a dinghy, or a bulkhead in a yacht.

B

backing plate A piece of wood, metal or fibreglass designed to fit under the deck beneath a fitting, and so spread the load.

backstay Part of the standing rigging that gives fore-and-aft support to the mast. The backstay runs from the back of the boat to the top of the mast.

ball valve A ball-shaped valve that opens or closes with a single 90-degree movement of a handle.

batten The leech of most mainsails is supported by horizontal battens (usually made of fibreglass) that improve the sail's aerodynamic shape and increase its lifespan by reducing flapping.

belt polisher A machine that can be fitted with different grades of sandpaper to progressively remove the rough 'as cast' finish of metal fittings.

bevel board A straight-edged board on which the angle of a bevel is recorded from a bevel gauge.

bevel gauge A device consisting of two straight-edged lengths of metal or wood that can be set to any angle. It is used to establish the angle between two fixed points, such as the side of a frame and a plank.

biaxial cloth A reinforcement material used with epoxy or polyester resins. The strands are woven in two distinct directions (two axis) for increased strength.

bilge keel A keel that is attached to the turn of the bilge in opposing pairs. This allows a yacht to take the ground upright.

blind rivet Technical term for a pop rivet.

boltrope Rope stitched along the edge of a sail, either to give protection against chafe, or to enable the sail to be set in a groove in the back of the mast, the top of the boom or the roller reefing system.

bottlescrew turnbuckle A threaded device located between the wire rigging supporting the mast and the chainplates on the hull. Used to tension the rig.

bow roller A roller assembly used for guiding the anchor chain (or rope) over the bow of the boat.

brushes Small carbon blocks that, in contact with a rotating shaft, are used to conduct electricity. The brushes, which are replaceable, are held in contact with the shaft by springs.

bulkhead A transverse full or partial 'wall' running across the boat, often used to separate different areas of accommodation. Bulkheads can be important structural members, especially on older boats.

C

carvel planking A method of wooden hull construction that uses planks of wood laid edge to edge. The joints are sealed with cotton or oakum and putty.

caulking A method of sealing the narrow gaps ('seams') between planks of wood laid edge to edge. Cotton or oakum is rammed into the seams and then sealed with putty.

centreboard A retractable keel made of wood, fibreglass, steel or other materials that pivots near its front edge. This allows it to swing upwards either directly under the hull, or within a case inside the hull.

chainplate The fitting that attaches the standing rigging (forestay, backstay and shrouds) to the vessel's hull and/or deck.

chroming The process of applying a thin layer of chromium to a metal fitting using electricity. The steps required before the layer of chromium can be applied will be determined by the condition and type of metal to be chromed.

clevis pin Typically a short pin with a large diameter, most commonly used to join rigging components together. May be made of galvanised or stainless steel.

clinker planking A method of wooden hull construction in which the lower edge of each plank overlaps the upper edge of the plank below it. The planks (strakes) may be glued or rely on direct contact to ensure they are watertight.

coachroof The cabin top, if it projects above deck level.

collet A two-part metal ring that fits around a groove in a shaft to hold it in place.

compounding The term used when applying an abrasive polish to a faded gel coat to restore its shine.

compression gauge Instrument used to determine the compression of each of an engine's cylinders.

compression joint A pipe joint consisting of a screwed coupling that compresses metal seals (olives) onto the pipe to achieve the seal.

contact adhesive A powerful glue that sticks to itself upon contact.

contact breaker points A mechanical low-voltage switch that supplies the power to create the spark needed to ignite the fuel of a petrol engine at the optimum moment.

copper-clenched hull A method of construction by which the planks are joined to the frames or timbers using a copper nail and rove (washer).

core Material that is used as a filler in a fibreglass sandwich laminate. Core material is usually made from lightweight materials, such as foam or balsa wood, and gives additional strength and insulation to a hull.

counter-bore A short hole of greater diameter than the main hole, to allow the head of a screw or bolt to be recessed.

crazing A collection of small fractures in resin or fibreglass caused by stress or impact damage. They are usually most evident in the gel coat around a deck fitting.

CSM Chopped Strand Mat, the most common form of reinforcement material used in fibreglass lay-up.

cutlass bearing The aftermost bearing that supports the propeller shaft.

cutting back Another term for compounding.

D

daggerboard A type of lifting keel that lifts vertically within a casing. Made of wood, fibreglass, metal or other materials, they can be ballasted or unballasted.

de-zincification The loss of zinc from a copper alloy due to galvanic action.

deck beam A transverse length of timber that supports the deck.

distributor Device that routes a high voltage pulse of electricity to the spark plugs of a multi-cylinder petrol engine in the correct order.

drift A length of metal rod that is used to apply force to a bolt when it is being driven through a thick piece of wood.

dry fit Trying a new piece of equipment or furniture for size or functionality before securing it in to place.

dummy stick A straight-edged rectangular piece of wood

Glossary

used to record the exact shape required for a new component on a rough template.

duo prop Volvo Penta's trade name – and now a generic term – for a system of counter-rotating propellers on an outdrive leg. The opposing blades cancel out propwalk (sideways movement) and deliver more power to the water.

E

end grain balsa A core material made up from squares of balsa wood butted together in a flexible sheet. The squares are assembled so the open-ended grain is joined to the square next to it, which makes the wood far less prone to absorbing water.

epoxy resin A type of resin that uses a hardener rather than a catalyst to promote curing. Epoxy resins have a far higher adhesive factor, and repel water far better than polyester resins, but are more expensive. They also need more precise mixing.

eye splice A loop that is formed at the end of a rope by turning the end back and splicing it to the standing part of the rope.

F

fairing The process of repeatedly filling and sanding a repair or other piece of work to create a perfectly smooth finish.

fenderstrip Made from wood, metal, rubber, or a combination of all three, a fenderstrip is a long piece of material along the hull that is designed to protect against knocks and bumps. Fenderstrips also have a decorative role.

flange The protruding lip of a hull or deck moulding that is used to join the two together. A rubber fenderstrip is often pushed over the flange to hide it.

flow coat A generic term for polyester resin infused with pigment and styrene wax. The resin is 'flowed' into bilges and locker bases as a decorative layer, as it behaves like a thick paint and dries with a slippery smooth surface.

foot Bottom edge of a sail. Mainsails may be set loose footed, with only either end of the foot attached to the mast and boom, or the foot may be attached to the boom along its entire length.

forestay Part of the standing rigging that gives fore and aft support to the mast. The forestay runs from the bow of the boat towards the top of the mast.

four-stroke engine An engine in which there is only one power stroke for every four up or downward movements of each piston. Lubrication is via oil stored in a sump, as with all modern car engines.

frame The frame is connected to the keel and gives a boat its shape and strength.

FRP Fibre Reinforced Plastic, another term for Glass Reinforced Plastic.

futtock One of the pieces of wood that makes up a sawn frame.

G

gaiter A rubber bellows used to protect the drive shafts between a gearbox and an outdrive leg.

galvanic corrosion The electrochemical action between two dissimilar metals that are in contact with each other or linked by a conductor, such as sea water. The more 'noble' metal (for example, bronze or stainless steel) will cause the less 'noble' metal (for example, aluminium or mild steel) to corrode. This can be avoided by isolating the metals, using

plastic gaskets or an insulating compound, or, if they are below water, linking them to a sacrificial zinc anode, which will be corroded instead.

galvanising The process of coating mild steel with a protective layer of zinc. It is applied by dipping the steel component into a vat of molten zinc.

garboard planks The planks of a traditionally constructed wooden boat immediately next to the keel.

gate valve A valve incorporating a 'gate' that is screwed into the pipework to block the flow of fluids. Not normally considered suitable for marine use, as it's not possible to tell visually whether the valve is open or shut.

gel coat Made from pigmented resin, gel coat is the decorative outer layer of a hull. It is usually only about the thickness of two business cards.

gland A seal on a rotating shaft used to prevent oil and water leaking past.

glassing Verb used to describe laying-up or bonding in fibreglass. A bulkhead would be 'glassed in' to a hull using resin and CSM.

graving piece A small piece of wood that is let into a larger piece of wood to fill a hole.

grommet A soft rubber or plastic ring that protects wiring or piping from the sharp edges of a hole through which the wire or pipe passes.

GRP Glass Reinforced Plastic, or fibreglass.

grub screw A screw with no head, so that it can be tightened into a threaded hole and have no projection outside.

gypsy A pulley with a pattern in its groove that grips the links of a chain – usually fitted to an anchor windlass. The chain and gypsy must be matched, because the wrong pattern size will cause the chain to jump off.

H

halyard Rope used to pull sails up the rig.

hard A drying-out berth where the muddy bottom has been

covered with a layer of shingle or gravel so that boats can be inspected or worked on below the waterline during the lower part of the tide.

head gasket The pressure-resistant seal between the engine block and cylinder head of an internal combustion engine, which keeps gasses and liquids such as coolant and lubricating oil in the right place.

headboard The top reinforced corner of a sail.

heads A generic term used for a boat's toilet compartment, or sometimes the toilet itself.

heat exchanger Device used to transfer heat from one fluid to another. Most frequently encountered on a boat in the cooling system of fresh water-cooled engines.

hood ends The forward or aft ends of a plank.

hounds Point at which the shrouds are attached to the mast.

HT lead Electrical cable that delivers the high-voltage (high tension) current to the spark plug of a petrol engine.

K

keel bolts A metal bolt that is used to secure a lead keel to the hull of a sailing boat

L

laid deck A deck where individual planks of wood are laid onto the deck beams or sub-deck. On fibreglass boats, the laid deck is often used for cosmetic purposes.

laminate Usually used in reference to fibreglass construction, the noun 'laminate' means the layers of fibreglass under the gel coat. The verb 'to laminate' is the process of laying-up a fibreglass hull with a series of wetted-out layers of reinforcement.

lands The overlapping edges of clinker planking.

leech Back edge of a sail.

lift pump A small low-pressure pump used on diesel engines to deliver fuel from the tank to the high-pressure injector pump. Usually has a small handle allowing the pump to be activated by hand to bleed air out of the fuel system.

LPG Liquefied Petroleum Gas. A fuel source that is stored as a liquid under pressure in a metal cylinder, but is returned to gaseous form as it passes through a regulator prior to being used in, for example, a cooker. The gas may be either butane or propane.

luff Front edge of a sail.

M

mandrel The shaft of an attachment that is inserted into the chuck of a drill. Also describes the shaft of a blind (pop) rivet.

mastic A flexible sealant made from a variety of substances according to use.

MDF Medium Density Fibreboard. A man-made material that is manufactured by combining wood fibre, wax and resin binder. The mixture is subjected to a combination of high pressure and temperature to form panels.

monel An alloy rich in nickel and copper. It has many uses in a marine environment due to its resistance to corrosion.

mop polisher A machine that can be fitted with 'mops' to polish off marks in the surface of a piece of metal. A compound is applied to the circular mop, the type of which is dictated by the standard of the metal's finish prior to polishing.

mould A mould is a hollow shape in which a fibreglass component – from a hatch to an entire hull – can be cast. Moulds are usually made from a plug.

mouse/messenger line A thin rope that is used to pull new ropes into a sealed channel, such as the groove for a halyard inside a wooden mast.

mousing The use of a light line to replace a rope such as a halyard when it's removed from the mast. Can also be used when replacing electrical wiring.

N

Nyloc nuts Nyloc is the trade name for nuts that have a nylon insert. This is designed to stop the nut from vibrating loose on a thread. Ideally, they should only be used once, as when removed the insert is compromised.

O

O-ring A small tubular ring, usually made of soft rubber, which acts as a seal.

olive A metal ring used to seal a compression joint.

osmosis The blistering on a fibreglass hull caused by a

Glossary

chemical reaction in the laminate between water vapour and unreacted pockets of styrene.

outdrive Alternative term for stern drive.

P

palm A strip of leather that goes round the hand, which is fitted with a metal disc to provide reinforcement so a sailmaker's needle can be forced through sailcloth or rope when stitching.

pintle The pin that forms the hinge on which a transom-hung rudder rotates.

plug A sculpted shape made from MDF, wood or some other soft material from which a mould is cast.

pop rivet Generic term for a blind rivet.

puller A three-armed tool used to press out bearings that are a tight fit in their mount.

R

rabbet A triangular-shaped groove in the stem, sternpost or keel of a wooden boat for the appropriate edge of the planking to fit into.

raw water The water in which the boat floats (for example, sea water), and used on board to cool the engine or flush the toilet.

reef point A reinforced eyelet in a sail. The reef points on some sails have short lengths of rope permanently attached, which can be used to tie down a reef when required. On other sails, a rope is threaded through the eyelet when the sail is reefed.

release wax A wax that is applied to the inside of a mould to ensure the moulding doesn't stick when cured.

RIB Rigid-hulled Inflatable Boat – typically a fibreglass hull with inflatable tubes.

rope clutch A lever-operated device that rope passes through, which can be used to secure or release a rope – usually a halyard – quickly.

router A power tool that can cut complex grooves in timber and other soft materials.

roving A 'knitted' reinforcement for polyester lay-ups. Rovings come in several different designs.

rubbing strake Usually a wooden strake at or near the top of the hull that provides protection from damage. In some cases it also helps to stiffen the structure.

running rigging Ropes used to raise and control sails or spars, such as booms and spinnaker poles.

S

scarph joint A long, tapered joint used to join two pieces of timber together. Scarphs should be at least eight times longer than the width of the timber being joined.

SDS drill A power tool that punches into brick or concrete without shattering the material. Recommended for use on ferro-cement boats rather than the hammer action of a DIY drill. SDS drills also have quick-change bayonet-style bits.

seam The longitudinal gap between two planks.

shaft drive A conventional propulsion system where the propeller shaft exits the hull towards the rear of the boat, usually at a small downwards angle.

shear pin A weak link between the propeller of some smaller or older outboard engines and the propeller shaft. If the propeller strikes a solid object the shear pin breaks, thereby protecting the gearbox from damage.

sheave A grooved wheel in which a rope runs, usually within a block or mast.

shroud Part of the standing rigging that gives lateral support to the mast. Cap shrouds are the rig's longest shrouds, running to the masthead; lower shrouds run from the deck to just below the mast spreaders.

single skin A term used to describe a hull that is made out of a single layer of fibreglass or epoxy only, as opposed to a sandwich or cored lay-up.

sistership For our purposes, a fibreglass hull that has been laid-up in the same mould so the hulls are identical.

skeg Appendage immediately forward of the rudder that helps support the foil. Fitted to many sailing yachts designed in the 1970s and 1980s.

skin fitting Through-hull fitting with a hole that passes through the hull from inside to outside. A valve must be fitted to through-hull fittings below the waterline, enabling inlet/outlet pipes to be sealed shut.

spade rudder Rudder of a sailing yacht that is hung on an internal shaft – which is usually made of stainless steel – rather than a skeg or on the back of the keel.

spars Collective term for masts, booms, gaffs, spinnaker poles, and so on.

spiling board The board on which the exact shape that is required to make a new component is recorded.

spiling The process of transferring the exact shape that is required to make a new component such as a plank or frame on to a template (the spiling board or spiling plank).

spline Thin strips of wood glued in the seams as an alternative to cotton and putty.

spreaders Struts projecting from the sides of the mast,

which spread the angle of the upper shrouds.

springing out a plank Detaching part of a plank from a boat's frames or timbers.

sprung plank A plank that is no longer attached to a boat's frames or timbers along its entire length.

stanchion (rail or post) An upright pillar or structure that supports the guardwires around a boat's decks.

standing rigging The wires that support the mast, usually made of stainless or galvanised steel.

stem The foremost part of the hull that rises up vertically from the forward end of the keel.

sternpost The vertical timber that rises up from the aft end of the keel.

stern drive A propulsion system where the drive unit on which the propeller is mounted passes through the transom at the rear of the boat. The drive unit is bolted to the engine/gearbox through the transom and can be removed for maintenance.

stock (rudder) The rudder stock is the shaft that enters the rudder blade, with the upper end attached to the steering gear.

swaged terminal Fitting attached to the end of a rigging wire in a hydraulic press, using enormous force.

T

T-hook A type of low profile rigging attachment connecting the top of a shroud to a mast.

tack rag (Tak rag) A wipe that is impregnated with glue so that the dust sticks to the rag when it is wiped across a surface.

tangs Fingers of metal that are attached to the rudder stock, and embedded in the rudder blade to provide leverage.

timbers Steamed frames on a wooden boat.

torque wrench Calibrated wrench that measures the amount of force used to tighten a nut.

transom A flat or gently curved surface that forms the stern of a boat. A transom can be mounted vertically or at an angle.

transom knee A right-angled piece of wood that is bolted to the transom and keel.

turnbuckle Another term for a bottlescrew.

two-stroke engine An engine in which there is one power stroke for every two up or downward movements of each piston. There is no sump for engine oil – two-stroke oil must be added to the fuel,

either directly in the tank, or via a built-in 'oil injection' system.

U

uncored deck A single-skin deck that lacks the sandwich construction of foam or balsa.

V

veneer A thin decorative layer of material that is bonded to a substrate.

W

waisting The term used to describe the corrosion of a keel bolt where sea water has gained access, usually through compromised sealant at the keel/hull interface. This gives the bolt a 'waist' and weakens the metal.

wetting out The physical application of activated resin to reinforcement material.

winding sticks Two or more identical lengths of straight-edged timber or metal, which are used to check the flatness of a surface.

windlass Mechanical or electrical device used to recover the anchor and chain or rope.

wooden cleats A length of wood that is used to hold a plank or spline in place temporarily while it's being fastened or glued in position.

woven roving A type of reinforcement that is particularly strong, as the strands are woven together like a fabric.

Index

A
A-brackets 199
acid washing 109
adhesives
  glue failure in wooden masts 232–3
  headlinings 117
  inflatable dinghy repairs 277
  interior laminates 115
  laminated deck beams 83
  shelf-life 21
  spar making 232–5, 263
aluminium fittings
  corrosion 62–3, 136
  upgrading 62–3
aluminium masts
  corrosion 231
  repairing dents 230–1
  replacing loose fittings 273
anchor windlasses see windlasses
angle grinders 19, 98, 100, 102, 105, 108
anodes
  engine 67
  outdrive 67, 223
  propeller 198
  replacing 66–7
  shaft 198
  skin fittings 66
anodising 231
antennae, communications 161
antifouling
  health and safety 13
  propellers 203
arc welding 98–9, 100
autopilots
  replacing below-deck autopilots 165
  and sail trim 164
  tiller pilots 164

B
backing pads
  for aluminium spars 273
  for fittings 108, 242, 272
  materials for 52–3, 63
ball valves 139
ballast 46
batten pocket repairs 247
batteries 152, 172, 209
beams, laminating deck 82–3
bearings
  cutlass bearings 192–3
  rudder bearings 44–5
  wheel bearings 278
bellows failure 222
belts, drive 178–9
bilge-keeled yachts 46
bilge pumps
  spares for 20
  stray current corrosion and 160–1
bilge runners 266–7
black pudding mix 73
bleeding hydraulic systems 147
blind rivets 254–5
blisters
  on ferro-cement hulls 109
  on fibreglass hulls 28, 32–3
  on wooden hulls 84
blocks, unseizing 236–7
bolt ropes 246

bow thrusters, wiring diameter 153
brackets, A- and P- 199
braided rope 229, 249
braking systems, trailers 279
brushes, starter motor 173
bulkheads
  delamination 17, 114–15
  repairing damaged 37, 50–1
buoyancy tank leaks 270–1

C
calipers, vernier 170
cam belts 179
carburettors 214, 284, 285
carvel hulls 86
cast fittings 64
caulking
  teak decks 88, 89
  wooden hulls 73, 86–7
centre-console boats 220–1
centreboards 48
chafe, sails 228
chemicals, and unseizing fittings 137
chisels 70, 114
choke, outboard engines 284
chopped strand mat (CSM) 27
chroming 65
clinker dinghies, repairing 274–5
clutches, replacing worn 223
coachroof, resurfacing 90–1
communications equipment, grounding 161
compression tests 171, 186
connectors, electrical 156–9
consoles, powerboat 220, 221
contamination
  of fuel 174–5, 184–5, 290–1
  of oil 186–7
  of water 186–7
controls
  inboard engines 190–1
  outboard engines 288–9
cooling systems 182, 208, 223
copper piping 123, 124
cored decks
  and installing new fittings 242
  re-bedding loose fittings 52, 53
  repairing 34–5
corrosion
  aluminium fittings 62
  aluminium masts 231
  and anodes 66–7
  forestay 240
  freeing seized fastenings 135
  freeing seized fittings 136–7
  keelbolts 46–7
  rigging 251
  signs of 231
  stray current and 160–1
  through-hull fittings 140
  trailers 280, 281
  underwater fittings 198
cosmetic repairs, fibreglass 28
crazing, fibreglass 30
crooks, wooden 81
CSM (chopped strand mat) 27
cushion foam 112, 113
cutlass bearings 192–3
cutting back (fibreglass repairs) 40–1
cylinder heads 186, 187

D
daggerboards 48
deck fittings
  aluminium 62–3
  dinghy 272–3
  on ferro-cement hulls 108
  re-bedding 16, 52–3
  removing welded 105
  on steel hulls 104–5
  surveying 16
  winches 238–9, 242–3
deck glands, fitting 153
decks 54–65
  core damage 34–5
  cracks in fibreglass decks 30–1
  deck leaks 50
  installing winches 242–3
  laminating deck beams 82–3
  ply sub-decks 74
  resealing hull to deck joints 36–7
  surveying 16
  teak-finished 54–5
  teak-laid 74–5, 88–9
  see also coachroof, resurfacing; deck fittings
delamination
  of fibreglass hulls 33
  of floorboards 114–15
  of washboards 114–15
dents, in aluminium masts 230–1
descaling
  heat exchangers 183
  marine toilets 128–9
  outboard engines 292–3
dezincification 198
diesel bug 175, 183
diesel engines
  bleeding 176
  decompression levers 208
  troubleshooting 208–9, 210–11
  see also engines
diesel heaters, troubleshooting 126–7
dinghies 266–81
  buoyancy tank leaks 270–1
  fibreglass dinghy repairs 266–9
  inflatable dinghy repairs 276–7
  replacing deck fittings on 272–3
  trailers 278–81
  wooden dinghy repairs 274–5
domestic repairs 112–31
doubler frames 80
dowels 77
drag, and propellers 197
drills 19, 108
drive belts 178–9
dummy sticks 79
duo props 224–5
dust, and health and safety 13

E
electrics 152–67
  autopilots 164–5
  batteries 152, 172, 209
  earth leaks 160–1
  electrical connections 156–7, 158–9
  essential spares 20
  health and safety 13
  lifting keel mechanisms 49
  marine toilets 130–1
  navigation instruments 162–3

petrol engines 212
replacing damaged wiring 154–5
resistance testing 158–9
starter motors 209
trim tabs 219
voltage drop testing 159
waterproofing 153, 163, 164
water pumps 118–19
windlasses 144
wiring diameter 153
electrolytic corrosion 140
engineering skills 170–1
engines, inboard 170–215
  A- and P-bracket damage 199
  adjusting the drive belt 178–9
  anodes 67
  bleeding 176–7, 210
  blocked fuel pipes 174, 175
  broken engine mounts 188–9, 194
  carburettors 214
  cleanliness and 171
  cutlass bearings 193
  damaged engine controls 190–1
  decompression levers 208
  descaling 292–3
  diesel 176, 208–9, 210–11
  engine beds and feet 206, 207
  essential spares 20
  fault codes 215
  heat exchanger problems 182–3
  horsepower 204, 207
  injector problems 211
  installing new 204–7
  monitoring wear 171
  overheating 208
  petrol 176, 212–15
  realigning 189, 206–7
  starter motors 172–3, 209
  surveying 17
  tools 170, 171
  torque settings 171
  troubleshooting 208–15
  upgrading your systems 207
  water in the fuel 174–5
  water and oil contamination 186–7
  water pump repair 180–1
  see also fuel systems; outboard engines; outdrives; propellers
epoxy
  epoxy resin 27
  epoxy sheathing 90, 91
  and ferro-cement hulls 109
  filleting 27
  and steel hulls 103
exhausts
  exhaust gas 126
  exhaust hoses 205, 208

F
fastenings
  on aluminium spars 273
  corroded 135, 160, 205
  loose deck fastenings 272–3
  on wooden boats 76–7, 275
feeler gauges 170
ferro-cement boats 106–9
  cutting apertures in 108
  filling holes in 107
  painting 108–9
  stanchions 61

water ingress and 106–7
fibreglass boats 26–67
  cored decks 34–5, 242
  cracks, voids and crazing 30–1, 199
  cutting and polishing 40–1
  damaged bulkheads 50–1
  delamination 33
  dinghy repairs 266–9
  fibreglass skills 26–7
  fuel and water tanks 143
  impact and surface damage repairs 28–9
  moulding from a sister ship 38–9
  osmosis 32–3
  repair materials 21
  resealing hull to deck joints 36–7
  teak-finished decks 54–5
  testing the soundness of 14–15
filleting, epoxy 27
filters, fuel
  blocked 185, 211
  fine filters 176
  outboard engines 290, 291
  petrol engines 215
  primary 176
fin-keeled yachts 46
fittings
  cast 64
  corrosion of 160–1
  dinghy 272–3
  on ferro-cement hulls 108
  on powerboats 221
  re-bedding deck fittings 52–3
  re-chroming 65
  refurbishing old 64–5
  re-galvanising 64–5
  seized 136–7
  on steel hulls 104–5
  surveying 16
  through-hull 140–1
  upgrading aluminium 62–3
  winches 238–9, 242–3
floorboards, delamination 114
flow-coat 26, 27
foam, cushion
  bolstering 113
  waterlogged 112
forestay corrosion 240
frames
  doubler 80
  fitting new 81
  laminating 80
  making a pattern 80
  sawn 80–1
fresh water pumps
  extending life of 119
  fixing 118–19
  leaks in 120
fuel systems
  bleeding 177
  blocked fuel lines 174, 175, 290
  cleaning 291
  contamination 290–1
  diesel bug 184–5
  diesel heaters 126
  filters 176, 185, 211, 215, 290, 291
  flooded carburettors 284
  fuel leaks 188
  injectors 176, 211
  outboard engines 290–1
  petrol engines 214

pumps 176, 211, 215
  tanks 142–3, 184–5, 291
  water in the fuel 174–5, 184
furling systems, headsail 240–1
fuses 153
futtocks, fitting new 81

G
galvanic corrosion 160, 161, 198
galvanising 64–5
gas installations
  copper tubing 123, 124
  flexible gas pipe 123, 124, 125
  gas alarms 122
  gas leaks 122–3
  gas regulators 122–3
  maintenance 124
gate valves 138
gearbox oil seals 286–7
gel coat 26, 27
  colour matching 31, 40–1
  and osmosis 32–3
  repairing cracks 31
genoa blocks 237
glass cloth 90
glow plugs 172
glues and gluing
  glue failure in wooden masts 232–3
  headlining replacement 117
  inflatable dinghy repairs 277
  interior laminates 115
  laminated deck beams 83
  spar making 234–5, 263
grab handles, powerboats 221
graving pieces
  laid decks 74
  wooden hulls 84–5
GRP see fibreglass
guardrails, bent 60–1

H
H-brackets 223
hacksaws 98
halyards 229
  eye splices in 249
  replacing 248
  seized sheaves 252
  sheered halyard pins 252
hammer drills 108
hand tools
  engineering 170, 171
  essential 18–19
  maintaining 18
  mechanical 134, 135, 137
  pop rivet guns 254–5
  seam rakes 86
  sharpening 70
  transporting 23
  woodworking 54–5, 70–1
hatches
  leaking 56–7
  non-slip surfaces on 59
  replacing 58–9
headlining, replacing 116–17
heads, electric
  laying-up/recommissioning 131
  replacing the impeller 131
  troubleshooting 130–1
  unblocking 130–1
heads, manual
  and limescale 128–9

troubleshooting 128–9
  unblocking 128
headsails
  blocks for 237
  roller furling systems 240–1
health and safety
  dust 13
  electrical dangers 13
  paints, solvents and resins 13, 103
  heat, use for unseizing fittings 136
heat exchangers
  descaling 183
  dismantling 183
  problems with 182–3, 186
heating systems, diesel 126–7
hood ends, refastening 275
hull repairs see dinghies;
  ferro-cement boats; fibreglass boats; steel boats; wooden boats
hydraulic systems
  bleeding 147
  leaking 146–7
  lifting keels 48–9
  trim tabs 219
Hypalon 276

I
impact damage
  fibreglass hulls 28–9
  guardrails 60–1
  keels 46
  rudders 42
  wooden hulls 78
impact drivers 135, 137
impellers
  electric marine toilets 130, 131
  water pumps 181, 208
inflatable dinghies
  care of 276–7
  repairing leaks 277
injectors, fuel 174, 176, 211

J
Japanese back-saws 71
jigs, making 83
jigsaws 19
joints
  compression joints 125
  scarph joints 50, 234, 260
  testing pipework joints for leaks 120, 123

K
keelbolts
  drawing 46, 92–3
  fitting 92–3
  surveying 14, 17
keels
  dropping 47
  impact damage to 46
  lifting keels 48–9
  long-keeled yachts 45, 46
  weeping keels 46–7

L
ladders 12
laminating
  cutting laminates 82
  deck beams 82–3
  frames 80
  gluing laminates together 82

relaminating interior surfaces 114–15
  removing laminates 114–15
leaks
  around shaft seals 194, 225
  buoyancy tanks 270–1
  in domestic water systems 120–1
  fuel 188, 211
  fuel lift pumps 175, 211
  gas 122–3, 125
  hydraulic systems 146–7
  marine toilets 128, 130
  oil 188
  stanchion bases 61
  stray current leaks 160–1
  through-hull fittings 140–1
  window and hatches 56–7, 58
  wooden boats 72–3, 275
  see also water ingress
lift pumps 175, 211
lifting keels 48–9
lightning 160
limescale
  dripless shaft seals 194
  heat exchangers 183
  marine toilets 128–9
  mechanical removal of 293
  outboard engines 292–3
linings, repairing and replacing interior 116–17
locking mechanisms, outdrives 222
LPG 122, 124
  see also gas installations

M
macerator pumps 130
mainsheet blocks 237
Marelon through-hull fittings 141
marine growth 203
mastic 72–3
masts
  aluminium mast repairs 230–1
  glue failure in wooden masts 232–3
  making a hollow wooden spar 262–3
  making a solid wooden spar 260–1
  mast boots 258–9
  pop riveting 254–5
  repairing rot in wooden masts 234–5
  replacing a halyard 248
  rigging terminal repairs 250–1
  sheaves 252
  standing rigging 256–7
mechanics
  general mechanical skills 134–49
  mechanical tools 134, 135
  trailer repairs 278–9
messenger lines 155, 246, 249, 272
metal
  corrosion 136
  cutting 98, 105
  metalworking skills 98–9
  pop riveting 254–5
  unseizing fittings and fastenings 134–7
  welding 98–9
  see also corrosion and individual metals

Index

micrometers 170
MIG (metal inert gas) welding 99
moisture meters 15, 32, 33, 50
Morse levers 190
motorboats 218–25
  centre-console boats 220–1
  duo props 224–5
  fittings 221
  propellers for 197
  RIBs 196, 220–1, 289
  seats 220
  servicing outdrives 222–3
  trim tabs 218–19
  see also engines, inboard;
  outboard engines; outdrives
mousing lines 155, 246, 249, 272
multimeters 152, 158

N

navigation instruments 162–3
non-slip surfaces, hatches 59
nuts, unseizing 135, 137

O

oil
  oil leaks 188
  water in the oil 186–7, 225, 286
osmosis
  on rudders 28
  signs of 14, 15, 28
  treating 32–3
outboard engines
  anodes 67
  blocked jets 285
  descaling waterways 292–3
  faulty outboard controls 288–9
  flooded carburettors 284
  fuel blockage and contamination
  290–1
  installing water separators 291
  propellers 198
  repairs 284–93
  replacing gearbox oil seals 286–7
  starting problems 284–5
  steering problems 289
  two-stroke engines 284, 285
outdrives
  anodes 67, 223
  bellows failure 222
  H-brackets 223
  locking mechanisms 222
  servicing 222–3
  water intake 223
  worn clutches 223
overheating engines 208
oxyacetylene cutting 98, 105

P

P-brackets 199
  galvanic corrosion of 198
paints and painting
  ferro-cement hulls 108–9
  fibreglass boats 40–1
  health and safety 13, 103
  steel boats 103, 104
  storing paints 21
  two-pack paints 103
  wooden boats 94–5, 274
panel saws 71
paying a deck 88, 89
percussion tests
  bulkheads 50

decks 16
  fibreglass hulls 14–15
  metalwork 280
  wooden hulls 84
petrol engines
  bleeding 176
  fuel filters 215
  fuel system 214
  outboards 290
  testing for a spark 213
  troubleshooting 212–15
  see also engines
pipes and pipework
  blocked fuel pipes 174, 175, 290
  copper 123, 124, 125
  flexible fuel pipes 174
  gas 122–3
  hydraulic systems 146, 147
  leaks in 120
  and limescale 128–9
  marine toilets 128–9
  pipe connections 125
  testing joints 123
pitch, for caulking 88
pitch, propeller 196
planes 71
planks and planking
  caulking seams 86–7
  deck planking 54–5, 74–5, 88–9
  dinghy repairs 275
  graving pieces 84–5
  hood ends 275
  refastening 76–7
  replanking 78–9
  scarph joints 78, 79
  spiling new 79
plasma cutters 98, 105
plastic tanks 143
polishing fibreglass 40–1
polyester resins 26, 27
pop riveting
  replacing rivets 255
  types of rivet 254
power tools 13, 19
powerboats 218–25
  centre-console boats 220–1
  duo props 224–5
  fitting trim tabs 218–19
  fittings 221
  grab handles 221
  RIBs 196, 220–1, 289
  seats 220, 221
  see also engines, inboard;
  outboard engines; outdrives
priming
  steel hulls 103
  wooden hulls 94–5
propellers
  clearing fouled 202–3
  damage to 198, 203, 225
  duo props 224–5
  fouled 286
  galvanic corrosion 198
  and marine growth 203
  pitch 196
  sailboat vs motorboat 197
  size 196
propshafts
  A- and P-brackets 199
  assessing the condition of 201
  dripless shaft seals 194–5
  galvanic corrosion 198

realigning 189
  removing 200–1
  replacing cutlass bearings 192–3
pumps
  bilge pumps 20, 160–1
  extending life of 119
  fuel 174, 175, 176, 215
  marine toilet pumps 128
  water pumps 118–19, 120, 142,
  180–1, 208
putty
  red lead putty 73
  replacing hardened 72
PVC dinghies 276

R

raw water systems 182
  overheating 208
rebates 89
re-bedding deck fittings 52–3
red lead putty 73
reefing points 247
reinforcement materials 27
remote controls, outboard engines
  288
resin
  activating 27
  epoxy resin 27
  filleting 27
  health and safety 13
  polyester resin 21, 26
  wetting out 27
resistance testing 158–9
RIBs
  attaching fittings to 220-1
  grab handles 221
  propeller pitch 196
  replacing fittings 221
  steering racks 289
  see also outboard engines
rigs and rigging
  braid on braid splices 249
  corrosion of 240, 251
  eye splices 229, 249
  halyards 229, 248, 249, 252
  loose rigging strands 250–1, 257
  rigging screws 250, 251
  rolled swage terminals 250, 257
  roller furling systems 240–1
  seized blocks 236–7
  seized sheaves 252
  shackles 253
  standing rigging 16, 229, 256–7
  see also masts
rivets 254–5
  on aluminium spars 273
roller furling systems 240–1
ropes and ropework
  braided lines 229
  braid on braid splices 229, 249
  eye splices 249
  halyard repairs 248–9
  seized sheaves 252
rot
  in wooden masts 234–5
  in wooden planking 84
routers, palm 89
rubbing strakes 266
rudders
  dropping 44–5
  fittings 15
  long-keeled yachts 45

modifying the design of 28
  repairing damage to 42–3
  replacing bearings 44–5
  spade 44–5
rust
  removing 100, 102
  rust streaks on ferro hulls 106,
  107
  and seized fittings 136–7
  on standing rigging 257
  on trailers 280

S

safety
  dust 13
  electrical dangers 13
  fibreglass repairs 26
  ladders and staging 12
  paints 13, 103
  windlasses 144
  working with metal 99
sailboats 228–63
  keels 46–7
  propellers 197
  see also dinghies; masts; rigs and
  rigging; sails and sailmaking
sails and sailmaking
  batten pocket repairs 247
  bolt ropes 246
  reefing points 247
  repairing chafe/holes 228, 244–5
  sail trim and autopilots 164
  sailmaking skills 228–9
  seized roller furling systems
  240–1
  shackles 253
salt water, and corrosion 162
sanders 19
sanding teak decks 88
sandwich construction, decks
  34–5, 242
saws 71
scarph joints
  bulkhead repairs 50
  hull planking 78, 79
  masts and spars 234, 260
scratches, in fibreglass hulls 29, 40
screwdrivers 19, 134, 135, 137
screws
  drilling out 137
  unseizing 135, 136, 137
SDS (Special Direct System)
  hammer drills 108
seacocks
  and anodes 66
  ball valves 139
  checking for corrosion 15
  in ferro-cement hulls 108
  freeing seized 138–9
  gate valves 138
  traditional cone-type 138
sealants
  re-sealing deck seams 88, 89
  re-sealing fittings 273
  shelf-life 21
seals
  dripless shaft seals 194–5
  duo props 225
  fixed windows 56
  gearbox oil seals 286–7
  replacing hatch seals 56–7, 59
  shaft seals 194–5, 201

seam rakes 54–5
seams
    caulking 73, 86–7
    cracks in seams 72
    leaking seams 72
    loose splines 73
    recaulking laid decks 88, 89
seats
    powerboats 220, 221
    repairing vinyl seat covers 112
self-steering, wind vane 148–9
shackles 253
shaft seals 201
    dripless shaft seals 194–5
shafts
    A- and P-brackets 199
    assessing the condition of 201
    dripless shaft seals 194–5
    galvanic corrosion 198
    realigning 189
    removing 200–1
    replacing cutlass bearings 192–3
sharpening blades 70
sheathing, epoxy 90, 91
sheaves 236, 252
shelters, building 23
shotblasting 100, 102
sister frames 80
skin fittings
    and anodes 66
    ball valves 139
    checking for corrosion 15
    in ferro-cement boats 108
    freeing seized 138–9
    gate valves 138
    traditional cone-type 138
slurry blasting 106–7, 109
soldering connections 156
solenoid valves 172, 173, 210
solvents 13
spanners 134
spar gauges 261
spares, essential 20–1
spark plugs 212, 213
spars
    aluminium mast repairs 230–1,
    273
    glue failure in wooden masts
    232–3
    making a hollow wooden spar
    262–3
    making a solid wooden spar
    260–1
    mast boots 258–9
    pop riveting 254–5
    repairing rot in wooden spars
    234–5
    shaping solid spars 261
    sheaves 252
spiling planks 79
spinnaker blocks 236
splices and splicing 229
    braid on braid splices 249
    eye splices 229, 249
splines
    replacing loose 73
    and wooden hull leaks 72
spokeshaves 71
staging 12
stainless steel, marine grade 62
stanchions
    accessing base bolts 60

bent or sheared 60–1
    checking your stanchion bases 61
standing rigging 16, 229, 256–7
starter motors
    brushes 173
    problems with 172–3, 209
steel
    corrosion 136
    cutting 98–9
    re-galvanising steel fittings 64–5
    use for fuel and water tanks 142
    welding 98, 100–1
steel boats 98–105
    painting 103, 104
    removing rust 100
    replacing deck fittings 104–5
    shotblasting 102
    stanchions 61
    welding new panels 100–1
steering
    problems with outboard engines
    289
    wind vane steering systems
    148–9
stopping compounds 72–3
stress cracks, fibreglass hulls 30
stuffing boxes 194
surveying your boat
    hull 14–15
    on board 16–17
swage terminals
    problems with 16
    rolled swage terminals 250, 257

T
T-hooks 257
tanks
    buoyancy 270–1
    flexible 143
    fuel 142–3, 291
    plastic 143
    water 121, 142–3
tar 88
teak decks
    refurbishing laid teak decks 88–9
    repairing laid teak decks 74–5
    repairing teak-finished decks
    54–5
tenders see dinghies
tenon saws 71
terminals, rolled swage 250, 257
through-hull fittings 140–1
TIG (tungsten inert gas) welding
    99
toe rails 61
toilets see heads, electric; heads,
    manual
tools
    electrical 152
    engineering 170, 171
    essential 18–19
    maintaining 18
    mechanical 134, 135, 137
    pop rivet guns 254–5
    power tools 13, 19
    sharpening 70
    transporting 23
    woodworking 54–5, 70–1, 86
topcoat resin 26, 27
torque 137, 171
trailers
    braked 279, 281

breakaway cables 281
    damage assessment 280
    mechanical repairs 278–9
    replacing wheel bearings 278
    security couplings 281
    storing 279
    suspension units 281
    tyres 278
transoms 275
trim tabs
    electric 219
    fitting new 219
    hydraulic 219
    size and position 218–19
two-pack polyurethane paints 103,
    109
two-stroke engines 284, 285
tyres, trailer 278

U
ultraviolet light 162, 277
upholstery
    bolstering cushion foam 113
    repairing upholstery 112–13
    repairing vinyl seat covers 112

V
veneered bulkheads 51
ventilation 17
vents, leaking 56–7
vernier calipers 170
vinyl
    inflatable dinghies 276
    interior linings 116–17
    upholstery 112
voids, filling fibreglass 31
voltage, battery 152, 172, 209
voltage drop testing 159
voltmeters 152

W
washboards, delamination of 114
water ingress
    around shaft seals 194, 225
    around stanchion bases 61
    and electrical systems 153, 154
    and ferro-cement hulls 106–7
    in engine oil 186–7, 225, 286
    in fuel 174–5, 184, 290–1
    and interior delamination 114–15
    and navigation instruments 162
    signs of 117
    through-hull fittings 140
    window and hatches 56–7, 58
    wooden boats 72–3, 275
water locks 207
water pumps
    electric 118–19
    extending life of 119
    impellers 181, 208
    leaks in 120
    manual 118, 142
    priming 180
    repairing 180–1
    spares 20
water separators 291
water systems, domestic 120–1
water tanks 142–3
waterproofing
    electrical systems 153
    tiller pilots 164
    waterproofing ratings 163

wear
    of cutlass bearings 192
    monitoring engine 171
welding 98–9
    arc welding 100
    deck gear 105
    fuel and water tanks 142
    MIG welding 99
    thin materials 99
    TIG welding 99
    welding new panels 100–1
wetting out (fibreglass) 27
wheel bearings 278
winches
    adding new 243
    location of 242
    reasons for failure 238
    seized 238–9
    stripping 238–9
wind vane self steering 148–9
windlasses
    electric 144
    stripping seized 144–5
    wiring diameter for 153
windows, replacing seals on 56–7
windscreen wipers
    repairing 166
    replacing arms and blades 167
    replacing wiper motors 167
wiring
    deck glands 153
    engine wiring 205
    resistance testing 158–9
    rewiring 154–5
    and stray current corrosion
    160–1
    tracing connection problems
    158–9
    types of connectors 156–7
    types of wire 154–5
    voltage drop testing 159
    waterproofing 153
    wiring diameter 153
wooden boats 70–95
    caulking hulls 86–7
    copper-clenched 78
    dinghy repairs 274–5
    drawing keel bolts 92–3
    graving pieces 84–5
    minor hull leaks 72–3
    refastening planking 76–7
    refastening tired hood ends 275
    removing old paint 274
    repainting 94–5
    replacing sawn frames 80–1
    replanking 78–9
    resealing leaking planks 275
    teak deck repairs 74–5
wooden masts
    glue failure in 232–3
    making a hollow wooden spar
    262–3
    making a solid wooden spar
    260–1
    repairing rot in 234–5
woodworking skills 70–1
workbenches 13
workshops, portable 22–3

Z
zips, seized 112

Acknowledgements

The publisher would like to thank the following for their kind permission to reproduce photographs in this book. (Abbreviations key: t = top, b = bottom, r = right, l = left)

Vanessa Bird 139, 220

Peter Caplen 13 (bl), 34, 35 (panel), 52, 59, 77 (b), 99, 101 (panel), 115 (panel), 126, 127 (tl), 130, 131, 134, 143 (b), 165, 167, 178 (r), 182, 183 (b), 192, 194 (l), 195, 197 (t), 198, 213 (b), 279 (b), 289 (panel), 292 (b), 296

Nic Compton 2–3, 6–7, 8 (b), 9 (t), 16, 17, 48 (b), 53, 58, 60, 96–97, 103 (t), 114, 115 (t), 168–169, 226–227, 228, 232, 233, 236 (b), 238, 240, 250, 252, 256, 264–265

Mark Goodacre (c/o J Kavanagh) 38, 42, 43, 49, 61 (tr & b)

Rupert Holmes 4–5, 15 (b), 18, 19, 20, 21, 22, 23, 32 (b), 33 (b), 44, 45, 48 (t), 50, 51, 56, 57, 98, 101 (tl), 104, 105, 118, 119, 120, 121, 122, 123, 127 (tl), 128, 129, 135 (b), 142, 144, 146, 147, 148, 149 (b), 150–151, 152, 153, 154, 155, 158, 159, 161, 162, 163, 164, 170 (t), 171, 172, 173, 174 (t), 175, 183 (t), 185, 187, 188, 189 (t), 190 (t), 193, 194 (r), 197 (b), 199 (t), 200, 201

(b), 202, 203, 208, 209, 210, 211, 212, 213 (t&r), 214, 215, 218, 219, 221, 229, 242, 243, 249 (t), 266, 267, 270, 271, 272, 273, 276, 277, 278, 279 (t), 280, 281, 282–283, 284, 285, 286, 287, 288, 289 (l), 290, 291, 292 (b), 293, 295, 299

Richard Johnstone-Bryden 10–11, 24–25, 38, 64, 65, 68–69, 70, 71, 72, 73, 74, 75, 76, 77 (panel), 78, 79, 80, 81, 82, 83, 84, 85, 86, 87, 88, 89, 90, 91, 92, 93, 94, 95, 140, 166, 189 (b), 190 (t), 191 (b), 196, 216–217, 234, 235, 244, 245, 246, 247, 248, 249 (panel), 251, 253, 260, 261, 262, 263, 274, 275, 297

Jake Kavanagh 8 (t), 9 (b), 12, 13 (t & br), 15 (tl), 26, 27, 28, 29, 30 (bl), 35 (b), 36. 37, 40, 41, 46, 47, 54 (b), 61 (tl), 62, 63, 66, 67, 100, 102, 103 (b), 106, 107, 108, 109, 113, 116, 117, 135 (t), 136, 137, 138, 143 (t), 148 (t), 170 (b), 174 (b), 201 (t), 205, 206, 207, 222, 223, 224, 225, 230, 231, 236 (t), 237, 239, 241, 254, 255, 257, 258, 259, 269, 294, 298

Pat Manley 14, 15 (tr), 30 (br), 31, 32 (t), 33 (t), 54 (t), 55, 124, 125, 141, 145, 156, 157, 176, 177, 178 (l), 179, 181

Joe McCarthy 110–111, 112, 132–133, 184, 190 (b)

istockphoto.com/ gaspr13 front cover

Photolibrary.com 268, Pierre-Paul Feyte 160, Anthony Moore 204

M Shepard (c/o P Manley) 180

Stuart Marine (c/o R Holmes): 186

T Norris Marine (c/o R Holmes) 199 (b)

All Illustrations by KJA Artists and Stuart Edwards

The authors would like to thank the following for their help in researching this book:

Rupert Holmes:
Alekos Steffan, Alison Molyneaux, Bembridge SC, Bennett Trim Tabs, British Keelboat Academy, David and Bob Groom, Glomex srl, Graham Sunderland, Kass Schmitt, Kevin Mole Outboards, Martin Morris and Roma Griffin, Mini B dive equipment, Royal Victoria YC, Stuart Marine (Anglesey), Sunsail, Tim Preddy, T Norris Marine (propeller repair), UKSA.

Jake Kavanagh:
Alan Rose of APAS Engineering Ltd, Alan Dring of Hawke House

Marine Upholstery, Phil Howard, Seals + Direct, Robert Lee of Hempel/ Blakes Paints, Richard Jerram of International Paints, Mark Goodacre of Goodacre Boat Repairs and Refits, Kieran Hill of Small Boat Services, and Motortech Marine Engineering.

Richard Johnstone-Bryden: Nat Wilson, Peter Graham, Jonathan Richardson and the students of the International Boatbuilding Training College, Moray MacPhail and the staff of Classic Marine, Chris Jeckells, Brian Saunders and the staff of Jeckells the Sailmakers, and Roger Hodds and the staff of ANH Yachting.

Thanks also to Andrew Simpson, Vanessa Bird and Anna Kisby.